£10

D0936770

KONOE FUMIMARO

KONOE FUMIMARO
A Political Biography

Yoshitake Oka

Translated by

Shumpei Okamoto and Patricia Murray

UNIVERSITY OF TOKYO PRESS

Translation supported by a grant from the Ministry of Education, Science and Culture, and publication supported by a grant from The Japan Foundation.

Translated from the Japanese oriignal
KONOE FUMIMARO—"UMMEI" NO SEIJIKA (Iwanami Shoten, 1972)
English translation © 1983 by UNIVERSITY OF TOKYO PRESS
UTP Number 3031-37095-5149
ISBN 0-86008-304-7

Printed in Japan

CONTENTS

PREFACE

F umimaro Konoe was born in 1891, one year after Japan's
first constitutional government was inaugurated. Born
into one of the nation's most prestigious families, Konoe
brought an aristocratic pedigree with him when he entered
politics as a young man starting out on his career. He was in his
prime when the accelerating turblence of the early 1930s began
to push Japanese politics and diplomacy toward aggression and
war, and it was during that stormy era that he was asked to
assume responsibility for leading the nation. Three times he
became prime minister and formed cabinets. During those
years he was always in the nation's spotlight. In him were
placed the political hopes of a public who adored him. The
upheavals of the ensuing years have pushed the decade of the
1930s into the far recesses of our memory. Those events seem
now to be much further in the past than they really are. This is
partly because Japan underwent profound changes in many
respects since 1945.

When the war ended in crushing defeat, public feeling
underwent a drastic change. Konoe was now the object of loud,
bitter attacks for his war responsibility. The criticism mounted,
finally culminating in his designation as a suspected war
criminal by the Allied Powers. To appear as a defendant before
the Far Eastern Military Tribunal, a suspected war criminal,
was to Konoe the height of humiliation. Rather than submit to
this cardinal insult, he poisoned himself and died the night
before he was to go into custody. It was the ultimate act of
self-defense to protect the proud name of his noble lineage.
Thirty-seven years have passed since Konoe's death. Now, his

life seem merely to bear witness to the dictum *Sic transit gloria mundi*.

Konoe often used the world "fate" and even called himself a fatalist. But the fate of a statesman is woven together with the vicissitudes of his times and the nature of his personality. This small biography is an attempt to reconsider the era in which Konoe lived and to trace the path he cut for himself through the era. In writing it I hoped that a reexamination of Konoe's approach to his own life and politics, and of the way he responded to the events before him would lead to an understanding of why his "fate" took the turns it did.

I also had another purpose behind this study. It was to suggest, even partially, the price of power: the costs paid by the person who is given power, and also the heavy sacrifices that are borne by the people for entrusting power to certain individuals at given times. I feel that a fresh look at the times and life of Fumimaro Konoe and the fate he carried provide some valuable suggestions regarding the important question of power.

I was assisted greatly in the preparation of this manuscript by Professor Michitaka Konoe of University of Tokyo. His cooperation and thoughtful advice enabled me to make maximum use of the private papers of his father, Fumimaro Konoe, and other documents. I am also indebted to Messrs. Tomohiko Ushiba and Morisada Hosokawa for their valuable suggestions and help. I also wish to express my deep gratitude to the many other individuals who assisted me in the collection and use of documents and by allowing me to interview them. Their willing cooperation was indispensable.

Some time after the publication of this book in Japanese, I received a kind letter from Professor Shumpei Okamoto of Temple University in Philadelphia asking if I would agree to an English translation of this book, to be published by the University of Tokyo Press. I would like to express special thanks to Professor Okamoto for his painstaking work on the translation. Finally, to Patricia Murray I owe my gratitude for her invaluable collaboration in the translation process.

March 1983   Yoshitake Oka

KONOE FUMIMARO

1

FUMIMARO'S YOUTH

In May 1893 a small, two-year-old boy was led through the gates of the imperial palace. He was accompanied by two women. This was Konoe Fumimaro, accepting his first invitation from the imperial family. One of the women was his grandmother, Mitsuko, and the other was Motoko, whom the young Fumimaro then thought was his mother. They were greeted by the empress with the warm hospitality of a relative. During the audience, the little boy, still unable to retain a formal sitting position, sat with his legs stretched out toward the empress.

It was fitting that Fumimaro should receive such an invitation, for he was the heir in a prestigious and noble family. The Konoe were directly descended from Fujiwara Kamatari, the seventh-century founder of a dynasty of regents which held dominant power in the court for centuries. The Fujiwara forged permanent ties with the court by providing consorts for the emperors, and so the Konoe, the foremost of the five main Fujiwara houses,[1] were intimately connected with the imperial family.

Konoe Fumimaro was born in Tokyo on October 12, 1891, at the family's Iidamachi mansion. He was the first child of Konoe Atsumaro and Sawako, daughter of Maeda Yoshiyasu, former lord of the Kaga clan. Just before Fumimaro was born, five tortoises had appeared in the garden. At this auspicious event, his 86-year-old grandfather, Tadahiro, named his grandson Ayamaro (文麿) after the term bunki (文亀) for "five tortoises" in the ancient Chinese dictionary Erh-ya (爾雅). For better euphony, however, Tadahiro adopted another reading of the Chinese character for bun (文), fumi.

Fumimaro was brought up with the attentive and respectful

3

care considered appropriate to a child of a noble family. But he never knew his mother. She died of puerperal fever eight days after his birth, and the following year Atsumaro married Motoko, his late wife's younger sister. Fumimaro grew up with a stepsister, Takeko, and three stepbrothers, Hidemaro, Naomaro, and Tadamaro. For many years he was led to believe that Motoko was his real mother, and it came as a shattering blow when he learned the truth. The deception convinced him, he is said to have mused later, that "the world is full of lies." In September 1897 Fumimaro entered the elementary division of Gakushūin (Peers School) and in 1903 advanced to Gakushūin's middle school. The following year his father died, and the fortunes of his family changed radically.

Prince Konoe Atsumaro had always been immensely proud of his Fujiwara lineage. He believed that the aristocrats were the bulwark of the throne and that their duty lay in dedicating themselves to their sovereign and country. It was not long before he established a reputation as an aristocratic politician with strong nationalistic convictions. During the early years of the Imperial Diet, when revision of the unequal treaties between Japan and the Western powers was one of the most incendiary topics of debate, Atsumaro was a leading member of the strong foreign policy faction that advocated strict observation of the existing treaties. This strategy did not mean acceptance of the status quo, rather, it was intended to create such problems for the powers that they would be compelled to give in to treaty revision. Atsumaro was also deeply concerned with East Asian affairs, for, like many of his fellow nationalists, he believed that the future of China and Korea would have a vital bearing on Japan's national sovereignty and independence. He urged the government to pursue a policy of maintaining China's territorial integrity and to support and protect Korea, and he was firmly behind greater Sino-Japanese cooperation. In 1891 he became vice-president of the Tōhō Kyōkai (Far Eastern Association), and in 1898 founded the Tōa Dōbunkai (East Asia Common Culture Association). Meanwhile, in October 1896, he was appointed president of the House of Peers. In recognition of his rising political influence, three prime ministers—Matsukata

Masayoshi in 1896 and Ōkuma Shigenobu and Yamagata Aritomo in 1898—asked Konoe to join their respective cabinets. However, each time he declined.

In 1900 when the Boxer Uprising broke out in China, Russian forces took advantage of the turmoil and occupied part of Manchuria. The Russian move provoked Konoe and several other activists into stirring up a campaign for a strong anti-Russia policy. For that purpose they organized the Kokumin Dōmeikai (People's Alliance), but, not long afterward, when it seemed to Konoe that the group's initial objective had been accomplished, he dissolved it. But Russia did not let up. Later, it resumed its thrust into Manchuria, and this time the Japanese protest resulted in the formation of the Tairo Dōshikai (Anti-Russia Society) in July 1903. Although bedridden by then, Konoe took part in the establishment of this nationalist association. Also in July, Saionji Kimmochi succeeded Itō Hirobumi as president of the Seiyūkai party.[2] In an article called "The New President of the Seiyūkai" published in the August 1903 issue of the journal *Taiyō*, Toyabe Shuntei, a political critic, wrote: "Those who search for able leaders among today's nobles agree that Marquis Saionji and Prince Konoe are among the most likely candidates for the prime ministership in the near future." But Konoe Atsumaro died in January 1904 at the prime of his life. He had just turned 40. Japan broke diplomatic relations with Russia one month later, and the Russo-Japanese War began.

Fumimaro was then 12 years old. He later wrote in an essay, "My Father," that his father had always been so preoccupied with public affairs that he had little time to relax at home, and he had been able to talk personally with his son on only a few occasions. Fumimaro bitterly mourned his father's untimely death. "My memories of my father are inexhaustible,"[3] he wrote. The boy was equally saddened by subsequent events at home. Years later, in another essay, he wrote: "When my father was alive, all sorts of people called on him from early morning well into the evening, and they always gave a lot of attention to me, too. But when he died, all that suddenly stopped. Even people who were politically deeply indebted to my late father changed overnight. Now they began pressing us to pay his debts. One wealthy man kept bringing back to us some scroll paintings, which we had given him as collateral on a debt that we were unable to pay right away."[4] Fumimaro's younger stepbrother, Hidemaro, who was then an infant, later recalled seeing strangers in the house on several occasions around that time. Although he was too young to understand what was happening, these men were friends and collaborators of Atsumaro, some of the *shina rōnin* (China activists) like Tōyama Mitsuru and Uchida Ryōhei. Sympathizing with the Konoe family tormented by creditors, they had come to help turn the creditors away from the mansion. In the end, the Konoe family paid off their debts by selling heirlooms, but for a time the family experienced serious financial difficulties. Hidemaro recalled that, young as he was, even he felt the beleaguered state of his family following his father's death.[5] Their financial crisis left traces on Fumimaro's thinking for the rest of his life. Later he confided, "I could never forget what we went through in those days."[6] Throughout his political career, Konoe remained suspicious of the rich and very cautious in monetary matters.

Fumimaro inherited his father's title of Prince, and the members of his household began to address him as "Lord," rather than "Young Master." In 1909 he completed middle school at Gakushūin and, having passed the entrance examination, joined the literature course of the First Higher School. Since he had been an outstanding runner on the Gakushūin team, the higher school athletic club urged the freshman prince to join. But his guardian, Baron Yamakawa Kenjirō, objected. When the club members called upon the baron to ask him to change his mind, Yamakawa indignantly dismissed his youthful visitors, shouting at them that the Konoe were the leading family of the five Fujiwara houses. "How dare you ask the prince of such a noble family to run like a horse!" That ended any chance of joining the athletic club.

To a classmate, Gotō Ryūnosuke, Konoe at first seemed aloof and full of aristocratic airs. However, Konoe remarked later, his family's financial troubles after Atsumaro's death "had made me rebellious against the whole world. During middle and higher school, I remained a jaundiced and melancholy youth who spent long hours reading European radical literature."[7] At higher school, Konoe suffered in Professor Iwamoto Tei's German class, but Iwamoto left a strong impression. "His teaching method was extremely rough," Konoe wrote, "but his personality impressed me deeply. . . . Plato was his ideal, and I felt as if he were the Greek philosopher incarnate. I became so absorbed by Professor Iwamoto that I began to believe in those days that the world's basest people were politicians and the noblest were philosophers."[8] To improve his German, Konoe was tutored by Professor Kazami Kenjirō, whom he apparently grew to trust and confide in. Kazami recalled that Konoe then harbored strong antagonism toward the privileged class. He talked about giving up his title and becoming a professor of philosophy. Kazami warned the young prince that he must not make such a weighty decision alone and asked professors Motora Yūjirō and Anezaki Masaharu to dissuade him. Apparently Konoe was hard to convince.[9] One day during the Pacific War, he told Tomita Kenji, "I just cannot practice religion. Philosophy suits me better," as he worked on translating into Japanese an English philosophical work on death.[10] It is hard to pinpoint why Konoe was drawn to philosophy, but experiences in his youth must have contributed to that predilection. Kazami mentions one occasion when Fumimaro complained that he was lonely. "My school friends pretend to treat me as though I were no different from them, but actually they set me apart because I am a prince. The professors are the same way." At home Konoe grumbled, even though they lived under the same roof, he saw his mother only about once a month. Konoe felt a profound loneliness then, and it afflicted him to the end of his life.

In 1912, upon graduating from higher school, Konoe entered the Philosophy Department of the Faculty of Literature of Tokyo Imperial University. Before long, however, he transferred to the Law Faculty of Kyoto Imperial University. Many years later Konoe explained that Professor Iwamoto had inspired him to study philosophy, but during his last year at higher school he became interested in social science. He began reading works by Yoneda Shōtarō, Kawakami Hajime, and others on the

faculty at Kyoto Imperial University. When at last he began
the study of philosophy at Tokyo Imperial University, he found
that the lectures by Inoue Tetsujirō and his other professors no
longer interested him. He transferred to Kyoto to study under
professors Yoneda and Kawakami,[11] but he made no close friends
among his fellow students there, either. In 1913, after he had
gone to Kyoto, he married Chiyoko, the second daughter of
Viscount Mōri Takanori, a descendant of the former lord of the
Saeki clan in Kyushu. Interestingly, this was not the traditional
arranged marriage; it was a marriage for love.

Soon after his marriage, however, Konoe, who already had a
considerable weakness for women, bought a geisha out of the
Gion gay quarters in Kyoto to become his mistress. They met for
the first time at a tea house, the woman recalled after his death.
The prince was in formal attire, drinking quietly, with some ten
geisha surrounding him. Rather than making merry, Konoe
seemed to enjoy just listening to the girls talk and sing. She described his party as so quiet that at first she mistook the prince
for a Buddhist monk. He was tall and dignified, and "he was
quite a dandy in a very Japanese way." Even after she had come
to know him intimately, Konoe told her little about himself.
Sometimes when they walked together he would take out a
Western book and read, which led her to suspect that he was a
student. Several months later, when she learned who he was,
she was shocked, she says in her memoir of the period with
Konoe as a young man.[12]

Looking back, Konoe acknowledged how grateful he was for
having had the opportunity to study under Nishida Kitarō and
Toda Kaiichi. Of his association with Kawakami Hajime in
particular, Konoe noted that "the professor was studying Marx
and he insisted time and again that we had to be able to read and
understand Marx. He had not yet turned toward radicalism at
that time. Whenever I visited his home he would invite me into
his study where we sat with a brazier between us. Smoking cut
tobacco, the professor talked quietly in leisurely conversation
with me. One day he gave me two books: J. Spargo's *Karl Marx,
His Life and Work*, and *Contemporary Social Problems* by Professor
A. Loria of the University of Turin in Italy. Handing me Loria's

book, he said, 'I found this one so interesting that I sat up all night reading it.' The book was fascinating to me, too, and I still remember reading the whole thing at one stretch. In those days Professor Kawakami seemed to be mainly involved in the study of Marxism. He was not yet politically active. Occasionally, however, he would declare, 'One should be always prepared to live in exile for one's convictions.' About a year after I began to visit his home he was ordered to study abroad and went to Europe."[13]

After Konoe's death, Hidemaro recalled that his elder brother often lectured him on socialism. He spoke of one occasion when he was in about the fourth grade and Fumimaro was in middle school: after dinner, Fumimaro remarked that again they had had more than enough to eat that evening while many people in the world were hungry, and he asked Hidemaro what he thought about that. Frightened by such talk, Hidemaro and his younger brothers bought some candies and passed them out to the less fortunate in their neighborhood. Konoe's lectures on socialism were probably deliberate, motivated by the growing hostility Fumimaro felt toward the world after his father's death. The same hostility must have been one factor that drew him to Professor Kawakami's study a few years later. While at Kyoto Imperial University, Konoe translated Oscar Wilde's *The Soul of Man Under Socialism* into Japanese, and it was published in the May and June 1914 issues of the third series of the journal *Shin Shichō*. The May issue was quickly banned, partly because of the radical contents of the essay.

During his time in Kyoto, Konoe became acquainted with Prince Saionji Kimmochi. In December 1912 the second Saionji cabinet fell when it rejected the army's demand for the creation of two additional divisions. The political turnover led to the rise of the Movement for Constitutional Government.[14] The movement grew in strength when Katsura Tarō replaced Saionji and formed his third cabinet. Until then the young Konoe had been antipathetic toward politics; it seemed to him vulgar. But as he daily learned more from the newspapers about the rising tide of the Movement for Constitutional Government, politics began to interest him. At the same time he developed a sympathetic

interest in Saionji and decided he wanted to meet him. Shortly
after Saionji's resignation, without even a letter of introduction, Konoe presented himself at Seifūsō, the statesman's
Kyoto villa. The Saionji family, like the Konoe, had a proud
pedigree deeply rooted in the high-ranking court aristocracy.
They were descended from one of the top noble families called
the nine Seiga houses.[15] The two families had other ties as well.
Before the fall of the Tokugawa regime, Saionji as a young
man had studied calligraphy under Konoe's grandfather, Tadahiro. In 1885, when Konoe's father, Atsumaro, went to study in
Germany and Austria, he was escorted by Saionji, the newly
appointed minister to Austria-Hungary. For these reasons
Konoe's visit was not completely out of order. In fact, during
their first meeting Saionji repeatedly addressed Konoe, still in
his student uniform, as "Your Excellency," which not only
embarrassed Konoe but also made him suspect that Saionji was
ridiculing him. Saionji was quite sincere, however, and was
simply acknowledging that the Konoe family ranked higher than
his own. He continued to address Konoe the same way in later
years. In any event, Konoe's first impression of Saionji was unfavorable, and he did not go back there for some time, although
he was told that the venerable statesman remained concerned
about him. After graduating from the university, Konoe called
on Saionji again. This time, Konoe wrote, Saionji received him
with a completely different attitude. Encouraged and disarmed,
Konoe indulged in youthful tall talk and sought Saionji's advice
on his career.[16]

In November 1918, the year after Konoe's graduation, the
first world war ended in victory for the Allies, and a peace conference was convened in Paris to plan the postwar reconstruction
of the world. Just before the war ended, Konoe had written an
essay entitled "Reject the Anglo-American–Centered Peace"
and published it in the December 15, 1918, issue of the leading
nationalistic journal *Nihon oyobi Nihonjin* (Japan and the Japanese). The article is worth describing at length, because it
reflects Konoe's view of the world at that time.

In the postwar world, Konoe wrote, the ideals of democracy

and humanitarianism will inevitably spread. These ideals are rooted in a sense of equality among men, which is an eternal, universal, and fundamental moral doctrine for the human community. Japan, too, should encourage these democratic and humanitarian trends within its own borders. Unfortunately, however, Japanese opinion leaders are so enthralled by the spectacular pronouncements of Anglo-American politicians that they cannot perceive the conscious and unconscious ways in which the democracy and humanitarianism put forward by Anglo-American spokesmen provide a mask for their own self-interest. Thus our opinion leaders stoop so far as to extol the Anglo-American–centered League of Nations, equating it with universal justice and humanity. The peace that the Anglo-American leaders are urging on us amounts to no more than maintaining a status quo that suits their interests. They are attempting merely to sanctify their own interest in the name of humanity. In declarations and speeches, they insist that this war is a war of democracy and humanitarianism against despotism and militarism; that it is a struggle between justice and violence, good and evil.

We also believe, Konoe continued, that Germany is primarily responsible for the war and was the violator of peace. When, however, the Anglo-American nations attempt to identify the violator of the prewar peace with the enemy of justice and humanity, they are manipulating logic in a cunning way. Only if the prewar European condition had been humane and just would their claims be grounded. But was Europe humane and just? The true nature of the present conflict is a struggle between the established powers and powers not yet established—a struggle between those nations that benefit by maintaining the status quo and those nations which would benefit by its destruction. The former call for peace, and the latter cry for war. In this case pacifism does not necessarily coincide with justice and humanity. Similarly, militarism does not necessarily transgress justice and humanity. The prewar European condition might have suited the Anglo-American powers best, but it never served justice and humanity. At an early stage Britain and France colonized the "less civilized" regions of the world, and monopolized their exploitation. As a result, Germany, and all the late-coming nations also, were left with no land to acquire and no space to expand. Such actions violated the principle of equal opportunity among men and threatened the equal right of existence for all nations. They totally controverted justice and humanity. One could sympathize with Germany, which has justifiably tried to redress the wrongs in this unfair situation.

In short, the pacifism that the Anglo-American powers advocate is a peace-at-any-price, which only those who wish to maintain the status quo would uphold. It has nothing to do with justice and humanity. In actual fact, the present position of Japan in the world, like that of Germany before the war, demands the destruction of the status quo. Nevertheless, our opinion leaders, spellbound by flowery Anglo-American proclamations, mistake peace for humanity. Contaminated by Anglo-American–centered pacifism, they welcome the League of Nations as if it were a gift from heaven. Their attitude represents the height of servility and runs completely contrary to the interests of justice and humanity. We would wholeheartedly welcome the League of Nations if it were established on the principle of true justice and humanity. However, our real fear is that the League of Nations might let the powerful nations dominate the weak nations economically, and condemn the late-coming nations to remain forever subordinate to the advanced nations.

In the coming peace conference, should we decide to join the League of Nations, we must demand as the minimum *sine qua non* the eradication of economic imperialism and discriminatory treatment of Asian peoples by Caucasians. Militarism is not the only force that violates justice and humanity. Economic imperialism, also, by enabling the most powerful to monopolize enormous amounts of capital and natural resources, prevents the free development of other nations and enriches the imperialists without requiring the use of force. Should the peace conference fail to suppress this rampant economic imperialism, the Anglo-American powers will become the economic masters of the world and, in the name of preserving the status quo, dominate it through the League of Nations and arms reduction, thus serving their own selfish interests. Many people in Britain, for example, are urging their country to become self-sufficient and to close its colonies to other nations. In such ways the Anglo-American powers say one thing and do another. Should their policy prevail, Japan, which is small, resource-poor, and unable to consume all its own industrial products, would have no resort but to destory the status quo for the sake of self-preservation, just like Germany. This is true not only of Japan but of all late-coming nations that are small and do not have colonial territories. That is why we must reject economic imperialism, not only for the sake of Japan, but to establish among all nations equally the right of existence based upon the principle of justice and humanity. We must require all the powers to open the doors of their colonies to others, so that all nations will have equal access to the markets and natural resources of the colonial areas. It is also imperative that Japan insist on the eradication of racial discrimination. At the coming peace conference we must demand this in the name of justice and humanity. Indeed, the peace conference will provide the opportunity to determine whether or not the human race is capable of reforming the world on those principles. Japan must not blindly submit to an Anglo-American–centered peace; it must struggle for the fulfillment of its own demands, which are grounded in justice and humanity.[17]

We do not know when and under whose influence Konoe formulated the positions explicit in this essay. But the beliefs stated there by the 27-year-old Konoe remained basically unchanged. They are important, for they continued to influence his entire political career.

After graduating from Kyoto Imperial University, Konoe worked briefly in the Local Affairs Bureau of the Home Ministry. Shortly thereafter Saionji was appointed head of the Japanese delegation to the Paris Peace Conference, which was to open in January 1919, and Konoe successfully petitioned Saionji for a place on it. When the old statesman escorted Konoe's father to Vienna, he probably never dreamed that some 34 years later he would take the younger Konoe to Paris. By the time the Japanese delegation arrived in Shanghai on the N.Y.K. liner *Tambamaru*, Konoe's article "Reject the Anglo-American–Centered Peace" had reached China, where it caused an uproar. Thomas F. Millard, the pro-Chinese American journalist and editor of *Millard's Review*, had taken sharp issue with Konoe's statements and had published a rebuttal in the journal. In it he warned that insofar as Konoe was a member of the Japanese delegation, his opinions merited careful attention. Learning of Millard's response to Konoe's article, Saionji reprimanded Konoe. As an internationalist he attached great importance to Japan's relations with Britain, France, and the United States, and he could not afford to have any member of his delegation stir up antagonism.

During the European trip, according to Konoe, Saionji admonished the young man on several other occasions, probably more out of concern for the future of the young prince than anger. When their ship called at Colombo, the Japanese delegates took a stroll in a park. Coming upon some flowers, Konoe and the others randomly picked a few and continued to chat, sniffing at the flowers in their hands. Outraged, Saionji declared, "How can you be so ill-mannered? Behave yourselves, or I shall never take you abroad again!" Later, in the dining hall, as the ship approached Marseilles, Saionji overheard Konoe and some of the other young men bantering about how to evade the customs inspector's questions. Saionji angrily lectured them: "With such an attitude, how can you pretend to be respectable gentlemen, dignitaries on the international stage?" One day in Paris, the chief delegates were called to a conference from which their aides were specifically barred. Konoe, however, learning that reporters were allowed, attended the conference posing as a reporter for a Japanese newspaper of which he was a stockholder. Saionji was furious. He summoned Konoe and issued an ultimatum: "If you continue to behave like this, I will have to dismiss you from the delegation." Konoe's recollections suggest that Saionji had indeed become a guardian for one of this illustrious family.

In an essay, "My Impressions of the Paris Peace Conference," Konoe wrote that the iron rule of "Power controls" still prevailed intact, and that the peace conference was the best proof of it. He stated that both its organization and operation clearly revealed the tyranny of the great powers. The hope to reform the world upon the principles of justice and equity was quashed at the outset of the conference. The League Covenant rejected the principle of racial equality and accommodated the Monroe Doctrine in the most brazen application of the rule "Power controls." Konoe continued that the League of Nations, ostensibly set up to maintain world peace based on justice, was morally obliged to incorporate the principle of racial equality into the Covenant, but the motion was defeated because Japan, a lesser power, had proposed it. On the other hand, the unjust Monroe Doctrine was codified in the League Covenant because the United States, a big power, demanded it. All the same, Konoe took issue with the view that power alone determined the entire course of the peace conference. President Woodrow Wilson's Fourteen Points, as one example, were trampled and largely dismissed by European politicians, who were concerned only with the interests of their own countries. Of the Fourteen Points, only the principle of national self-determination seemed to affect the conference proceedings to some degree. But the acceptance of this principle gave hope for a brighter future to many small, oppressed powers. The League was far from perfect, but without Wilson's efforts and dedication it would never have come into being at all, and, for this alone, he would be remembered forever in the chronicles of human history. We must not, Konoe concluded,declare "the end of idealism" judging only from the outcome of the Paris Peace Conference. We must remember that world politics is at the point of transition, and it is too soon to make such conclusions.[18]

On the whole, Konoe seems to have believed that the negative results of the peace conference amply vindicated the views he expounded in his controversial "Reject the Anglo-American–Centered Peace" article.

After signing the Treaty of Versailles, Saionji and his retinue left for home. Instead of going straight back, Konoe parted with the delegation and traveled in France and Germany. On his way he stopped to visit Bonn. In an article, "My Rhine Trip," he wrote: "I arrived at Bonn in the evening. As one might expect of a university town, Bonn was not boisterous like other cities.

I found it quiet and restful. An ideal place for study. . . . In 1885 [actually 1886] my father and his two younger brothers, Tsugaru Fusamaro and Tokiwai Gyōyū, came all the way from Japan to attend the university here. Like a dream, more than 30 years has elapsed since then. My father has passed away, and this last spring Uncle Tsugaru followed him. I was shocked when I received the sad news of his death while I was in Paris. As students, the three brothers lived at the house of [Johann Justus] Rein. Mr. Rein was a professor at the University of Bonn. In early Meiji he visited our country and published a book entitled *Japan* in German. . . . Since my childhood I had heard much about Bonn and felt a longing to know the stranger who had been my father's teacher in that distant foreign country. And so when I arrived at the town, I went to the university to inquire about the old professor, only to learn that he also had passed away in January of last year. Saddened, I wanted at least to meet Mrs. Rein and offer my condolences. On the morning of the 25th, I took some flowers and called at the widow's residence. So pleased was she to see me, she virtually hugged me and led me to a parlor, where she tearfully talked to me about the good old days. She told me that her present residence was not the place my father had lived, and that the old house was still standing at such and such a street. After half an hour, I wished her the best of health and bade her farewell. That afternoon, I left the town and its poignant associations, and went on to Cologne."[19]

Konoe deeply missed his late father, and the visit to Bonn was evidently a moving experience for the young prince. He then went on to England and returned to Japan via the United States in November 1919.

His first-hand observation of Europe and America greatly affected Konoe. Many of the traditions he had grown up with, customs and manners in Japan's aristocratic society, as well as the complex conventions and ceremonies long established within the Konoe family, now seemed irrational and meaningless. As he began to express this new sentiment in speech and action, a rumor spread that Konoe was planning to emigrate with his family to the United States. Then the March 1920 issue of the leading women's monthly magazine *Fujin Kōron* published an article under Konoe's name, entitled "As I Leave Unpleasant Japan," in which he said that he planned to take a trip abroad with his family in the near future. The newspapers erroneously reported that Konoe found Japan so inimical that he had decided to emigrate permanently. All he really wanted to do, as he said in the article, was to go abroad and to send his family home in due time, while he himself would stay behind for one to two years more. However unpleasant Japan might be, so long as he was a Japanese and had a career to carry on, he could not leave the country forever. Quite honestly, he said, Japan was not a comfortable place to live. "Should I be asked what I am unhappy about in our country, I would readily answer that 'everything I see and hear makes me unhappy,' not to mention the mundane matters of food, clothing, and residence; everything is bound by tradition, imperfection, and artificiality. I think they need reform from top to bottom." Praising the British royal family for their democratic manners, he said he hated social conventions and deplored the cumbersome customs of Japan's aristocratic society. He asserted: "Nobody, aristocrat or commoner, should raise an eyebrow or consider it unnatural if an aristocrat behaves like a commoner, in whatever matter it may be." He urged his countrymen to change their rice diet and to improve their housing and clothing. "I sorely miss life in the West," he said, "where I could put on my shoes as soon as I got out of bed in the morning. Back in Japan, I had to wear a kimono, because I frequently attended banquets and other functions where one had to sit or kneel on *tatami*. Our half-Japanese and half-Western life strains us. Without that duality our life would be much better." He went on to discuss the orderly European and American transportation systems. Because everything was so organized in the West and people were so well disciplined, life was comfortable. He added that Western workers enjoyed high social status and received good treatment from their employers.

There was more to this article, which was based on an interview with a reporter. It contained some misrepresentations, but it was probably to some extant a reflection of Konoe's state of mind immediately after his European trip. The next issue of

Fujin Kōron, however, carried a short "Apologia" in Konoe's name. After the March issue came out, it said, Konoe was harrassed by political bullies and threatening letters. He held to his opinion, it went on, that life in Japan could be very uncomfortable, but at the same time he believed it his duty to help make the country a place worth living in. In fact, the more discontented he became with things Japanese, the more patriotic he grew. We cannot, he said, demand the Japanese people to close their eyes to the shortcomings of their country and convince themselves of its perfection. Only a hopelessly narrow-minded or prejudiced pseudopatriot could impose such a demand.

Both Konoe's interview and "Apologia" leave the impression of a lively, straightforward, and self-confident youth. Konoe was then 29 years old. Incidentally, his plan for another trip abroad did not materialize at that time.

2

A NEW STAR IN POLITICS

Konoe returned from his trip invigorated with new and progressive ideas, and he soon made a name for himself as an energetic young noble who promised to inject new life into politics. His title had assured him a hereditary seat in the House of Peers, and he had been a member since October 1916, when he was still a Kyoto University student. In December 1921, when the 45th Imperial Diet convened, the upper house elected the 30-year-old prince acting president.

Increasingly, Konoe was regarded as the hope of the aristocratic class in politics. Nevertheless, his activities in the House of Peers were not always beyond reprehension. When he was made acting president, he had been critical of certain practices and procedures in the upper house, and he had advocated reform. But then in September 1922, he joined the Kenkyūkai, a powerful faction in the upper house since the early 1890s, the first years of the Imperial Diet. Konoe's affiliation with the Kenkyūkai stirred up a torrent of outrage and criticism. The faction had created a very bad public reputation for questionable dealings with the successive cabinets and widespread corruption among its members. In fact, Konoe's demand for reform in the House of Peers was originally directed at the dubious activities of the Kenkyūkai. Konoe later admitted that he was opening himself to attack when he joined the faction.

Some time before he joined, Konoe had become acquainted with Viscount Mizuno Naoshi, a leading member of the Kenkyūkai. According to Konoe, he was very close to Mizuno until he left the faction. Mizuno was not only one of the most influential leaders of the Kenkyūkai but was also widely known as a political strategist and intriguer. The close association they formed, and Konoe's motives in joining the Kenkyūkai in the first place, pose interesting questions. Mindful of Konoe's growing reputation and his intimate connections with the Genrō Saionji,[1] Mizuno seems to have sought collaboration with the young prince in order to strengthen both his own position within the Kenkyūkai and the political influence of the faction. On the other hand, Konoe probably joined the Kenkyūkai with the hope of some day controlling the faction, as Izawa Takio, member of the House of Peers, later surmised.[2] If so, Mizuno and Konoe both were using each other for their own objectives.[3] In that light, Konoe's approaches to Mizuno and his decision to join the Kenkyūkai reflected a thirst for power and a penchant for political intrigue.

In January 1924, Emperor Taishō, in accordance with the recommendation of the Genrō, ordered Viscount Kiyoura Keigo to form a cabinet. Manipulated by Kenkyūkai leaders, Kiyoura filled all the cabinet posts except those of the army, navy, and foreign ministers with factional and independent members of the House of Peers. Naturally Kenkyūkai members were among the new ministers. The subsequent public outcry spurred three political parties, the Seiyūkai, the Kenseikai, and the Kakushin Kurabu,[4] to launch another Movement for Constitutional Government. Konoe did not stand back but condemned the Kenkyūkai's maneuver for power, stating that it undermined the proper functioning of the upper house. In any case, the Kiyoura cabinet was defeated in a general election and was replaced by the first Katō cabinet in June 1924. This was a coalition cabinet of the three parties mentioned above under Prime Minister Katō Takaaki, president of the Kenseikai, which had emerged as the leading party in the general election.

Saionji, who had great hopes for Konoe's political future, continued to keep a protective watch over his political activities. One day just before the Kiyoura cabinet was replaced, Konoe called on Saionji in Kyoto and asked him to introduce him to Matsumoto Gōkichi. Matsumoto was what might be called a political purveyor (*seikai rōnin*), an independent operator privy to many confidential, behind-the-scenes political moves. He had won the confidence of the genrō Yamagata Aritomo by providing him from time to time with useful political information. After Yamagata's death in 1922, Matsumoto began to frequent the Saionji residence, performing the same service. Saionji personally conveyed Konoe's wish to Matsumoto, who recorded verbatim in his diary what the Genrō said to him that day:

> "The other day [Saionji related] Prince Konoe came to see me and spoke of various ill-informed matters. At the end of his talk, the prince said that he wanted to meet Matsumoto Gōkichi, whom he understood to be a frequent visitor to me, and the prince asked me to introduce him to you. I told the prince, 'It would be a good idea. Matsumoto is a man conversant with political affairs. You might as well receive some guidance in politics directly from him. . . .' I am under the impression that Konoe will one day be a leader of the Kenkyūkai, but he is still young and inexperienced. Actually, we are relatives and his father was a person of fine character. Some years ago, I took the young prince along when I attended the Paris Peace Conference. After graduation from university, he must have dabbled in new novels. I understand that some people suspected him of harboring dangerous leftist thoughts. But he is no fool, and of late he seems to be behaving quite prudently."
>
> At this point, believing Konoe to be still in Kyoto, Prince Saionji telephoned to ask him to join us for dinner. But the young prince had already left for Tokyo by the morning special express. The Genrō then asked me to see Prince Konoe, as he would visit me one of these days. . . . I assured Prince Saionji that I would call on the young prince.[5]

Among other things, this entry in the Matsumoto diary reveals the affectionate concern Saionji felt for the young prince. Shortly afterward Matsumoto met with Konoe, thus beginning their political contact.

About the time when the first Katō cabinet was formed in June 1924, Konoe assumed a post on the standing committee of the Kenkyūkai. While Konoe's advancement was decided through a special election held to fill committee vacancies, it greatly pleased Saionji. Meanwhile, the membership of the entire standing committee was scheduled for reelection in November 1924. In October Saionji asked Matsumoto to see that measures be taken to boost the authority of the Kenkyūkai by retaining Konoe on the standing committee and to include Mizuno Naoshi and Viscount Aoki Nobumitsu on the committee as support for the young prince.[6] Konoe was subsequently reelected to the standing committee.

As Konoe's political standing rose, some of those who had deserted the family after the death of Atsumaro began now to court his favor, reasserting their old ties with his late father. In the meantime, in July 1924, some of Atsumaro's old associates erected a monument in his memory at the Konoe mansion in Mejiro, where he had died. At its unveiling, Fumimaro addressed the gathering, using notes written himself:

> I am sincerely grateful for the kind gesture you have made in dedicating this monument to my father. When he was with us, he was blessed with your warm friendship and support. Unfortunately in 1904, he met an untimely death here—at the place where this monument stands. Two decades have passed since then, like a dream. During these many years, your friendship toward my late father has never changed, and today it bears fruit in this splendid monument erected at this place where my father passed away. I am deeply moved by your loyal friendship. Friends often drift away from one another, and friendship can be a changeable thing. In this world, where, sad to say, the proverb "Out of sight, out of mind" so often prevails, I will cherish the memory of my father at this monument, which symbolizes the beautiful friendship you have extended to us over these long twenty years.

While this short and sentimental address conveys the longing Konoe still felt for his father, it also vents some of his indignation at human unreliability. Atsumaro's widow, Motoko, later commented about the address, "It must have stung, for some of those attending the ceremony had turned away from us. I thought Fumimaro said what ought to be said."[7]

The first Katō cabinet was a product of the Movement for

Constitutional Government and that circumstance strained the relationship between the cabinet and the Kenkyūkai enough to create considerable trouble for the prime minister. This prompted Konoe, in collaboration with Mizuno, to act as a liaison between the Katō cabinet and the Kenkyūkai. The government presented a universal manhood suffrage bill to the 50th Imperial Diet session in 1925. The bill encountered strong opposition in the House of Peers, which obstructed deliberation, but Konoe supported it, arguing that the house, in its proper function as the second house of the Diet, was bound to take up the bill. His contribution to its passage attracted wide public attention.

About when the suffrage bill was being debated in the Diet, Matsumoto Gōkichi called on Saionji. He remarked to the Genrō that no one could tell what the next cabinet would be like, but if anyone from the Kenkyūkai was to have a place in it, Prince Konoe should be recommended so long as his health permitted. Konoe was still young, Matsumoto further noted, and the times seemed to favor the young. Saionji emphatically agreed.[8]

Konoe's action in joining the Kenkyūkai was not the only incident in which his behavior was questioned. In January 1926, when Prime Minister Katō died, Wakatsuki Reijirō became president of the Kenseikai and was asked to form a new cabinet. Shortly afterward, Wakatsuki attempted a cabinet reshuffle in order to strengthen his government by setting up a coalition with the Seiyūhontō, a party created by former Seiyūkai members who had broken away in opposition to the Movement for Constitutional Government. Aligning himself with Mizuno, Aoki, and other Kenkyūkai leaders, Konoe stood behind the attempted coalition government, and in so doing he once more opened himself to attack. Critics pounced on the Kenkyūkai and Konoe, too, recalling with distaste the faction's scheming for advantage when the Kiyoura cabinet was formed. It was an ironic turn of events for Konoe, who had condemned the action of the Kenkyūkai at that time. The Kenkyūkai-Seiyūhontō coalition, in any case, did not materialize.

In December 1926, the Kenkyūkai held another election to choose new standing committee members, but before the election took place Konoe was appointed to a newly created post of advisor. Details are not known, but evidently his change of position was designed to remove him from the power center of the faction. A year later he left the Kenkyūkai. He must have realized that it was impossible for him to wield influence in, much less control, a faction that suffered from such serious internal dissension. At that point Konoe formed a new political faction, the Kayōkai ("Tuesday Club"), consisting of all upper house members with the title of prince or marquis. In February 1928 Konoe announced that his purpose in the Kayōkai was to help guide the upper house in performing what he called its proper function.

Three months later, in May, Konoe became involved in what is known as the Imperial Message Incident. When Prime Minister Tanaka Giichi announced his decision to appoint Kuhara Fusanosuke to a post in his Seiyūkai cabinet, Mizuno Rentarō, the minister of education, tendered his resignation in protest, only to change his mind almost immediately and withdraw his resignation. The decision to remain in his post was made, ostensibly, in deference to the express wish of the Emperor. Mizuno was censured for his vacillation and in the end forced to resign, and Tanaka's handling of the incident also became a political issue. Konoe's Kayōkai joined other upper house factions in pressing Tanaka to assume responsibility. In February 1929, during the 56th Imperial Diet session, the House of Peers took the extraordinary step of passing a bill of censure against the prime minister. Konoe had been instrumental in moving the upper house to pass this almost unprecedented bill.

Tanaka resigned in July 1929, and he was succeeded by Hamaguchi Osachi, president of the Minseitō.[9] In making its political appointments, the newly formed Hamaguchi government wanted to appoint Izawa Takio governor-general of Korea, which was then a Japanese colony. Izawa gave his informal consent. While he disapproved of Konoe's less than proper social life and frequent games of golf, he wanted Konoe to accompany him to Korea, where the prince could acquire political and administrative experience. Izawa planned to have Konoe succeed him as governor-general after a few years and make Gotō Fumio, who would be appointed chief of the Korean Political Affairs Board, Konoe's principal aide. Saionji liked the idea, but army opposition blocked Izawa's appointment, and he never became governor-general of Korea.[10]

In January 1931, Konoe was elected vice president of the House of Peers. He was 39 years old. There occurred that year the first in a series of crises for Japan, domestic and international, that would go on and would escalate for many years to come. The so-called March Incident[11] centered on events in Manchuria, the area to the north of China where Japan already had a large financial and political stake. Chiang Kai-shek's National Revolutionary Army had reached Peking and completed the Northern Expedition by June 1928. In December 1929, the Manchurian warlord Chang Hsüeh-liang announced his allegiance to the Nationalist government, finally bringing about the long-sought, but only temporary, unification of China. Urged on by the Nationalist party's cry for "Down with Imperialist Powers," the Chinese people grew increasingly more agitated in their demands for the recovery of their national sovereignty. Japanese were all too aware that the vast rights and interests they had accumulated over many years in China, above all in Manchuria and Mongolia, now faced a precarious future. The effects of the Great Depression which was triggered by the Wall Street crash of October 1929, reached Japan the following January. By accelerating the formation of tight economic blocs throughout the world, the depression put Japanese industry and foreign trade into dire jeopardy. At the same time it dealt a devastating blow to Japanese farmers and small- and medium-scale urban industrialists. Public distrust of both the party in power and the cabinet grew steadily deeper as the effects of the depression at home and in the world economy took their toll. Much of the population was in urgent straits and nerves were already frayed when the army, the young officers in particular, began to demand a military solution for the Manchurian-Mongolian problem as well as immediate political reform and national reconstruction. Unwilling to wait any longer, a group of young army officers planned a coup d'état in March 1931, but it was exposed before any action had occurred.

Two months later, with tension mounting daily, Konoe and

Mori Kaku, former chief secretary of the Seiyūkai, met at the Komazawa golf course. Konoe had become acquainted with Mori some ten years before, and together they had formed the Kempō Kenkyūkai (Constitution Study Group), whose members included several other young members of both houses of the Diet. The group discussed various issues in foreign and domestic politics, but above all upper house reform. Konoe had had little contact with Mori for a number of years before the meeting at the golf course, and he found him to be no longer an advocate of party politics, according to Konoe's memory of the reunion. Mori said something to the effect that "the world is changing drastically. We simply cannot afford to remain caught up with such trivia as party politics and the House of Peers."

At the time, Konoe was so blissfully unaware of what was going on even right around him that he did not know about the March Incident[11] until Arima Yoriyasu[12] told him what had happened long after the event. Because of Mori's remark, Konoe recalled, "I began to take note of current trends and events."[13] Thereafter, Konoe often visited Mori, who was beginning to lean toward fascism. Konoe also began setting up contacts with some of the young army officers and their sympathizers, mainly right-wing activists, to learn of their views. Konoe's principal intermediaries in establishing contacts with the right wing were Mori Kaku and Shiga Naokata. Shiga had been a student at the Peers School when Konoe Atsumaro was its president. Later he became a professional soldier and was wounded in the Russo-Japanese War, at last retiring from the army with the rank of captain. Out of a lasting sense of indebtedness to Atsumaro, he wanted to assist Fumimaro in achieving political success, and he helped him expand his connections with the reformist camp, as the political Right was called at the time. Konoe became particularly intimate with the army officers who were soon to become the core of the Kōdōha (Imperial Way faction),[14] and with the so-called idealist right wingers (*kannen uyoku*)[15] from Hiranuma Kiichirō on down, who aligned themselves with the Kōdōha. Konoe seems to have been interested in these groups partly because he found their fervent clamor to realize Japan's "national polity" (*kokutai*)[16] reassuring. Also, Shiga, his intermediary, was associated closely with Araki Sadao, a central figure in the Kōdōha.

In September 1931, the Manchurian Incident erupted and that led into the Shanghai Incident the following January. In March the "independent" state of Manchukuo was proclaimed. As events followed one after another, heightening tension charged the atmosphere in and around Japan. One month after the outbreak of the Manchurian Incident, a plot by young officers to carry out another coup d'état, commonly known as the October Incident,[17] was exposed. Then in 1932, the nation was shocked when a rightist terrorist group, the Ketsumeidan, assassinated former finance minister Inoue Junnosuke of the Minseitō in February, and a top Mitsui zaibatsu executive, Dan Takuma, in March. The May 15th Incident[18] followed two months later.

Konoe's position regarding these events is made quite clear in an article he wrote in 1933 entitled, "Improving Our World." Konoe wrote to the effect that:

> since the Manchurian Incident, Japanese actions in the region have been questioned many times by the League of Nations. Japan seems to be in the position of a defendant being tried in the name of world peace before an international court. It is time now that we explain to the world why Japan's national survival compels us to act this way, and state our honest convictions about how true world peace can be achieved. It is important that the so-called pacifists in the West reflect upon our position. War breaks out because unreasonable conditions exist among nations. A distribution of land can hardly be called reasonable when it confines some nations with growing populations and a capacity for expansion within narrow territory, while other sparsely populated nations enjoy vast territories and abundant resources. Should the wishes of these self-styled pacifists prevail, nothing will change. No nation dissatisfied with the present state of the world will tolerate that.

World War I had little to do with justice versus brute force. It was a conflict between the advanced nations that would benefit from maintaining the status quo and the less developed nations that sought to destroy it. Therefore it is not only futile, but unreasonable and unjust to try to eliminate war, while the real cause of conflict, the unfair conditions of the world, remain intact. What can we do to remove these conditions and achieve true peace? At the least, freedom of economic transactions must be secured, and freedom of migration must be recognized. But Japan's economic life is threatened by a population that is growing by almost one million annually. We must find a means of survival immediately. We cannot simply wait until we have the freedom of economic transactions and migration. However, Europeans and Americans condemn the Japanese actions in Manchuria and Mongolia in the name of world peace. They criticize us by invoking the Convenant of the League of Nations and the Kellogg-Briand Pact, and some even call us, the Japanese, the public enemy of peace and humanity. It is, in fact, the Europeans and Americans who are the unmovable block to world peace. They are in no position to judge us. Japan knew that there were no immediate prospects of establishing the foundations for the true peace, freedom of economic transactions and migration, and we had no choice but to advance into Manchuria and Mongolia. It was a matter of national survival. The peoples of Europe and America must cease attempting to incriminate us for action taken solely for national survival. They should, rather, do everything in their power to realize true world peace.[19]

Using the same argument in this article that he set forth in "Reject the Anglo-American–Centered Peace," Konoe vigorously defended the Japanese conquest of Manchuria. That support gained him wide popularity among military officers and right-wing activists, but they valued his political usefulness to them as much as his political views. He was of noble birth, he was young, and he had intimate connections with the court, the Genrō, and the senior statesmen; he would be extremely useful in the promotion of their foreign and domestic programs, they reasoned. Thus the ultranationalist and rightist groups began to count Konoe, along with Araki and Hiranuma, among their future candidates for prime minister.

Konoe's situation was precarious. Japan's activities, particularly since the Manchurian Incident, had generated enough suspicion abroad that the court, the Genrō, and senior statesmen were all deeply concerned about the future. Konoe, on the other hand, despite being intimately bound to the ruling elite, showed a certain sympathy toward the military and rightists who supported expansionist policies. Konoe's recommendations and opinions often perplexed his superiors and elders. In February 1932, when Inukai Tsuyoshi was prime minister, Konoe told Baron Harada Kumao, Saionji's secretary,[20] that it was vital to prevent Hiranuma Kiichirō from pushing Imperial Prince Fushimi Hiroyasu for the post of Lord Keeper of the Privy Seal, if Hiranuma himself could not assume the post; he would be able to manipulate the prince and carry his scheming into the court. This posed a dangerous possibility, Konoe said, and he recommended that they seize the initiative and appoint the imperial prince to the post of Privy Seal themselves and make Hiranuma, Makino Nobuaki, Ichiki Kitokurō, and Saitō Makoto his aides. Konoe suggested that only by moving first and rearranging the personnel around the throne could Hiranuma's intrigue be forestalled.

Later, Konoe made the same suggestion directly to Saionji. He must have been thinking that the court representatives had to adopt a policy of appeasement and comply with some of the demands of the extreme right, which had been growing rapidly stronger since the Manchurian Incident. Such a move—'seizing the initiative'—would be the only way to keep those forces from penetrating the court itself. When in March Konoe visited Saionji at Zagyosō, his villa in Okitsu, Shizuoka Prefecture, he remarked that the Emperor's liberalism might have been the main cause of his clash with the army. To Saionji this sounded very much like a criticism of the Emperor for his liberalism. Konoe kept stressing also that future prime ministers must reject any temporizing and carry out drastic innovation. He further suggested that the Genrō 'seize the initiative' and recommend Hiranuma or Araki as prime minister. Soon afterward, Mori Kaku also expounded his stand against 'temporizing measures' to Saionji, making him suspect that Konoe had been manipulated by Mori.

Unlike Konoe, Saionji was deeply troubled by developments since the Manchurian Incident. He was particularly discouraged around the time when Konoe came to propose his idea on the Privy Seal post. Saionji told Konoe that Japanese politics were moving against his long-cherished ideal. In selecting prime ministers, he could not bear to recommend someone from the military. Unless he acted with utmost prudence and resolution, he would bring eternal shame on himself, and so he was seriously contemplating giving up his role as Genrō and his title. The senior court officials were astonished when they learned of this from Konoe. It was only with some difficulty that they managed to convince Saionji to change his mind. He was, in any case, in no frame of mind to condone Konoe and his obvious shift toward the extreme Right.

Nevertheless, Saionji was still the guardian, holding great expectations for his protégé. In March 1932, he told Harada that it might be wise to make Konoe president of the House of Peers at the earliest possible chance, thus removing him from the reach of various political movements, and only when it became necessary have him take the reins of government. The following month, however, Saionji confided to Harada that it would be better both for the court and the nation to appoint Konoe president of the upper house as quickly as possible and then some time later promote him to the post of Privy Seal, not prime minister. Whoever the prime minister, no one could successfully manage the present political situation. Saionji had decided that Konoe should wait for a better day to form his own cabinet.

In May 1932, the May 15th Incident brought down the Inukai cabinet. Saionji was summoned to the imperial palace from Okitsu. He recommended to Emperor Hirohito that the former governor-general of Korea, Admiral Saitō Makoto, be appointed as Inukai's successor. Saitō formed a cabinet and included members of the two major political parties, the Seiyūkai and the Minseitō, among his ministers.

Immediately after the May 15th Incident and before Saionji was summoned to the palace, Konoe visited him at Okitsu. At a press conference afterward, Konoe emphatically rejected the conjecture that he had represented to Prince Saionji the interests of Baron Hiranuma and the military. The very strength of his denial, however, suggests that Konoe's behavior at the time had actually generated considerable suspicion. At that meeting, Konoe later recollected, he had told Saionji that he had but two choices: one, to instruct the majority party leader to form a cabinet with the intention of upholding party politics and parliamentary government; the other, to take the heavy risk of letting the military lead the government. Should he choose the latter, Konoe argued, the military would cease to interfere with politics as a "government outside the government." Moreover, once they tried to take on the full burden of governing, the military would certainly fail and, as a result, lose all their political standing.

Saionji silently listened, but shortly afterward, rejecting both choices, asked Saitō Makoto to form an interim cabinet. Prince Saionji, Konoe wrote, believed in the principle of party government, but he feared that another party cabinet which lacked public confidence would only produce greater friction with the military. He also feared that if the military took charge of the government, their radical policies might be carried out of control. Saionji hoped, Konoe wrote, that even if the interim cabinet could not halt the military altogether, it would slow them down as much as possible. "It would yield, only when circumstances rendered it impossible to restrain the military. Even then, the cabinet would endeavor to delay and minimize the baneful effects of concession."[21]

Konoe was sharply critical of Saionji's choice of an interim government. He wrote about this in another of his memoirs: Prince Saionji insisted that the young officers were delirious at the time and that it would be wisest to avoid inciting them and wait for them to calm down. Then Japanese diplomacy would get back on track, following the principles of international cooperation advanced by Foreign Minister Shidehara Kijūrō.[22] Konoe believed that Japan's course of action was determined by events in the world; the nation had to follow "an unavoidable fate," regardless of the young officers' demands or occurrences like the Manchurian Incident. Prince Saionji urged government leaders to wait until the military grew less excitable, but the army officers were not going to calm down as long as politicians failed to understand the nation's destiny, argued Konoe. On the contrary, his memoir continued, they would drive the nation even harder in the "direction that destiny dictates." Granted, it would be extremely dangerous to let the soldiers direct national policy. Therefore, Konoe wrote, he told Saionji that the only way politicians could swiftly recover control of government was by perceiving the nation's destiny and meeting it squarely. Civilian leaders must carry out the necessary reforms if they wished to impede the political rise of the military.[23]

Saionji remained convinced that Konoe's best course was to become president of the House of Peers first. He told Harada that if Konoe went directly into the office of Privy Seal or prime minister, he would inevitably suffer a political setback and his service to the Emperor would be foreshortened. Then in June 1933, Tokugawa Iesato finally left the office after 30 years, and Konoe became president of the upper house. Konoe Atsumaro was Tokugawa's predecessor. Thus with 30 years intervening, Fumimaro followed his father into the post.

In October, when Kido Kōichi, chief secretary to the Lord Keeper of the Privy Seal, visited Okitsu, Saionji declared that as far as he was concerned, Konoe was unusually competent and practically irreplaceable. This opinion, he said, was not based on their close family ties or affection. He wanted to protect Konoe from being battered and bruised in the fray of politics, but would not stop him if he wanted to go forward with clear objectives. Kido agreed with Saionji's suggestion that Konoe remain for two or three years as president of the House of Peers, and then take the office of Privy Seal or president of the Privy Council. Saionji added that there were only two options in deciding the course of Japanese politics: to surrender the government to a military dictatorship or to take gradual steps to improve the situation until parliamentary government should be restored. If a military dictatorship won the support even of people like

Konoe, Saionji declared, he could not accept that; he would have no alternative but to fade away, a man of the past. Saionji still had great hopes for Konoe and a solid future for him in politics. If Konoe plunged into the current political thicket at this point, when he was already inclined toward the extreme Right, Saionji feared he would quickly become a puppet of the military and the right wing. For the sake of both Konoe and the nation, Saionji wanted to keep him away from the center of politics for the time being. He hoped that as the political situation calmed down, Konoe himself would begin to think and act more prudently.

In the spring of 1934, Prime Minister Saitō decided that to turn the premiership over to Konoe would revive the nation politically. Saionji opposed the idea when he learned of it from Harada; Konoe should go as intended to the United States and have a chance to look at Japan from the outside. Thus when Saitō called on Saionji in April to convey his wish to resign, the Genrō persuaded him to remain in office.

In May Konoe left for America. Ostensibly, the purpose of his trip was to attend the high school commencement ceremony of his eldest son, Fumitaka. But his real objective was to explain Japan's position to American leaders and gain their understanding for the Japanese viewpoint in recent years. Before he left, Konoe paid formal respects at the Imperial Sanctuary and then reported the details of his trip to the Emperor. Just as he was about to take leave, the Emperor said in a moving personal gesture, "Take good care of yourself." Saionji happened to visit the empress dowager's palace the same day. He told her that some of the nobility must dedicate themselves to the service of the imperial nation, and that Prince Konoe seemed to be the most promising candidate. The empress dowager seemed exceedingly pleased by his remark. She also, apparently, had high expectations for Konoe. Harada heard about this episode from Saionji and recorded in his diary, "How I wish that the expectations of such people would guide Konoe to be more prudent."

Konoe stayed in America for almost fifty days, and during that time he perceived strong antipathy and distrust toward Japan. Japanese-American relations had steadily deteriorated

since September 1932, when the Saitō government had recognized Manchukuo, particularly after Japan announced its
withdrawal from the League of Nations in March 1933. Americans were growing increasingly wary of Japan.

In July 1934, when Konoe was still abroad, a scandal commonly known as the Teikoku Jinken Incident[24] brought the
Saitō cabinet down. It was succeeded by another interim government under Admiral Okada Keisuke, whom Saionji had recommended to the Emperor for the same reason for which he
had presented Saitō as candidate. Saionji confided to Kido
after Okada had formed a cabinet that for the time being they
probably could do nothing to avoid being dragged along by the
military. It was important not to strain the situation any more
than it was. Like handling an unruly horse, he said, we must
keep to our principles but we cannot help being dragged around
a little. "It is nevertheless unpleasant indeed," he declared.
When Konoe heard of the change of government, once more
he strongly disapproved of setting up an interim cabinet. He
returned to Japan in early August. Konoe had been sent off to
the United States by Prime Minister Saitō at Yokohama pier,
and on his return he was met at Tokyo station by Prime
Minister Okada, Privy Council President Ichiki, and the cabinet
ministers. This was indeed a prestigious group of dignitaries,
symbolizing the status that Konoe then enjoyed among the
ruling elite.

The following month Konoe told Harada that the general
public, particularly the right wing, criticized the Genrō, the
Privy Seal, and others around the throne as being westernizers.
Now Konoe suggested placing someone known to have rightist
leanings in the Emperor's personal advisory group in order to
ward off criticism directed at the Imperial Court. This was the
same line of thinking that earlier prompted him to recommend
Hiranuma Kiichirō as aide to the Emperor on the Privy Seal
secretariat. Saionji responded to Konoe's suggestion, related
to him by Harada, with adamant opposition. He rejected the
appointment of a rightist, whom he declared to be generally
fanatical, to the Imperial Court or to the Ministry of the
Imperial Household. It was both unreasonable and undesirable,

he stated, to ask sensible people to accommodate themselves to right-wing demands. Knowing that he would not live much longer, Saionji adjured Konoe, Kido, and Harada to cooperate in keeping the fanatical element well away from the court and the Imperial Household.

Saionji's unmoving opposition rankled the increasingly dissatisfied Konoe. He began to vent his frustration in critical remarks about the Genrō. In the autumn of 1934, Tomita Kenji, then head of Ishikawa Prefecture's police department, met Konoe for the first time and commented on the inertia and corruption among party politicians, their blindness to current public distrust of the established parties, and the palpable discontent among the young officers and the people as a whole. Konoe startled Tomita by replying that the political parties were useless. The Imperial Diet—both houses—was helpless. He could understand very well, he said, the young army officers' impatience with the inertia and obtuseness of the parliamentarians. He voiced doubts that parliamentary government was equipped to pull the nation out of the crisis. If it was not, he concluded, parliamentarism should be destroyed, and the guardian of parliamentary government was Saionji. "He is the citadel," he said.

Some two years later, Harada recorded in his diary something he heard from Yanagida Seijirō, an official of the Bank of Japan: In late 1935, Iijima Hanji, head of the economic department of the *Osaka Asahi* newspaper, attended a private meeting with Konoe in Kyoto. Iijima later told Yanagida that Konoe did not sound as radical as Kuhara Fusanosuke, who was openly advocating the destruction of the "Genrō–senior statesmen bloc." But Konoe commented that Saionji was old and he tired easily from meeting people. He said that the Genrō's understanding of current affairs was considerably out of date, and the senior statesmen were more or less the same. In the final analysis, he concluded, they were "obstacles" to the national policy. According to Iijima, this remark made a very strange impression on the audience. They found it hard to understand why he had expressed such an opinion. Harada added in his diary that perhaps because Konoe mingled with "all sorts of extremists," their sentiments sometimes rubbed off on him.

In October 1934, a preliminary meeting before the Naval Disarmament Conference of 1935 had been held in London. Under heavy pressure from the navy, the Okada cabinet decided to reject any agreements based on ratio and instructed the Japanese delegation to the London talks to demand absolute parity with the British and American navies. As a result, the preliminary meeting broke up with Japan in sharp opposition to the United States and Britain. Shortly thereafter Japan notified the other parties that it would not renew either the Washington or London Naval Disarmament treaties at the expiration of their terms. The naval conference convened as planned in December 1935, but it was abruptly adjourned in January 1936, when the Japanese delegation walked out. The following December both the Washington and London treaties were terminated, beginning an era of unrestricted arms escalation on both sides of the Pacific and further deterioration in Japan's international relations.

Meanwhile, in November 1935, Konoe delivered a speech entitled "The Basic Issue in International Peace" at the Nihon Seinen Kan. In it, he summarized an article by Colonel Edward M. House on the need for an international New Deal, which had appeared in the September issue of the American journal *Liberty*. According to Konoe's article, Colonel House had written that the world was divided between nations with huge territories and abundant resources and those without either. The summary continued: Just as social peace within a nation cannot be sustained if the present capitalistic economic system is not modified to some extent, international peace, too, is threatened unless nations with abundant territories and resources share some of their wealth with nations less well endowed. Britain, the United States, the Soviet Union, and France are 'monopolizing' much of the world. Their peoples should heed the demands of the three great peoples of Japan, Germany, and Italy, and share their huge holdings under some appropriate terms.

Konoe added that Colonel House was an elder statesman of the Democratic party, and his views were important. Similar views were advocated, he said, by Viscount Philip Snowden, Sir Samuel Hoare, and other influential British politicians. Konoe then stated his own opinion. There are two basic causes of war, he began. One is the unfair distribution of territories among nations and the other, the maldistribution of resources. The first precondition for lasting world peace is to rectify that imbalance among nations. But the tendency so far has been to seek only the eradication of war without doing anything to remove the unjust conditions of the world. The Allies, especially Britain and the United States, called World War I a struggle between pacifism and militarism, but it was actually a war between the advanced nations, which wanted to maintain the status quo, and the late-comers, which demanded its destruction. In short, the former turned to pacifism and the latter aggression. The war ended in victory for the Allied Powers, and they established a peace structure in the League of Nations that would serve to support the status quo. If nothing is done, the late-coming nations will be forever subordinated to the advanced nations. Even if the territorial distribution remains unchanged, world peace could be achieved by establishing true freedom of migration and trade. But as long as these two basic conditions are not realized, it is right to question the maintenance of the territorial status quo.

Konoe continued: as Colonel House recognizes, Japan, like Germany and Italy, is in a position that is not always compatible with the peace structure built to keep the status quo firm. It is unfortunate that many Japanese have gone along with that principle of peace in the belief that it is supported by most of the world. But no such world opinion has developed spontaneously; it has been artificially molded, sometimes by England or the United States and at other times by Russia, France, or some other country. They do what they want or believe in the name of world opinion. And we Japanese have accepted this opinion as if it were a divine command, lacking the will and spirit to examine it and correct it when necessary. Our leaders cannot seem to come out and declare the need for territorial expansion by acquisition, unlike German and Italian politicians. We have been so brainwashed by the virtually sacred Anglo-American idea of a peace structure based on the status quo that we defended our action in the Manchurian Incident like the accused standing before a judge. World peace can no longer be guaranteed by this peace structure.

Japan and the other late-coming nations should have demanded a worldwide "new deal" long ago. But when such progressive views arise even among the British and American politicians, we know that times are changing. I hope Japan will vigorously encourage this change until the remarkable views of Colonel House and others become the views of the world.[25]

House's concept of an international New Deal coincided with Konoe's long-cherished idea outlined in his essay "Reject the Anglo-American–Centered Peace." In an enthusiastic response Konoe sent in to *Liberty* a piece praising House's stand as far-sighted. The time has come, he wrote, when the United States, Britain, France, and the Soviet Union must think seriously about the future and courageously bring this New Deal into being. Konoe urged Colonel House to help push the Powers into action by providing them with his own concrete program.

About this time another political scheme was launched. Collaborating with the right wing, a group of politicians worked behind the scenes to have Konoe replace Okada as prime minister. Right-wing activists, on their part, challenged the idea, rooted in legal theory, that the Emperor was merely an organ of government[26] and in so doing ignited a national controversy. That, in addition to their movement to "clarify the national polity"—which meant, among other things, to explicitly recognize a sacred mission for Japan—brought the government to the brink of collapse. Again, in December 1935, a plan was conceived to form a new political party with Konoe as president by combining part of the Seiyūkai with the Minseitō. It was hoped that, if Konoe were made president, his high standing among the military and the political Right would help the parties regain some of their influence, which had declined after the May 15th Incident. Konoe expressed no interest in the idea, however, and it never got off the ground.

About then Makino, then in the office of Privy Seal, and Privy Council President Ichiki were both trying to relinquish their posts for reasons of health. Saionji, who was determined to keep Japan's domestic and foreign policies from falling completely into the hands of the military and right wing, sought any possible means to prevent those forces from penetrating the Imperial

Court. He regarded the offices then occupied by Makino
and Ichiki as crucial; a personnel change at that juncture would
be very dangerous. Saionji requested Makino and Ichiki to
remain in their posts. Some of the senior statesmen recommended
that Konoe succeed Makino, but Saionji was reluctant to appoint
Konoe to that post because of his right-wing associations. In the
end, Makino resigned in December 1935 and Saitō Makoto
succeeded him. Ichiki changed his mind and remained in office.

Two months later, Saionji was horrified to learn that former
finance minister Takahashi Korekiyo, Saitō Makoto, and
General Watanabe Jōtarō had been assassinated, and Grand
Chamberlain Suzuki Kantarō had been wounded by fanatical
right-wing junior army officers. This was the February 26th
Incident.[27] Once again Saionji traveled from Okitsu to the
imperial palace to recommend to the Emperor a new prime
minister for a government now in shambles. Speaking with
Harada, Saionji said he had no choice but to follow his con-
science; he could recommend no one except Konoe. Harada
replied that Konoe's health could be a problem, but, even if he
became prime minister, Konoe's intimate connections with the
military should cause less concern at present, for both Mazaki
Jinzaburō and Araki Sadao were considered part of the rebel
army and their influence in the military had declined. Nonetheless Konoe must be assisted by a stout aide, someone he must
choose carefully, in consideration of all the complex elements
behind his appointment.

The February 26th Incident so shocked Saionji that he
changed his stand. Now it seemed that the only way to avert an
immediate and total takeover of the government by the military
was to recommend Konoe as prime minister. Although Saionji
had strongly criticized Konoe's popularity among the military
and right wing, the uprising forced the Genrō to try to use that
popularity. Konoe was Saionji's last—and not altogether dependable—trump card. He could only hope that Konoe's ancient and
intimate relationships with the imperial family and his innate
intelligence would guide him in dealing with the rising extremist
groups. Some of the senior statesmen shared the Genrō's desperate
wish.

Saionji summoned Konoe and asked him to form a cabinet, stating that no one but himself, in good standing among army and navy groups as well as in the political and financial communities, would be able to manage the current crisis. Pleading poor health, Konoe declined. That he was popular among various different groups, he added, actually meant that he enjoyed no real support anywhere. Without powerful support, no one could possibly handle a situation as critical as the present one. Konoe was adamant in his refusal. After the meeting, Saionji sent for Harada and Kido and informed them that he was going to recommend the prince to the Emperor anyway, and it was up to Konoe whether or not to comply with the imperial order. Soon thereafter in an audience with the Emperor Saionji recommended Konoe as the next premier, deliberately adding that there was no other suitable candidate.

The Emperor summoned Konoe and told him to assume the office of prime minister, that it was important for him to accept. Konoe requested time to think and withdrew from the imperial presence. Shaken by the Emperor's order, Konoe later said that he could not even walk straight as he left by the long palace corridor. When Kido, too, urged him to obey the imperial order, Konoe again pleaded poor health. How would he respond, Kido asked, if the Emperor repeated his order? In that case, Konoe answered, he would have no choice but to surrender his title. Konoe told Saionji once more that he would decline the imperial request for reasons of health, and then he reported his decision directly to the throne.

In one of his memoirs Konoe explained that his sharp disagreement with Saionji on political issues was an important factor in his decision to decline the premiership at that time.[28] After the Pacific War, Konoe wrote that the entire membership of the Kōdōha had exercised a moderating influence on Japanese policies toward the United States and China, but they were implicated for involvement in the February 26th Incident and expelled from the army. What the military would do without the dampening effect of the Kōdōha greatly worried him. That, he said, is why he told Saionji that he had no confidence to run the government and declined the premiership, ostensibly for reasons of ill health. Saionji, on the other hand, believed that suppressing the Kōdōha, which he saw as the most serious threat to both foreign and domestic politics of Japan, would help the military to put its house in order. Saionji therefore took issue with Konoe. In his postwar memoirs, Konoe used the series of events between the Sino-Japanese War and the Pacific War to prove that he had been right in 1936.[29] He tried hard in his memoirs to justify his earlier stand from the point of view he later embraced, as will be discussed later. Hirota Kōki, foreign minister under Okada, was appointed prime minister. Throughout its tenure, the Hirota cabinet was subjected to unrelenting pressure from the military.

By declining the imperial request to become prime minister in the chaotic aftermath of the February 26th Incident, Konoe became even more conspicuous in the Japanese political world, and people now held even higher expectations for this aristocratic young politician. Yet Konoe continued to worry Saionji and the senior statesmen by frequent utterances that betrayed close alignment with the military and the extreme Right. In August 1936, for example, Konoe visited Saionji to discuss a plan for government reorganization that Army Minister Terauchi Hisaichi was contemplating. A few days later, Harada also consulted Saionji, informing him that Terauchi might demand Prime Minister Hirota to carry out the proposed reform. Saionji mentioned Konoe's visit. He now suspected that some young officers had told Konoe what they were demanding of Terauchi. Further, Konoe argued in defense of Araki and Mazaki. It was difficult to understand why he talked the way he did. Was it out of conviction? Was he compelled to talk like that? Or was it because he was frightened? Did he think it would enhance his position in the present situation? "I deplore a man of his ability and birth acting as he does," Saionji said. "If only we could somehow bring him back to a reasonable course." Harada replied that Konoe would understand if they spoke to him about his behavior, but that he lacked courage and worried too much about his popularity.[30]

Harada suggested that since Konoe was not receptive to Saionji's advice, the Emperor might be induced to instruct him briefly to behave more prudently, for Konoe's sake and for the nation. Saionji agreed. Harada reported this to the minister of the Imperial Household, Matsudaira Tsuneo, and consulted Lord Keeper of the Privy Seal Yuasa Kurahei on the matter. Yuasa told Harada that he also was deeply concerned about Prince Konoe. Some time before the prince had suggested that Hiraizumi Kiyoshi, an extreme rightist ideologue, should be allowed greater access to the court so that the Emperor could benefit from his talks. Yuasa described a recent lecture given by Hiraizumi before the Emperor on the rule of Emperor Godaigo (1288–1339).[31] Hiraizumi had praised the revolutionary fervor of Godaigo so extravagantly that he seemed to insinuate that the present Emperor was not radical enough. The Emperor obviously did not enjoy hearing Hiraizumi's accolades to Godaigo. Yuasa also wondered why Konoe wanted the court to forge closer ties with people like Hiraizumi, and he promised to discuss Saionji's suggestion with Matsudaira.[32]

Shortly afterward Yuasa reported the matter to the Emperor, who remarked that he would like to talk casually with Konoe, perhaps while playing golf, but, since Konoe no longer played the game, he might invite the prince to his biological laboratory and use that as an opportunity to talk. He noted that Konoe was older than he, and hesitated to order him to do this or that. According to Yuasa, the Emperor wanted to remind Konoe that when one assumes a position of responsibility, he must realize that matters are more complex than they were when he was an outside critic. Saionji thought this was a fine idea.[33] We do not know whether the Emperor actually ever had such a talk with Konoe.

For a time during the crisis immediately after the February 26th Incident, Saionji was convinced that only Konoe could save the situation, but his earlier reservations had not disappeared. Late in 1936 when Harada reported rumors of an imminent government change, Saionji said that Konoe would not do. Under the circumstances, the prime minister would inevitably become a mere robot, whoever he might be. We must restrain Konoe for the time being, said Saionji. When Hirota resigned in January 1937, Saionji recommended General Ugaki Kazushige as his successor. But some army officers objected to Ugaki and successfully blocked the formation of his cabinet by refusing to provide a candidate for the post of army minister. Saionji consulted Yuasa and then recommended to the Emperor General Hayashi Senjūrō, who managed to form a cabinet.

During Hirota's tenure, there was considerable backing for Konoe as prime minister, but he himself was determined not to be appointed, apparently for the same reasons he declined the earlier offer after the February 26th Incident. But if the Emperor were to ask him a second time, he could hardly decline. As the end of the Hirota cabinet approached, Konoe virtually pleaded with Kido and Harada to make certain that he was not nominated. "I do not want the job," he told them. When Ugaki's effort to form a cabinet was deadlocked, Konoe secretly sent his secretary to Okitsu to tell Saionji that, despite all sorts of rumors, he did not want the premiership. Konoe complained that whenever he explained to people that he did not want the nomination because this time he could not refuse an imperial request, they interpreted that to mean he was prepared to accept the task. "Please see that I am not nominated," Konoe said. Harada's diary notes that "when he is urged on by people around him, he will not silence them simply by declaring, 'I do not want the job.' Instead, he ends up saying, 'Should the Emperor command me, I must obey him, even if it costs me my life.' As a result, the rumor spreads that he is willing to accept the imperial order. People even suspect that Kido, I, and above all, Prince Saionji are deliberately blocking Konoe, because we do not wish to see him become prime minister."[34]

3

THE FIRST KONOE CABINET

Soon after the Hayashi cabinet was formed in February 1937, it dissolved the House of Representatives with the hope of pulling the recalcitrant political parties into line. The strategy backfired, and, instead, Hayashi found himself out on a limb with little prospect of regaining the necessary support. The question of who should replace him began to crop up among everyone with an interest in the political leadership. Continuing to plead ill health, Konoe refused to be considered. Eventually Yuasa, Hayashi, Kido, Harada, and Konoe together came to an agreement that Sugiyama Hajime, Hayashi's army minister, should be the next prime minister. Saionji vehemently opposed the choice when Harada informed him of it. Why not Konoe? he asked. Originally Saionji had wanted to avoid recommending Konoe if at all possible, but now, he told Harada, if the Emperor sought his opinion, he could not recommend anyone who did not come up to his standards, and that left no one but Konoe. It seemed unfair to ask Konoe to perform in such intractable circumstances, but there was no other suitable candidate.

Ever since the May 15th Incident, Saionji had been careful to recommend for the office of prime minister only men he believed would try to restrain military interference in government. But not many could meet this requirement. Each time the government changed, Saionji and his close associates were faced with an increasingly difficult task. Finally, learning that Yuasa and his colleagues had been compelled to nominate Army Minister Sugiyama, Saionji began to reconsider the possibility of Konoe. Although he apparently did not have complete confidence in Konoe, Saionji believed that at least he would be able to keep a more effective brake on the military than Sugiyama. Kido at last persuaded Konoe to accede to Saionji's wish and secured his informal consent. In May 1937, the Hayashi cabinet resigned. By that time, at Saionji's long-standing request, the procedures for recommending the succeeding prime minister had been modified. Under the new procedures the Emperor commanded the Lord Keeper of the Privy Seal to make the recommendation, but only after consulting with the Genrō. Accordingly, Yuasa consulted Saionji and then recommended Konoe to the Emperor, who commanded the prince to form a cabinet.

The public gave an enthusiastic welcome to Konoe's new cabinet. He was extraordinarily well liked. At 45 he was in the prime of life and conspicuously young for a Japanese prime minister. His ancient lineage and noble birth, his tall, imposing stature, and his nonchalant manner all worked to give him an enchanting aura of elegance. He was known to have superior intellectual ability, and so his never-failing courtesy and lack of arrogance were all the more appealing. He appeared as a democratic presence, in sharp contrast to the profound aristocratic pride hidden within him. Konoe's popularity was generated to a large extent by the popular tendency to adore the powerful, but his congenial deportment projected an air of intimacy and only made the people push him higher up on his pedestal.

Konoe's personality had undeniable appeal, which helped his rise in politics at a time when the country was yearning for a deliverer. The domestic and international crises that had rocked the nation since the Manchurian Incident had aroused a feverish chauvinism; Japan was "divine," "superior to all the nations of the world." The public was beginning to believe that Imperial Japan indeed was ordained to fulfill a sublime mission. But any visions of a glorious future were counterbalanced by the profound anxiety everyone felt at the increasingly grave prospects that lay before their country. Thus when Konoe became head of government, he was welcomed as a long-awaited leader who would guide the nation through those turbulent times.

Once when he was asked for a sample of his calligraphy, Konoe complied by writing with brush and ink, "I am a man of the

Land of the Rising Sun. The time has come for me to perform my duty as a man of the Land of the Rising Sun." To many people the new prime minister personified the gallant figure that these words suggest. They were awed by his pedigree and its ancient ties with the imperial family; he seemed to offer the chance for a new start under his youthful leadership and refreshing sense of the times. The people admired his serenity, his self-possession, and prudence, and they trusted his acute intelligence. Rather quickly Konoe became a national savior, who people believed could successfully tackle the difficult problems of the present and future where others had failed.

The lineup of the first Konoe cabinet, formed in June 1937, was as follows: Hirota Kōki, minister for foreign affairs; Baba Eichi, home minister; Kaya Okinori, minister of finance; Sugiyama Hajime, retained as minister of the army; Yonai Mitsumasa, retained as minister of the navy; Shiono Suehiko, retained as minister of justice; Yasui Eiji, minister of education; Arima Yoriyasu, minister of agriculture; Yoshino Shinji, minister of commerce; Nagai Ryūtarō, minister of communications; Nakajima Chikuhei, minister of railways; Ōtani Son'yū, minister of overseas development; and Kazami Akira, chief cabinet secretary.

The appointment of Konoe also satisfied army personnel. They had been hoping for just this development, but it was not because they expected a great deal from him or had any great confidence in him, nor because he had approved the foreign policy the army had been promoting since 1931. The army intended to utilize his popularity for its own ends. Even before Konoe had decided on all the cabinet appointments, the army clearly made its wishes known to him and interfered with his selection of ministers. In a typical move, they demanded the appointment of Baba Eiichi as finance minister, a man known for the unpopular and strongly pro-military financial policy he had introduced as finance minister in the Hirota cabinet just one year earlier. Konoe was aware of Baba's low standing in the business community, and he rejected the army demand. Instead he appointed Baba home minister.

When the members of the new cabinet were announced, the

Tokyo Asahi newspaper, in an editorial entitled "What We Expect of the Konoe Cabinet," wrote, "The enormous popularity that Prince Konoe enjoyed after he accepted the imperial order seems to be dwindling as his selection of cabinet ministers proceeds." His appointments so far "fail to reflect the basic beliefs that one would expect a cabinet under Konoe to stand for. Rather, they give the impression that someone is manipulating the process of selecting ministers. As a politician, Prince Konoe is as yet an unknown quantity, which is one of the main factors in his wide, general appeal. But that makes it all the more disillusioning that he should have selected for a post that is virtually equivalent to vice-premier—so quickly and so decisively—a man who is, in contrast, politically notorious: Mr. Baba, who engineered the infamous Baba financial policy." The editorial urged the Konoe government to correct the impression that it was a Konoe cabinet in form only, and, in substance, a Baba cabinet. Appointing former Prime Minister Hirota to the post of foreign minister, the *Asahi* editorial concluded, had to mean that the new cabinet would not carry on the disreputable Arita Hachirō diplomacy of the last days of the Hirota cabinet, but that it would uphold the Hirota foreign policy, which so bravely replaced the reckless scorched-earth policies of Uchida Yasuya.[1]

At a press conference following the inauguration of the new cabinet, Konoe stated that he would try to minimize any domestic conflicts and problems that might invite the contempt of other nations. He said that certain guiding principles were necessary and that strong government leadership would be important in upholding those principles. Concrete policies and programs would be established through cabinet deliberation. But his underlying goal was, he said, to strive for a true peace based on international justice, a genuine peace, not merely the maintenance of the status quo. Within Japan, he would do everything possible to build systems based on social justice so that all citizens, hand in hand, would contribute to the reform and progress of their country.

What he meant by international justice was undoubtedly the idea he first expressed in "Reject the Anglo-American–Centered Peace" (1918), and returned to in "Improving Our World"

(1933) and "The Basic Issue in International Peace" (1935).[2] In the long run, it may be that his aspirations for true social justice together with international justice contained a later, more focused expression of the deep interest he showed in his youth in socialism and social problems.

Few were more pleased than the Emperor that Konoe finally had accepted the appointment. Harada told Navy Minister Yonai that the Emperor had been in an exceptionally good frame of mind since Konoe became prime minister, despite the gloomy outlook for any political breakthrough and a deteriorating situation abroad. Apparently the Emperor was confident that Konoe, unlike his predecessor, would observe the Constitution, for, at the time of his appointment, he told Yuasa, the Privy Seal, "I don't need to talk about the Constitution to Konoe, do I?" An attendant reported that during meetings with Konoe, His Majesty was calm and spoke easily. It was very reassuring, he said, and added that Vice-Grand Chamberlain Hirohata Tadataka and others were very pleased to see the Emperor so relaxed with the new prime minister.

It was probably natural that, given the ancient ties between their families, the Emperor should have felt at ease with Konoe. Konoe shared the sense of intimacy. Tomita Kenji, chief secretary in the second and third Konoe cabinets, records the following episode. A chamberlain once complained to one of Tomita's subordinates that Konoe's manner in the presence of the Emperor seemed to lack the proper respect, and he wondered if anything could be done about it. The chamberlain remarked that while all senior statesmen punctiliously observed the proper decorum when reporting to the Emperor, Premier Konoe greeted His Majesty as a commoner would do a friend, asking "How are you? It's been quite a while, hasn't it!" Then Konoe would seat himself on a chair before the throne. Tomita was told that others rarely sat in the presence of the Emperor, but Konoe, seated and his long legs casually crossed, would report to His Majesty at length. The chamberlain added that he never doubted Konoe's loyalty, but his manner before the Emperor was a little disturbing. Konoe not only reported on the affairs of the state, but routinely told the Emperor whatever else came to mind, bantering on lightly about a variety of matters. As a result the Emperor often mistook Konoe's off-the-cuff remarks to be official statements.

At the press conference held immediately after all cabinet appointments had been made, Konoe expressed his hope that the domestic crises Japan had weathered could be resolved. Asserting that impoverished political policy and leadership lay at the root of the nation's political conflicts, Konoe told the reporters that he hoped the Emperor would grant a general pardon to all those convicted for political crimes during the Ketsumeidan,[3] May 15th, and February 26th incidents, and that amnesty might be extended to those convicted for leftist activities also. This idea was not originally Konoe's. In the autumn of 1933, Araki Sadao, army minister in the Saitō cabinet, proposed to Saitō and Konoe, who was then president of the House of Peers, that a general amnesty be granted by imperial decree to rightists convicted for their involvement in the Ketsumeidan and May 15th incidents, and that those convicted or on trial for communist activities also receive an imperial pardon. Araki argued that such a grand gesture would stir those receiving a pardon with His Majesty's benevolence and inspire the nation to unite and make a new start. Convinced that this would clear the depression that hung over the nation, Araki put forth his proposal with almost missionary vehemence. His argument, based at least in principle on his own ideal of national polity (*kokutai*), was tinged with spiritual fervor. Thereafter the idealist right wingers, including Araki's close associate Hiranuma Kiichirō, then vice president of the Privy Council, began to push the same idea. At first Konoe was shocked, but gradually he shifted ground, and by the time he became prime minister he wanted to carry it out.

In considering why he changed his stand on Araki's proposal, we must recall that Konoe had established close associations with Kōdōha members and sympathizers. After Araki left the post of army minister shortly before the resignation of the Saitō cabinet, the influence of the Kōdōha within the army declined rapidly, and was overtaken by the Tōseiha (Control Faction).[4] The February 26th Incident represented an attempt by the Kōdōha to turn the tide back, but in the end that group was suppressed and completely discredited. Taking into account the events and

Konoe's own ideas, his proposal for an imperial amnesty was clearly aimed at restoring the Kōdōha to its earlier position of strength in the army.

Konoe's intention is revealed in a cabinet document which he himself revised. It states:

Since about 1929 social unrest has mounted as people in farming, mountain, and fishing villages, and small business-men and industrialists in the cities have become increasingly impoverished. A growing number of young army officers and their civilian supporters are convinced that this dis-tress is caused by government leaders, party politicians, and zaibatsu executives who have manipulated political power to advance their interests at the expense of others. Some military officers and their civilian sympathizers have turned to unlawful means to try to destroy these powerful groups and reconstruct the state under a military govern-ment. The state has been seriously harmed by a trying series of incidents that have followed one upon another since 1931. The March and October plots, the Ketsumeidan, May 15th, and Shimpeitai[5] incidents and the February 26th attacks have a common thread. The root cause of them all lies in the government's failure to take drastic preventive measures, especially after the March and the October plots were exposed. The punishment of those involved in the February 26th Incident was so harsh as to be unjustifiable, when compared with the earlier cases. General Ugaki, who was considered the ringleader of the March Incident, not only went unpunished, but some time ago even received an imperial order to form a cabinet, while General Mazaki was indicted on the charge of aiding the rebels in the up-rising of February 26. The cases have been handled so unfairly that conflict within the army has only become worse. To take no effective measures risks not only another outbreak of deplorable incidents, but also the compromise of the Imperial Virtue.

Our government is guided by the imperative to manifest His Majesty's Virtue to the world, and the duty of those who assist the imperial rule ultimately lies therein. The state of our nation is, furthermore, critical; it requires reform of government policy in a spirit of national unity and enhancement of the national prestige overseas. It is, therefore, most urgent that we eradicate both the conflicts within the national military forces and any ideology that advocates national reconstruction through unlawful means. "For more than fifty days since I received the imperial order [to form a cabinet], I have contemplated measures to resolve this most pressing problem. I have at last arrived at a final decision. It is no other than to ask the Emperor to proclaim a general amnesty to the offenders in rebellions and uprisings and release them completely from the responsibilities of their crimes, thus moving them deeply by the vast imperial benevolence and letting them leave their resentment in the past. In this way we can eradicate the root of domestic conflicts."[6]

In October 1937, when Konoe was busy mustering support for the amnesty idea, Harada met Foreign Minister Hirota. The foreign minister told Harada in strict confidence that when he talked with Konoe about the amnesty issue, he inquired if the prime minister was confident that amnesty would insure the restoration of discipline within the army. Konoe answered that he was not. This episode, which Harada recorded in his diary, strengthens the argument that in pushing a general amnesty, Konoe was primarily interested in the salvation of the Kōdōha.

Konoe backed the idea of an amnesty vigorously and stubbornly, at one point even threatening to resign if he failed to have his way. Such tenacious behavior was unusual for him. It is obvious that he was motivated by his close ties with the Kōdōha and the idealist right-wing radicals, and he was probably under unceasing pressure from them. Mazaki Jinzaburō, together with Araki, was regarded as a ringleader of the Kōdōha. When Konoe became prime minister, Mazaki was being court-martialed for his part in the February 26th Incident, and the Kōdōha coterie was covertly campaigning for his acquittal. It seemed as though Konoe would be drawn into the campaign.

Harada approached Chief Cabinet Secretary Kazami Akira and told him that he knew Konoe would not be able to resist the pressure if he were confronted by Mazaki's supporters. He asked Kazami to try to keep those people away. Konoe always consented to meet anyone who asked to see him, and he was, as Harada feared, susceptible to the suggestions and information they presented to him. All sorts of people were constantly trying to push him this way and that, and it grew worse after Konoe became prime minister. Within the cabinet, Home Minister Baba, Justice Minister Shiono, who aligned himself with Hiranuma, and Education Minister Yasui, who showed a strong right-wing inclination, enthusiatically supported Konoe's amnesty scheme. The senior army officials who belonged to the Tōseiha were strongly opposed. The high court officials, the Genrō, and the senior statesmen objected to it. Above all, Saionji stood pitted against it from the very start.

When Araki first proposed the idea of a general amnesty, Harada reported the meeting to Saionji, who responded with despair. He declared that Araki was proposing nothing short of revolution. Why, he groaned, didn't Konoe flatly tell Araki it would be impossible. Learning from Harada that Konoe was insisting on the anmesty, Saionji declared that Konoe should quit rather than commit such an outrage. The prime minister does not have to be him, he stormed. The Genrō remained seriously concerned about the outcome of the amnesty issue. He told Harada that if an imperial edict of amnesty were issued, that would be the end of the Constitution and the destruction of the state order and social discipline.

For the sake of Konoe's future also, Saionji wanted him to give up. An imperial edict of amnesty must be prevented, no matter what, Saionji told Harada. It would dwarf Konoe's future and make him nothing more than a tool of the right wing. Konoe must grow, he said and become the champion of an enlightened government. In the end Konoe put forth the proposal for a general amnesty, but the Emperor did not approve it. Opposition from high-ranking army officers and court officials, Saionji, and the senior statesmen finally compelled Konoe to give up entirely.

Just when the commotion over the general amnesty had

reached a peak, Konoe was confronted with a grave international problem—the outbreak of the China Incident. Anti-Japanese feeling had been building in China ever since the Manchurian Incident but it reached a new intensity as Japan, or more precisely the Kwantung army, began in earnest to detach North China from the rest of the country with the aim of setting it up as an autonomous region. On July 7, 1937, when the Konoe cabinet was only one month old, Japanese troops exchanged fire with Chinese near Lukouch'iao in the suburbs of Peking. Army Minister Sugiyama immediately requested the cabinet council to approve sending three home divisions to the trouble spot. Konoe was worried about the international repercussions and the popular dismay that the dispatch of the home divisions would create, and he turned down the request. As succeeding clashes were reported, negotiations with the Chinese local authorities for a settlement dragged on until Sugiyama demanded the cabinet to authorize sending a total of five divisions (of which three would be sent immediately). On July 11, Konoe yielded and approved the dispatch of troops as the army minister deemed necessary, on the condition that the military authorities adhere to the policy of non-escalation and endeavor to settle the dispute locally.

Immediately after the July 11 cabinet decision, Konoe issued a declaration. In it, he stated that since the "unwarranted attack" by the Chinese troops at Lukouch'iao, Japan had made every effort to avoid escalation and settle the issue locally, but China had failed to demonstrate a sincere desire to negotiate a settlement. That indicated, said Konoe, that the recent clash, provoked by the Chinese, was a premeditated, armed attack against Japan. He stated that peace in North China was vital to the security of Japan and Manchukuo, and that the government had therefore decided to dispatch troops to the disturbed region.

After making this announcement Konoe invited representatives of both houses of the Diet, the press, and the business community to his official residence, where he solicited their support for the government position. The atmosphere was already charged, but the press caused greater agitation by standing unanimously behind the government. They competed, in fact, to appear more vehement than the others in their appeals for decisive action against China.

The cabinet's rigid position alarmed the Chinese and provoked Chiang Kai-shek to stress, in a speech made at Lushan, China's determination to stand strong. Six years had passed, he said, since Manchuria was plundered, and now the confrontation with Japan had shifted to Lukouch'iao, the gate of Peking. Should Lukouch'iao fall into Japanese hands, China's ancient capital of Peking would become a second Shenyang (Mukden).[7] The capital at Nanking might meet the same fate as Peking. The fate of China hung on the solution of the Lukouch'iao incident. Even if China stood on the brink of annihilation, they would fight, said Chiang, no matter what the sacrifice. China was a weak power, but the Chinese people would protect their country and carry out the responsibility their ancestors had bestowed upon them.

Negotiations between the local Japanese and the Chinese authorities grew ever more tangled and further skirmishes ensued. The cabinet decided to go ahead with the immediate dispatch of three divisions to North China. Hearing that reinforcements were coming, the Japanese expeditionary army (Tientsin army) launched a general assault on the Chinese forces. By July 29, the Japanese army had occupied the Peking-Tientsin area north of the Yungting River, and fighting was spreading rapidly over North China.

We have no way of knowing Konoe's inner thoughts during the course of these critical events, but at one point he sounded as though he personally was not happy about sending part of the home army to North China. After the cabinet decision had been made, Konoe warned Yuasa that if he tried to block the army demand, Sugiyama would resign and the cabinet would fall. Anyone who replaced Konoe would face the same dilemma. As there was no one who could possibly control the military, Konoe said that he felt compelled to act as he did.[8] However, in August after fighting had spread over the Peking-Tientsin area, Konoe conferred with a China expert, Nashimoto Yūhei, who had returned briefly from North China. During their meeting, Konoe said that he and his cabinet expected the Chinese resistance to crumble once the Japanese resolve to fight was made clear by the decision to send additional troops. Nashimoto responded that the cabinet had misjudged the situation. The conflict between the two nations in North China was, he said, a matter of survival for China; China was in no position to play with tactics and yield if Japan took a hard line. Nashimoto criticized the short-sighted attempt to settle the matter by threat and intimidation.

Konoe explained to Nashimoto that he had begun to worry when the situation failed to improve, and he had therefore consulted a staff officer stationed in China. The officer maintained that the Chinese would interpret any hesitation on the part of Japan as a sign of weakness and would grow bolder. Konoe thus had concluded that the conflict could still be resolved without escalating if Japan dispatched reinforcements at once.[9]

Since the outbreak of the Lukouch'iao Incident, the army was divided on how to resolve the conflict. While the army ministry quickly became the core of strong-policy advocates, the army general staff constituted the stronghold for those who supported a policy of conciliation. The hard-liners believed that if Japan took a resolute stance, the Chinese would be intimidated into seeking compromise or surrender. They did not anticipate escalation into a full-scale war. The conciliatory policy, on the other hand, derived from strategic considerations for the defense of Manchukuo against the Soviet Union. Its supporters sought to avoid any large-scale military involvement with China. Konoe's statement to Nashimoto indicates that he was in basic agreement with the strong-policy advocates within the army.

It must not be assumed, however, that Konoe's inclination after the Lukouch'iao Incident to counsel restraint had completely evaporated, and that he now tended toward wholehearted cooperation with the army's strong policy faction. His inability to control the army continued to frustrate him, and the prospects for the situation in North China seemed increasingly ominous. The memory of his father, Atsumaro, who had so tirelessly tried to make Japanese see the need for Sino-Japanese cooperation, also motivated Konoe to seek ways to achieve a rapid settlement of the issue.[10] For a time, Konoe seriously contemplated going to Nanking and settling the matter through direct negotiations with Chiang Kai-shek. However, considering developments since the Lukouch'iao Incident, Kazami Akira later wrote, the government saw that it could not trust the army's ability to control its own troops. It was feared that even if an agreement were reached between Konoe and Chiang, the local Japanese forces might disobey, destroying not only Konoe's prestige but also Japan's national honor. Konoe's idea was not accepted, and so he decided that at least he should send Miyazaki Ryūsuke to Nanking to sound out the Nationalist government on the possibilities for Konoe-Chiang talks.

Sugiyama consented, but strong-policy advocates in the army intervened by having the police arrest Miyazaki before he could leave Japan. Even then Konoe still sought some way to establish direct contact with Chiang. At one point he contemplated sending Tōyama Mitsuru[11] to Nanking. Tōyama and Chiang had been close friends for many years, Konoe explained to Harada, and, if he could strike a deal with Chiang through Tōyama, he would have gained a small victory over the right-wing activists scheming to set up a new Chinese regime in North China. "To fight poison with poison," as Konoe put it, Tōyama would be a good agent. This plan did not materialize either, possibly because of the outbreak of the Shanghai Incident.

Shanghai had been the vital center of Chinese anti-imperialist, above all, anti-Japanese, movements. Since the Lukouch'iao Incident, the metropolis had grown threateningly tense, and in August 1937 two members of the Japanese marine corps, an officer and a soldier, were murdered by the Chinese peace preservation corps. At the request of the army minister, the Konoe cabinet swiftly approved sending two home divisions to Shanghai, where, on the same day, fighting broke out between Japanese and Chinese forces. The battle was carried from North to Central China. On August 15 the cabinet issued a declaration that was much more strongly worded than that of July 11: "Imperial Japan, desirous of eternal peace in East Asia, has long endeavored to foster friendship and cooperation between Japan and China. However, the Nanking government [the Nationalist government] adopted an anti-Japanese policy as a means of agitating the

Chinese people and enhancing its political power. The Chinese government has been overconfident of its own strength and has underestimated Japan's strength. In collusion with communist forces, it has assumed an increasingly provocative and insulting attitude toward Japan, and now it threatens hostile action against Imperial Japan.

The declaration continued that since the Lukouch'iao Incident Japan had tried, with infinite patience, to bring about a peaceful, localized settlement of the dispute, and had requested the Nanking government to cease its provocations and refrain from interfering with a settlement. It accused the Chinese government of ignoring Japan's requests and advancing war preparations, and of threatening the Japanese garrison army by sending reinforcements from the south in blatant violation of military agreements between the two nations. In Shanghai the Chinese had opened fire on Japanese troops and bombarded Japanese warships. The declaration concluded: In this matter the Chinese contemptuously have inflicted every sort of unlawful outrage upon Imperial Japan and threatened the life and property of Japanese residents all over China. Imperial Japan has at long last exhausted its patience and is now compelled to take resolute action to punish the atrocious Chinese army and to bring the Nanking government to its senses.

It was Army Minister Sugiyama who actually initiated the August 15 declaration. At a cabinet meeting, he demanded a new declaration and presented a fully prepared draft, which the cabinet quickly approved after a slight change in wording. Kazami Akira, who attended as chief cabinet secretary, later wrote that the cabinet session began in the evening and lasted until 1 A.M. "The public assumed that, truly worthy of a cabinet council in the midst of grave crisis, the ministers must have earnestly deliberated the situation in China. The truth was far from it. We just wasted time with little serious discussion." The fact was, Kazami continued, when the army minister distributed copies of his draft, everyone began to read it silently. Then Foreign Minister Hirota commented on a sentence at the beginning, "The Nanking government in collusion with the Bolsheviks has assumed an increasingly provocative and insulting attitude toward Japan." He feared that it might imply that Japan was accusing the Soviets of complicity. The foreign minister called for a revision that would avoid such a misunderstanding. As other ministers responded with their own ideas, the council's attention gradually shifted from the draft into leisurely, aimless conversation. By the time they agreed to replace "Bolsheviks" with "communist forces," it was already midnight.

In the meantime, no formal debate was conducted on the policy Japan should pursue. Railways Minister Nakajima and Communications Minister Nagai urged the government to use the situation as an opportunity to thoroughly punish the Chinese forces. The other ministers were silent, offering no discussion. "Prime Minister Konoe," Kazami recorded, "as usual just patiently listened to the others. When no one, not even the foreign or navy ministers, raised any objections to Sugiyama's draft declaration, he simply approved it."[12] It may have been a passive action, but by approving the official declaration, Konoe once again sided with the army hard-liners.

In the Shanghai region, despite reinforcements of two divisions, the Japanese army continued to fight against fierce Chinese resistance, and Japan was soon forced to send more troops. Early in September, the Konoe government announced that the North China Incident (a term in official use since the skirmish at Lukouch'iao) would henceforth be called the China Incident, acknowledging that the local clash had expanded into the full-scale conflict between the nations that is now often referred to as the China War.

The day after that announcement, the 72nd Imperial Diet session convened. In his policy address to the Diet, Konoe stated that since the Lukouch'iao Incident Japan's basic policy had been to encourage the Chinese government to abandon its anti-Japanese stance in order to improve relations. The Japanese government had tried to prevent the escalation of the conflict and settle the dispute locally, he said.

The Chinese had not only failed to understand the "sincere intent" of the Japanese government, but had fanned a spirit of

contempt and resistance against Japan, and fighting had already
spread over Central and South China. The Japanese government
could no longer patiently wait for a local settlement to come
about. Japan was compelled to deal a full and decisive blow
against the Chinese forces. He continued that "in point of fact,
for one country to adopt antagonism toward a particular country
as its national policy and to make that the underlying principle
of national education, implanting such ideas in the minds of the
young, is unprecedented in the history of the world."

Konoe went on that the Japanese government had repeatedly
requested the Chinese government to reconsider its attitude, but
in vain; the present crisis must therefore be considered China's
responsibility. Japan firmly believed, he said, that to deal a
decisive blow to China was now justified in the name of self-
defense, and justice and humanity. Imperial Japan's only alternative was to destroy the will to fight of the Chinese army. If
China failed to see its mistakes and persisted in its stubborn resistance, Japan was prepared to execute a protracted war. Serious difficulties lay ahead before the great mission of bringing peace
to East Asia could be fulfilled, and, in order to overcome them,
Japan must proceed steadily in its task, persevering with forti-
tude as a united people. Konoe concluded by stressing to the
Diet the momentous responsibility of assisting imperial rule
and the need for unity.

Some two weeks after the Konoe speech, Koyama Kango
visited him at his private residence at Nagatachō. Koyama
recorded their conversation in his diary.[13]

> The prince looked haggard and said that the government
> had no idea how the situation in China would develop.
> With a deep sigh of despair, the prince complained, "I
> accepted a daunting job at an unfortunate time. I should
> have known better, for the situation was actually better right
> after the May 15th Incident. Right now the civilian govern-
> ment is too weak to do anything. Worse, the military is so
> divided that we do not know who to deal with. . . . " He
> seemed so discouraged that I tried to lift his spirits; he had
> undertaken the task, I told him, and he owed it to the coun-
> try to carry it out to the finish. I warned him that publicly

he must appear to be fully confident; otherwise he would cause harmful rumors that the prime minister was disheartened by the China problem. As for the future of China, would Chiang Kai-shek be able to maintain his position and negotiate peace with Japan? Or, would he fall, and with his defeat throw China into utter confusion? If Chiang would only concede at an appropriate moment and seek peace, Japan could avoid a protracted war. If he refused to surrender even after ignominious defeat and persisted in drawing out the hostilities, there would be no way of knowing how the situation would develop. The prince confessed that he had no idea at all which way the war would take us.

The diary shows a privately dejected and uncertain Konoe behind the façade of the firm, confident prime minister who had addressed China so uncompromisingly. Konoe recollected in his postwar memoirs that when the non-escalation policy began to crumble, especially after the fighting spread to Shanghai:

> I considered dissolving the cabinet to show that the expanding war was contrary to the government's wish, but that it would nevertheless take full responsibility for the unfortunate turn of events. In fact we seriously discussed it. But what would that have accomplished? Would it have led those who actually controlled the military—whether young officers or local army—to rethink what they were doing and begin to seek a solution to the China problem? Would they not, on the contrary, have set up a puppet regime and driven Japan further down the wrong course? I concluded that my task was to restrain the military by every possible means, being scrupulous to avoid inciting it any further. Toward this objective, I did my very best.[14]

This passage, although couched in self-justification, is noteworthy for its portrayal of Konoe's dilemma, in his own words, at the time of the Shanghai Incident.

In October after the 72nd Diet adjourned, the cabinet adopted a cabinet counselor system, which was designed to bring in outside individuals who would participate in deliberations on important policies related to the China War. Counselors were appointed personally by the Emperor and were accorded the privileges of minister of state. Those appointed were, from the army, Ugaki Kazushige and Araki Sadao; from the navy, Suetsugu Nobumasa and Abo Kiyokazu; from the political parties, Machida Chūji (Minseitō president), Maeda Yonezō (Seiyūkai), and Akita Kiyoshi (Daiichi Giinkurabu); from business, Gō Seinosuke and Ikeda Shigeaki; and from the diplomatic corps, Matsuoka Yōsuke (South Manchuria Railway president). The cabinet counselor system was initiated by Home Minister Baba as a means of reinforcing the cabinet. While it was still being set up, Konoe told Harada about the plan and counselor candidates, adding that "it is nothing more than a gesture [for national unity?—author]. I don't expect much of it, but what do you think?" Apparently Konoe had no great hopes for its success. Nevertheless, the selection of counselors clearly reflected Konoe's wish to represent as far as possible the various power centers. Following Kido's suggestion, Konoe arranged scheduled meetings with all the counselors, but they accomplished little more than bringing together representatives of the several power elites in one room. Konoe displayed no leadership in the conference. Any deliberation in conference without leadership is destined to ramble and be fruitless, and the cabinet counselor system was no exception. It achieved little.

Shortly after the outbreak of the Lukouch'iao Incident, Konoe had complained to Harada that, although many of his cabinet colleagues were able administrators, there was virtually no one among them whom he thought could be his confidante on policy matters. For some time Harada had suspected that Konoe needed someone in the cabinet he trusted and could consult without reserve. Thus when Kido Kōichi resigned the presidency of the Bureau of Peerage and Heraldry of the Imperial Household Ministry in October, Harada urged Konoe to enlist his help. Consequently, when Education Minister Yasui resigned the same October for reasons of illness, Konoe asked Kido to take over his cabinet post.

As Konoe's political status rose during his career, more and more people vied for his time. Some came with suggestions, but many others to seek favors or exploit him in some way. Konoe made himself available to as many as he could, and so he was always besieged with visitors. He was a good listener. He rarely expressed an opinion, but silently listened to what his callers had on their minds, and his attentive reception elated them. The questions Konoe asked from time to time were unfailingly to the point and incisive enough to inspire even greater admiration. His insight, attention, and gracious manner itself encouraged more visitors.

But no matter how wide his personal contacts and associations, he had few intimate friends whom he could fully trust. In his public life he remained as alone as he had been as a student. His loneliness may have been largely self-inflicted, the result of his tendency to distrust others and to regard them merely as a means, while being suspicious and wary of being used. Arima Yoriyasu, an old friend since Gakushūin days, speculated that Konoe's essential distrust of others was rooted in the temperament of a court noble. A daimyō family, such as Arima's, traditionally trusted its close retainers, but a peer descendant from court nobility more often remained aloof from everyone else. Aside from Arima's theory, Konoe's penchant to use others as tools and his fear of being exploited by them were rooted above all in a profound but concealed pride in his noble birth.

While Kido Kōichi was one of the few close friends that Konoe had, the contrast was striking. Konoe was weak in character and often vacillated, whereas Kido expressed his opinions firmly and his likes and dislikes clearly. Konoe had had no practical experience in administration and was attracted by vague ideas, while Kido had served in the Agriculture and the Commerce and Industry ministries as well as the Privy Seal secretariat and was more interested and better trained in practical solutions than abstract ideas. Regardless of, or perhaps because of, their differences, Kido was an indispensable, loyal friend, and he willingly joined the cabinet when Konoe called upon him. Saionji had always wished to see Kido assist Konoe and was pleased with the turn of events. The Emperor also, in approving Kido's resignation from the Imperial Household Ministry, told Imperial Household Minister Matsudaira Tsuneo that the ministry would miss Kido, but the government needed him even more, and as a cabinet minister he would be able to dissuade Konoe from promoting the far-fetched idea of issuing a general amnesty.

Meanwhile, the Japanese forces continued their frustrating struggle against the superior Chinese army in the Shanghai area. Then in November Japanese troops landed unexpectedly at Hangchow Bay, south of Shanghai, and with this move Japan successfully attacked the Chinese forces in the flank and brought the deadlocked battle to a quick end. The routed Chinese army fled, Japanese forces in hot pursuit. Ever since the beginning of the China War the military had asserted the independent right of supreme command and had kept the civilian government only sparsely informed of operational plans. Even the army and navy ministers had made only perfunctory war reports to the cabinet meetings. Thus, following the landing operation at Hangchow Bay, the Imperial Headquarters was established to facilitate communication. Konoe hoped that the Imperial Headquarters would improve liaison and coordination between the civilian government and the military command, and would help speed a settlement.

Both army and navy consented to the formation of the Imperial Headquarters, but the military insisted on retaining independence of supreme command. It ignored the precedents established during the Meiji era and stubbornly refused to allow the prime minister or other ministers to become working members of the Imperial Headquarters. In order to coordinate diplomacy and military operations, the Imperial Headquarters–Cabinet Liaison Conference was formed, but it failed to meet its original expectations. Konoe was so discouraged by the squabble over the Imperial Headquarters that he contemplated resigning.

In the midst of this dispute, Sugiyama complained to Konoe that the army was seriously hampered by secret information leaking through sources close to the prime minister and demanded a cabinet reorganization and the establishment of an inner cabinet system. Since the outbreak of the war, Konoe had been dragged along by the military and frustrated by its disregard for liaison with the civilian government on operational matters. Army Minister Sugiyama was of little help; incapable of controlling his own ministry and swayed by his subordinates' opinions, he often blandly retracted statements he had made in earlier cabinet meetings, causing additional problems. Konoe rejected Sugiyama's demand for an inner cabinet system and resolved at that point to resign, requesting Kido to explain the necessity for his resignation to Saionji and Yuasa. When he became prime minister, he said, he never dreamed that he would face such a serious incident and that it was an opportune moment to resign, with the Imperial Headquarters to be set up in a few days.[15]

Kido retorted that the mere thought of resignation was unconscionable just then. He would become a miserable, weak dropout in the eyes of the public, and he would have no way to explain himself to the Emperor. Kido impressed upon him the trust he inspired in the people and their expectations, and the necessity to reassure them by staying where he was. Kido pleaded with Konoe to reconsider. A sudden cabinet resignation just then might cause a financial panic, and any major fall in foreign exchange would make it difficult to procure goods from abroad, Kido told him. Furthermore, while morale was high among soldiers in the field through successive victories, a sudden change of government would invite contempt from the Chinese and damage Japan's national prestige, possibly undermining the troops' will to fight on. Resignation at the present juncture was out of the question.

When Harada reported Konoe's wish to Saionji at Okitsu, the Genrō fumed that Konoe was utterly impossible. "This is a fine pass! I thought he had some intelligence," raged Saionji, "but he seems to have no ideas of his own." Harada himself agreed that Konoe had good sense, but when attacked, he caved in. Harada commented that Konoe seemed to have no opinions of his own. In the end Saionji acknowledged that there was no choice but for Harada and Kido to encourage Konoe to remain in his post.

The Japanese forces continued in pursuit of the Chinese army retreating from the Shanghai area. By December, the army central command in Tokyo, yielding to the demand of Matsui Iwane, commander of Shanghai Expeditionary Army, decided to drive on to Nanking, the Nationalists' capital, and Konoe began to contemplate a cabinet reshuffle. Gotō Ryūnosuke, a close associate of Konoe, advised him to conclude a peace before the fall of Nanking, but Konoe reluctantly admitted that such a move was completely beyond his control.[16] The war was taking a course independent of Konoe's wishes, and Konoe insisted that he wanted to resign. To Harada he confessed that the situation had become unbearable. He predicted that the conquest of Nanking would topple the Chiang government, and Japan would repudiate the regime. That would be the opportune moment for him to resign, he said. He seemed unable to face an interminable war and being dragged along in the political maneuverings behind it. Again he announced that he wanted to resign. Harada and Kido barely managed to persuade him to stay in office.

In December, Home Minister Baba resigned for reasons of health, and Konoe filled the post with the cabinet counselor Suetsugu Nobumasa, who was a leading navy spokesman for the strong foreign policy and intimately associated with Hiranuma and the idealist right wingers. The appointment of Suetsugu as home minister, whose task was to preserve public peace, naturally provoked objections. Arima Yoriyasu recalled in his memoirs that in January 1937 Konoe told him that the Emperor might once more order Konoe to become prime minister, but he would not accept unless a condition—the appointment of General Itagaki Seishirō and Admiral Suetsugu Nobumasa as army and navy ministers—was met. Arima asked why Konoe thought so highly of Itagaki and Suetsugu. The prince replied that he did not really know how capable they were, but he had been told that both were widely trusted in the army and navy respectively. Without service ministers such as these who could control the army and the navy, particularly the young officers, the cabinet could not return the politically agitated military to normalcy, he said.[17] Konoe hoped that Suetsugu would restrain the rightist forces and appointed him first a cabinet counselor and now home minister. In Konoe's favorite phrase, he hoped to fight poison with poison.

Konoe had a habit of making personnel decisions casually, on the basis of hearsay or whims. He was also prone to making novel appointments and was often disappointed or embarrassed because the people he had chosen failed to come up to standard. Sometimes he was even tormented by the very persons whom he had promoted. As a result, Konoe was forced more than once to request his handpicked cabinet ministers to resign. The frequent changes in the ministerial roster during all his cabinets were largely the result of careless appointments.

In China, the Japanese forces pursued the Chinese until December 13, when they finally conquered Nanking. But it was no longer possible to make peace with the Nationalists. When the fighting threatened to escalate drastically following the Shanghai Incident, the Konoe government, still trying to avoid a total war with China, requested the German ambassador to China, Oskar P. Trautmann, to mediate peace. This came to be known as the Trautmann mediation, and it had the full support of the military. Only when the fall of Nanking was imminent did the Nationalist government consent to negotiate with Japan on the basis of the terms Japan had transmitted through Trautmann. Conveying the Chinese wishes to Japan, the ambassador inquired if Japan would revise the terms of peace, in view of drastic changes in the war situation. The Japanese government subsequently decided to reexamine the terms at the Imperial Headquarters–Cabinet Liaison Conference. But the conference did not convene until immediately after the fall of Nanking, at which point the entire nation was lightheaded over the victory. Within the exultant military and government, some argued that because the loss of the capital had reduced the Nationalist government to a local regime, there was no need now to negotiate a peace with it. Rather, Japan should wait for the emergence of a new Chinese regime that would accept Japan's demands. Under these circumstances, the liaison conference revised the terms of peace.

The new terms that the conference agreed upon were, in sum, that: 1) China would officially recognize Manchukuo; 2) China would cease all collaboration with communism, abandon its anti-Japan and anti-Manchukuo policy, and support the anti-communist policy of Japan and Manchukuo; 3) China would agree to establish in North China a new political organization

under Chinese sovereignty which would be suitable to the realization of co-prosperity among Japan, Manchukuo, and China
and have wide-ranging powers to achieve, above all, close economic cooperation among the three. In addition, China would
agree to the creation of demilitarized zones in North China and
Inner Mongolia; 4) China would agree to the formation of an
anti-communist and autonomous government in Inner Mongolia;
5) China would agree to the establishment of demilitarized zones
in Central China under Japanese occupation. In the greater
Shanghai area, China would cooperate with Japan in the maintenance of public order and economic development; 6) Japan,
Manchukuo, and China would agree on such matters as resources exploitation, customs, trade, aviation, and communications; 7) China would pay reparations to Japan; 8) the Japanese
forces would occupy specified areas in North and Central China
as well as Inner Mongolia as long as necessary. These peace
terms, which branded China as a vanquished nation, were the
product of the heady taste of success that intoxicated Japan at
that time. The liaison conference sought to stiffen the terms,
but Konoe remained silent and let the matter take its own
course.[18] In December his cabinet approved the new terms of
peace and delivered them to Ambassador Trautmann.

Chiang Kai-shek was in a quandary when he received the new
Japanese terms. The Nanking government's response was slow
in coming. As the days went by, the Japanese attitude hardened
further, and in January 1938 the imperial conference drew up a
Fundamental Policy for the Disposition of the China Incident,
which stated: If the Nationalist government reflected deeply and
seriously sought peace, Japan would negotiate with it on the
basis of the above peace terms, but, if China failed to seek peace,
Japan would promote a new regime in China with which Japan
would normalize relations between the two nations and cooperate
in the rejuvenation of a new China. Japan would proceed to annihilate the present Chinese central government and make
certain that it was absorbed under the control of the new central
government. Several days later, the Nationalist government
responded to Japan through the German ambassador and
demanded concrete stipulations. They claimed that the Japanese

peace terms were too abstract. Clearly, the Chinese demand reflected their deep-rooted suspicion of Japan.

At the Imperial Headquarters–Cabinet Liaison Conference convened to discuss the Chinese reply, the army was divided. While the general staff office asserted that Japan's Soviet policy required the continuation of the peace negotiations to end hostilities as soon as possible, the army ministry demanded that negotiations be cut off. Cabinet members, including Konoe and Foreign Minister Hirota, supported the army ministry position. Harada wrote in his diary that both Konoe and Kido said that they understood why the general staff office sought an early peace, but they insisted, having pushed the war successfully that far, that "Japan, as the victor, has no need to humble itself like a defeated nation, allowing China to dictate, or to meekly ask, if the terms are acceptable. Giving China such leeway would invite other nations to see through our design and conclude that 'Japan is in a terrible fix, maybe on the verge of collapse!' And it might seriously damage our economy."[19] The liaison conference again debated whether or not to continue negotiations, and once again Konoe was silent. In the end the general staff members, fearing their insistence would bring the cabinet down, agreed to terminate the negotiations. Thus ended the Trautmann mediation.

On January 16, 1938, the day after the liaison conference, the Japanese government issued a declaration in the name of Prime Minister Konoe stating that it would cease henceforth to deal with the Nationalist government. Even after the capture of Nanking, the declaration said, the Imperial Japanese government had patiently waited, giving the Nationalist government time to reconsider its attitude. However, the Nationalist government has not appreciated the good intentions of Japan and persisted in their opposition, showing no regard for either the miserable plight of their own people or for the peace and tranquility of all East Asia. Accordingly, the declaration said, the Japanese government would cease to deal with that government and look forward to the establishment and growth of a new Chinese regime, on which Japan could rely for harmonious cooperation. The Japanese government would cooperate fully with that regime in the adjustment of Sino-Japanese relations and the rejuvenation of China.

Later the Konoe government issued a strongly worded supplementary declaration. It stated that to refuse to deal with the Nationalist government was a stronger action than simply to refuse recognition. Under established international law, it continued, all Japan had to do to refuse recognition was to recognize a new Chinese regime. But since it was still premature to give formal recognition to the provisional government of the Republic of China, Japan would establish a new precedent in international law "by both refusing to recognize the Nationalist government and simultaneously trying to destroy it." The provisional government was no more than a puppet regime set up by the Japanese North China district army in Peking after the fall of Nanking. The army was scheming to install it as the central government of China.

Konoe and his government appeared to be sure and triumphant, but the fact was that they had no confidence at all as to how to conclude the war. Immediately after the Konoe declaration was made, a writer who knew Konoe well excitedly asked Kiya Ikusaburō why he had issued such a foolish declaration. Because of Konoe's reputed good sense, people expected him to act judiciously, but that declaration should have betrayed all confidence in him, he expostulated. When Kiya reported the criticism to Konoe, he listened silently and then managed to say only, "I have very little control over things."[20] Konoe had decided to terminate negotiations with the Nationalist government and issued the repudiation. But later when he weighed the prospects for the war, he was probably beset by profound misgivings.

When the 73rd session of the Imperial Diet convened in December 1937, the Konoe cabinet presented bills empowering the state to take over electric power and begin national mobilization. The Diet was thrown into a turmoil. By placing the generation and transmission of electric power under state control, the government sought to place the electric power industry on a wartime footing, to be at the disposal of national economic needs. The implications of this bill were serious for business.

Together with the political parties, business interests strongly opposed it. The mobilization bill would have delegated to the government wide-ranging powers of "control and use of manpower and material resources to assure the most effective mobilization of national strength for defense in times of war (including incidents that corresponded to war . . .)." With this legislation the government, if it so desired, could render the Imperial Diet impotent in times of war. But the government failed to clarify whether or not the China Incident "corresponded to war." Both of the major parties, the Seiyūkai and Minseitō, were opposed to the national general mobilization bill.

Despite opposition by the parties, the army was determined to push the measures through. Going along with the army, the minor rightist parties, including the Kokumin Dōmei and the Tōhōkai, supported the bills. In this uneasy atmosphere, the rumor spread that a group of young officers was plotting to carry out another coup d'état on the second anniversary of the February 26th Incident. Some right-wing activists occupied the Seiyūkai and the Minseitō headquarters, and Abe Isoo, chairman of the Shakai Taishūtō, was wounded by a rightist. More rumors followed that the Diet was about to be dissolved. These unsettling events and the army's relentless pressure intimidated the two political parties into submission, and in March the Diet passed the national mobilization bill without amendment and the electric power state control bill with partial revision.

Confronting the uproar when the bills came up for deliberation, Konoe announced to Harada that all he wanted to do was quit. Wouldn't Kido or Hirota do? he asked, noting that Hirota had no serious shortcomings and had made no major blunders. Konoe could not positively endorse Hirota but suggested that he might not be a bad choice. Konoe seemed determined to have the entire cabinet resign when the Diet session was over, and as soon as the Diet had adjourned, he went to the imperial palace and informed the Emperor that for someone like himself, who was popular but had no real power, it was extremely difficult to continue to serve as prime minister. A few days later, he told the Emperor that he felt like a mannequin—dragged along without being informed of anything.

Konoe's associates, however, could think of no suitable successor and urged him to remain in office. Saionji told Harada that it would be outrageous for Konoe to resign then. If it were a health problem, he said, Konoe could choose someone to fill in temporarily and take a good rest. If he were a little stronger, Saionji said, he would try to assist him himself. If Konoe were dissatisfied with any of his cabinet, he should obtain the Emperor's permission and replace them. But he must brace himself up and carry on; they should have the Emperor tell Konoe more pointedly that he must not resign now. Saionji bemoaned the situation to Harada and asked him to convey his opinion to the Privy Seal, who would, he hoped, report it to the Emperor. Harada informed Konoe, also, of what Saionji had said. Konoe finally agreed to stay in office, at least temporarily.

Konoe remained deeply discouraged. One day in May Ugaki Kazushige told Harada that several days earlier he had advised Konoe to take the initiative and push the policies he supported. He should remain passive no longer, he told the prime minister. Soon thereafter, Harada visited Saionji to report on the political situation, and at that time the Genrō commented that Konoe was conducting himself like a domestic servant. He needed more self-awareness and a sense of responsibility for the destiny of the nation, said Saionji. He must realize that he is responsible for the conduct of the imperial government; if only he would be more decisive and lead the nation positively. Konoe can never develop the spirit of strong leadership as long as he plays the servant, he quipped.

While his associates urged Konoe to stay on, they also feared that to remain prime minister any longer might cause such damage to his career that he would be unable to recover later. Some time after Konoe had agreed not to resign, Saionji confided second thoughts to Harada. It might be wiser for Konoe to resign at an appropriate time, he said. Although his term as prime minister had been a good experience for him, he might do better by waiting for another opportunity.

The fighting in China continued to spread. War requirements began to overshadow private needs, causing more and more hardship in daily life. In the autumn of 1937 the Konoe government launched a national spirit mobilization movement. With clamorous rallying cries the government tried to secure nation-wide support for and cooperation in the escalating war. Every-where one heard "Persevere and persist!" "One soup and one side dish (per meal)!" "Away with frivolous entertainment!" and "Luxury is an enemy!" At the same time the government drastically curtailed the freedom of speech and press.

In April and May of 1938 Japanese troops launched an opera-tion to capture Hsuchow, the junction of the main railways just below the border of Shantung. One of the objectives was to encircle and annihilate a large number of Chinese troops in the region and thus induce the Nationalist government to seek peace. Hsuchow was overtaken in May, but the Chinese army managed to evade the Japanese and retreat.

Soon after the capture of Hsuchow, Konoe carried out a major cabinet reshuffle. By that time he was painfully aware that his declaration earlier to cease dealing with the Nationalist govern-ment had been a serious mistake. He hoped the cabinet reorgani-zation would facilitate formation of a new policy that might somehow bring the war to a close. To begin with, Konoe re-placed Army Minister Sugiyama with Lieutenant-General Itagaki Seishirō. For some time Konoe had been deeply dissat-isfied with Sugiyama, and he worked hard to get Itagaki in the post. First, Itagaki advocated an early termination of the war in China. Second, Konoe knew that Itagaki enjoyed great popu-larity within the army; Konoe hoped that he would be able to lead the army in full cooperation with the effort to conclude hostilities quickly. But replacing the army minister was not easy. Not only did Sugiyama have no intention of resigning, but it had been a long-standing custom for the three army chiefs (army minister, chief of the army general staff, and inspector general of military education) to choose the new minister. The Emperor knew why Konoe wished to replace Sugiyama, and he learned that the army general staff concurred. Thereupon, in an act that had a direct bearing on Sugiyama's resignation, the Emperor conveyed Konoe's wish to Prince Kan'in Kotohito, chief of the army general staff, and asked him to cooperate. The Emperor also interceded for Itagaki's appointment by informing the three

army chiefs of his desire for their cooperation. When Privy Seal
Yuasa told the Emperor that Konoe might resign unless Itagaki
joined his cabinet, the Emperor urged Prince Kan'in again to
try and help secure Itagaki's appointment. This covert assistance
from the Emperor and its successful outcome pleased Konoe
exceedingly. Vice Army Minister, Umezu Yoshijirō, was also
replaced by Tōjō Hideki, an appointment Konoe welcomed.
Even before Tōjō was chosen, Konoe had remarked to Harada
that it would be ideal to have an exacting person like Tōjō assist
Itagaki, who had a tendency to be vague. Konoe replaced
Foreign Minister Hirota with Ugaki Kazushige. Ironically,
Konoe had been sharply critical of Hirota for the same tendency
he himself shared, a passive and indecisive stance toward the
military. In appointing Ugaki, Konoe pinned great hopes on him
to restrain the military and help terminate the war. For his part,
Ugaki was confidently ambitious, wanting to play the principal
role in resolving the China War. He submitted several conditions pending his acceptance. One was that he would not be
bound by the Konoe declaration—the statement that Japan
would not deal with the Nationalist government. Konoe reportedly told Ugaki, "The January 16th declaration was admittedly
uncalled for—do retract it, tactfully. . . ."[21]

Konoe appointed Araki Sadao education minister and reap-
pointed Kido, who had held the posts of education and public
welfare ministers concurrently, as full-time welfare minister.
Finance Minister Kaya and Commerce Minister Yoshino, both of
whom had been career bureaucrats, were replaced by Ikeda
Shigeaki of the Mitsui zaibatsu. Konoe hoped that by appointing
Ikeda to both economic posts concurrently, he could secure
greater support from business circles. He would need their cooperation in tackling the economic and financial problems of the
interminable war.

Through this sweeping cabinet reorganization, Konoe aspired
to break the deadlock of war. But the new army minister, Itagaki,
whose entry into the cabinet had troubled even the Emperor,
soon proved to be a disappointment. Although Konoe had been
adamant in his choice of Itagaki, his appraisal of the general
had been based on hearsay and reputation, and Konoe scarcely

knew him. They had the chance to talk intimately for the first time when Itagaki returned to Tokyo from the China front to assume his new post. The meeting was acutely disappointing to Konoe. Two days after the interviews, Matsudaira Yasumasa, chief secretary to the Privy Seal, told Harada in confidence that the Emperor had laughingly told the Privy Seal about Konoe's report on Itagaki. Apparently Konoe had told the Emperor that he found Itagaki rather thick-headed. The Emperor had added that Konoe certainly changed his mind easily. Soon after Itagaki became army minister, the army made the decision to move on Hankow and take Canton, which they did in October, further expanding the battlelines.

Konoe's disillusionment with Itagaki was the fruit of his own action. To begin with, Itagaki was not what Konoe had assumed him to be. Itagaki did not make his opinions clear nor act on definite convictions, and he did not command full respect from his subordinates. He was an indistinct personality, content to be a mouthpiece for those under him, and that was why he was so popular within the army. As army minister, he tended to be swayed by subordinates' opinions and often retracted his own statements. Konoe was particularly disappointed at Itagaki's failure to bring the army to cooperate with the government in a settlement of the war. To borrow Konoe's words from his memoirs, he had no idea who commanded army opinion, and the government continued to be manipulated by the shadow of a phantom supreme command. Konoe made no secret of his frustration: "I am thoroughly disgusted with playing the role of a robot," he declared.

Konoe expected much of his cabinet colleagues, but he himself exerted little leadership. When the drastic cabinet change failed to produce the anticipated results, once more he began to talk of resignation. In September, about three months after the cabinet reshuffle, Konoe told Kido that the capture of Hankow might give an opportunity for peace talks with Chiang Kai-shek. The China Incident had erupted suddenly, after he had formed his cabinet, and his subsequent efforts to achieve a settlement had often been stymied. If Japan was to negotiate peace with Chiang, Konoe continued, he had to resign to take responsibility for what had occurred. Kido urged Konoe to remain in office. A few days afterward, however, Konoe repeated his wish to resign to Harada, suggesting that he might perhaps change his post, if not resign altogether. If the Privy Seal became ill, for example, he could be transferred to that post and request Kido to run the government. Konoe proposed that he serve as Privy Seal for a year or so, and then be relieved from duty.

At the end of September, Ugaki resigned after serving as foreign minister for only four months. During his short tenure he had tried to restore peace with the Nationalist government, but a powerful sector of the army had thrown up barriers that thwarted his ability to act. He was deeply frustrated when the army proposed an Asia Development Board, which, with the prime minister as its president, would directly control all matters concerning China. The objective was to deprive the foreign minister of the power to form policy that could affect the China War. Such an organization would obviously undermine the function for which Ugaki had accepted the post of foreign minister, and naturally he objected strenuously to the Asia Development Board. Ugaki was also deeply dissatisfied that Konoe had never given any explicit support to the foreign minister's opinions and policy proposals within the cabinet council. And so, when the army proposed the Asia Development Board and Konoe approved it, Ugaki resigned.

Konoe tried to use Ugaki's resignation as an opportunity to have the cabinet resign en masse. The Emperor, Yuasa, Kido, and Harada all disapproved, and only after much persuasion, Kido barely managed to steer Konoe away from that move. In the end Konoe appointed Arita Hachirō as Ugaki's successor. But Konoe's spirits did not pick up, and he went through his duties only in a perfunctory way. Quietly he sought the first chance to resign.

On October 21 Japanese forces took Canton, and by the 27th the so-called three bastions of Wuhan—Wuchang, Hankow, and Hanyang—had also fallen into Japanese hands. The completion of the Wuhan operation brought the Japanese offensive to its conclusion: their forces had captured all the major cities of China. But defense of the Manchurian border against Soviet forces might require additional troops; on the other hand, the Nationalist government, having retreated to Chungking before Hankow fell, showed no inclination to seek peace through surrender. Faced with a stalemate, the army, including both the ministry and the general staff, became impatient for an early settlement.

Just before the fall of Hankow, Konoe told Harada that he would not resign immediately, for a change of government just then would have bad repercussions inside and outside the country. Further, he did not want his resignation to be considered irresponsible. He had carefully considered the matter, he said. If it was true that the Privy Seal was anxious to retire, Konoe would succeed him. If it appeared that no one but Konoe could succeed to the office of Privy Seal, Navy Minister Yonai, as the senior cabinet member, could become prime minister and continue the present cabinet without change. That is how Konoe wished to have matters arranged, and he asked Harada his opinion.

When Harada reported all this to Saionji, the Genrō retorted that it made no sense at all. He understood how trying it must have been for Konoe to maintain his government through such difficult days, but it was army support that had guaranteed the Konoe cabinet any tenure at all. If Konoe were appointed privy seal and placed near the throne, army influence would intrude into the Imperial Court, and that must be avoided at all costs. At present the government was run virtually at the will of the army, but the court had to be protected. Saionji asked Harada to inform only Yuasa in strict confidence that for the present the Genrō was strongly opposed to appointing Konoe to the Privy Seal post. If Konoe really wished to resign, Saionji continued, he should do so in a statesman-like manner, at an appropriate time after the conquest of Hankow, without resorting to petty schemes, to avoid being criticized as irresponsible. Harada was to convey to Konoe the Genrō's views on the course of action that the premier should take. For Privy Seal Yuasa the Genrō had the following message: However hard it may be, do not leave your post until death. Sacrifice yourself to His Majesty's cause. Once more, admonished by Saionji, Konoe remained in his post.

Shortly afterward Konoe told Harada apathetically that people still seemed to overestimate him; he was not the caliber of man to be prime minister, and he felt presumptuous. Harada sensed that Konoe was near despair. Under Konoe's flaccid leadership the cabinet quickly began to develop internal divisions, and they grew only more pronounced as Konoe's spirits fell. In November, Saionji joked to Harada that the cabinet was more like a federation than a united body. Chief Cabinet Secretary Kazami later commented to Harada that the members of the Konoe cabinet acted like Chinese warlords, each representing the different opinions of their constituents. Kazami lamented that although the people still trusted Konoe as they perceived him and were reassured by him, actually the government had accomplished precious little.

As if the Itagaki debacle were not enough, now Konoe was sorely embarrassed by another of his appointees. He had made Suetsugu home minister expecting him to restrain the right-wing forces. It came as a jolt therefore, when, upon assuming his post, Suetsugu began acting as a spokesman for the right wing. Konoe was angered by Suetsugu's behavior, but he took no action, and the government was left with no way to control the Right. In November the bewildered Konoe reported to the Emperor that Suetsugu was the scourge of his administration.

Business groups were apprehensive of the radical right wing and their anti-British, anti-Soviet slogans. They were unsettled by their noisy demands for a national socialist reconstruction of the country. By December the Right had grown so strident that Finance Minister Ikeda Shigeaki complained to Harada. He had accepted his cabinet appointment despite fragile health, he said, but he placed his official duties above his personal well-being. As long as the prime minister was resolved to work together with him in his efforts to fulfill his duties, he would be more than willing serve Konoe, Ikeda went on. To his deep regret, however, the prime minister seemed impassive when army officers and right wingers interfered with the execution of the duties of the finance minister. Ikeda needed the prime minister's full support. He would meet Konoe to inquire whether he was prepared to give such support, and, if not, Ikeda had no choice but to resign.

Earlier, on November 3, still having no clear prospect on the future of the war, Konoe proclaimed the establishment of the so-called New Order in East Asia. Behind the proclamation were expectations from a secret move in China. The previous January when Konoe had declared no more dealing with the Nationalist government, the Japanese government had intended to nurture the provisional government of the Republic of China to become a new Chinese regime. But this soon proved futile. The Japanese government and military, by then impatient for a settlement, had subsequently made several attempts to contact influential members of the Nationalist government for peace negotiations.

The kidnapping of Chiang Kai-shek at Sian in December 1936 gave rise to a short-lived collaboration between the Kuomintang and the Chinese Communist party in the form of a national united front against Japan. But Kuomingtang distrust of the Communists remained as strong as ever. The Japanese exploited the latent rift between the two by inducing Kuomintang leaders to seek peace with Japan. Of the various clandestine peace overtures by Japan, together known as the Chungking maneuvers, the one that came into the open was the Japanese collaboration with the vice president of the Kuomingtang, Wang Ching-wei. Wang had his differences with Chiang Kai-shek. He had long believed that China must conciliate Japan, and he had not changed his opinion even after the China Incident. He believed that to fight Japan to the bitter end would only result in the expansion of communist influence in China. He argued that as long as the Japanese peace terms did not jeopardize China's survival and independence, they should be accepted. The Japanese overture to Wang in the autumn of 1938, the so-called Wang Ching-wei maneuver, looked promising.

Konoe's proclamation on November 3 represented a revision of the policy of refusing to deal with the Nationalists. The Japanese army had already captured Canton and the three bastions of Wuhan, the proclamation began, and all the vital areas of China had fallen under Japanese control. The Nationalist government was now no more than a local regime. But if the Nationalist government persisted in its anti-Japanese and pro-

Communist policy, Japan would not lay down arms until the Chinese regime was crushed. Japan sought the establishment of a new order which would insure the permanent stability of East Asia; this was the ultimate purpose of Japan's military campaign. The new order would be founded on a tripartite relationship of mutual aid and cooperation among Japan, Manchukuo, and China in political, economic, cultural, and other areas. Its objective was to secure international justice, to build up a joint defense against communism, create a new "culture," and to realize close economic cooperation throughout East Asia. Japan wished China to share in the task of bringing about the New Order in East Asia. Even the participation of the Kuomintang government would not have been rejected, Konoe's proclamation added, significantly, if it repudiated past policies and improved the quality of its leadership, so that it could fully participate in the establishment of the New Order.

Late in November a group of Japanese, including Kagesa Sadaaki, chief of the Military Affairs Section, Military Affairs Bureau of the Army Ministry, and Imai Takeo, chief of the China Section, Army General Staff, met close associates of Wang, including Kao Tsung-wu and Mei Ssu-ping, in Shanghai. They reached an agreement on peace terms, which were recorded in two documents: the Minutes of Sino-Japanese Consultations and the Items of Understanding. Subsequently the Konoe cabinet submitted the Sino-Japanese agreement with some modifications to the Imperial Conference, which approved it as a document entitled Policy for the Adjustment of New Sino-Japanese Relations. At that time, instead of a new regime independent of the Nationalist government in Chungking, Wang Ching-wei and his associates were planning to set up a neutral zone in China. There they would entrench themselves with sufficient military power and rally the Nationalist government and the people to a policy of national recovery through peace and anti-communism. In that way they intended to restore total peace between China and Japan.

In December Konoe again expressed his desire to resign to Kido. He said that the army's secret plots [such as the Wang Ching-wei maneuver?—author] did not promise to yield much, and in every quarter he could see only an impasse. Now that the China Incident had become de facto a long-term engagement, Konoe explained, he wanted to seize the opportunity and resign. Kido replied that the man who carried the heaviest burden was the army minister, with over one and one-half million soldiers fighting under him on the continent. It would be unfair for Konoe to resign without the army minister's full understanding. Furthermore, Kido argued, his resignation would only cause more political instability within Japan, just when Wang Ching-wei was reportedly on the verge of defecting from the Chungking regime. Konoe gave in when Kido proposed to handle the matter, as he intended to confer with the army minister about Konoe's wish to resign. Learning of Konoe's intention from Kido, Itagaki was determined to stop him, arguing that the war was at a critical stage and Wang's defection was imminent.

In further discussion with Kido on the course of action of his cabinet, Konoe brought up the issue of strengthening the Anti-Comintern Pact of November 1936 as an additional reason for his resignation. Since early 1938 Japan and Germany had been discussing the possibility of strengthening the pact. At first, unable to smoothly extricate itself from the China War, Japan saw a way to check the Soviet Union more effectively in close ties with Germany. Germany, however, wanted to expand the new pact so that it would apply not only to the Soviet Union, but to Britain and France as well. Itagaki, who represented the dominant group in the army, wholeheartedly endorsed the German proposal, but Foreign Minister Arita, Navy Minister Yonai, and Finance Minister Ikeda flatly rejected it. The issue split the Konoe cabinet and threatened to throw it into turmoil, moving Konoe closer to actually resigning.

Wang Ching-wei had left Chungking and arrived in Hanoi on December 20. On December 22, corresponding with Wang's move, Konoe issued a statement which came to be known as the Konoe Declaration. It declared that the Japanese government was resolved, as had been made clear before, to carry on military operations until the anti-Japanese Kuomintang government was exterminated. At the same time, together with those far-sighted Chinese who shared Japan's ideals and aspirations, it would strive for the establishment of a New Order in East Asia. A spirit of rebirth was sweeping over all China, and enthusiasm for reconstruction was mounting ever higher. The Japanese government wished to make public its basic policy for relations with China in order that its intentions be thoroughly understood. Japan, Manchukuo, and China would be united by the common aim of establishing the New Order in East Asia and of realizing a good neighbor relationship, common defense against communism, and economic cooperation. To this end, Japan wished China to enter into full diplomatic relations with Manchukuo. Comintern influence in East Asia could not be tolerated, and Japan therefore considered it an essential condition that an anti-Comintern agreement between Japan and China be concluded.

In order to accomplish its purpose, the declaration continued, Japan demanded that its own troops be stationed as an anti-communist defense at specified points during the time the said agreement was in force, and also that the region of Inner Mongolia be designated as a special anti-communist area. As regards economic relations between the two countries, Japan did not intend to exercise economic monopoly in China, nor did Japan intend to demand China to restrict the interests of third countries. Plainly, the declaration went on, Japan only sought cooperation and collaboration between the two countries, not territory or military indemnities. It demanded only the minimum guarantee from China as a participant in the establishment of the New Order.

The Konoe Declaration recapitulated the Policy for the Adjustment of New Sino-Japanese Relations, with some modifications, but it is significant that the peace terms had become increasingly severe with each new pronouncement. From their first elaboration in the Minutes of Sino-Japanese Consultations and the Items of Understanding, to the Policy for the Adjustment of New Sino-Japanese Relations, and finally the Konoe Declaration, the terms grew steadily stiffer. That was the result of army pressure. The army was demanding an early settlement, but each time the opportunity for peace seemed imminent, the army reached out to grab a little more, wanting the maximum for its efforts. If Wang Ching-wei's collaboration with Japan was to succeed, the Japanese peace terms should have been kept moderate enough to induce the Nationalists and the Chinese people to seek the restoration of peace. Consequently Japan's increasingly harsh peace demands rendered Wang's political future even more precarious.

One may question how serious Konoe was in the first place about the Wang Ching-wei maneuver. One indication of his attitude can be seen when he expressed to Kido his desire to resign immediately before Wang's defection from Chungking. Harada later told Inukai Takeru that from the outset, Konoe was not very interested in the Wang affair. When Wang twice changed the date of his departure from Chungking, Konoe remarked, "After all he is only another Chinese. We might have been taken in by him." Harada understood this to reflect Konoe's basic distrust of the Chinese.[22] Konoe was by nature suspicious of others, and his attitude toward Wang Ching-wei seems to have been no exception.

On several occasions Kido managed to dissuade Konoe from resigning. By the time the Konoe Declaration was issued, however, Kido concluded that it was no longer meaningful to encourage Konoe to stay in office. Finally he told Harada that Konoe appeared so thoroughly dejected and apathetic that there was no point in urging him on. He may as well resign, he said. As for his successor, there seemed no choice but Hiranuma Kiichirō. Shortly afterward, Kido said to Koyama Kango that Prince Konoe had neither principles nor opinions, but only eccentric tastes [his penchant for novel appointments—author]. His cabinet is therefore hopelessly disunited, said Kido. Konoe is aware that people have begun to criticize his dissolute conduct, and he has no will to bring himself back. Kido concluded that resignation was the only choice left.

About that time Harada called on Saionji at Okitsu to report the imminent fall of the Konoe cabinet. Saionji remarked that at first Konoe must have hoped to lead the government by mobilizing and coordinating the many different forces at work. It had become clear that Konoe had failed in his initial objective and had become a victim of these very forces. It may be the fault of the times, said Saionji, "but I still wonder what he has been trying to do." A few days later the Genrō repeated to Harada that he had no idea what Konoe had tried to accomplish as prime minister. Perhaps, because of circumstances, he could not help what had happened. Saionji remarked that he was profoundly sorry for His Majesty. Precisely because His Majesty was so perceptive, he deeply sympathized with him. Saionji added that he was sorry for the Privy Seal and Konoe, too. His current predicament was a product of the times. Yes, no one could possibly escape that. Saionji had known Konoe since his youth and looked forward to witnessing his protégé achieve political success. He was greatly disappointed by Konoe as prime minister. But Saionji's affection for Konoe remained untouched.

Finally, on January 5, 1939, the Konoe cabinet resigned. The army deemed it highly undesirable for Konoe to resign when Wang Ching-wei had taken his decisive step and the Konoe Declaration had only just been issued. The army tried various moves to keep the cabinet intact, but in vain. They wanted the Konoe cabinet to continue—but not because they genuinely trusted Konoe. They had intended to utilize him as a puppet as long as his popularity remained. Soon after Konoe had formed his cabinet, Kiya Ikusaburō remarked to the premier that his cabinet enjoyed the enthusiastic support of the army. Konoe cooly replied, "To them I am a camouflage for their militaristic aims," and added, "I don't intend to become their robot."[23] In the final analysis, throughout its one and one-half years, the first Konoe cabinet had been continuously manipulated by the army.

How did Konoe see the China Incident, which escalated into a full-scale war during his tenure? His view can be gleaned from memoirs which Konoe seems to have written in 1940, during the Yonai cabinet era. The course on which the young officers drove Japan after the Manchurian Incident was, Konoe wrote, an "inevitable fate" that Japan was destined to meet. At that time the Powers were attempting to isolate Japan by means of an economic blockade. That would have deprived the country of overseas markets and raw materials, threatening the economy. It was the Manchurian Incident that broke the blockade. Even if the incident had not occurred then and in that manner, sooner or later some attempt to free Japan from the blockade would have certainly been made. The China Incident, like the Manchurian Incident, was destined ultimately to lead toward the establishment of the Greater East Asia Co-prosperity Sphere.[24] Thus, Konoe approved as natural and inevitable the course of overseas expansionism that Japan had taken from the Manchurian Incident through the China Incident, arriving at the construction of the Greater East Asia Co-prosperity Sphere. To the last, Konoe kept to the argument in his article, "Reject the Anglo-American–Centered Peace."

4

PURSUIT OF AN ILLUSION

For some time Saionji had been asking to be released from his duties as Genrō. He said he was getting too old and out of touch to be able to keep up with all the new faces and currents in politics. Partly to accommodate that wish, it was decided that the Genrō would no longer be responsible for recommending candidates for prime minister. Instead, the Lord Keeper of the Privy Seal would recommend the candidate after consultation with the Genrō. So it was that Yuasa was commanded to recommend Konoe's successor. Yuasa submitted to the Emperor the name of Hiranuma Kiichirō, president of the Privy Council. It was a virtual trade-off, for when Hiranuma became prime minister, Konoe took over as president of the Privy Council and concurrently became minister without portfolio in the new cabinet, ostensibly to remain responsible for the Wang Ching-wei maneuver.

The Hiranuma cabinet did not last long. From the start it was plagued by the issue of the Japanese-German Anti-Comintern Pact inherited from the Konoe government. Then in August 1939, Germany made a total about-face and concluded a non-aggression pact with the Soviet Union. After only eight months in office, Hiranuma resigned, declaring that the intricate and baffling turn of events in Europe required a new foreign policy that his cabinet could not provide.

To the Japanese army, which had collaborated closely with Germany to strengthen the Anti-Comintern Pact, the non-aggression pact with the Soviet Union represented a stunning betrayal. It was an ironic setback for the army, one that Saionji and Yuasa quickly sought to exploit. They turned to Ikeda Shigeaki,

who was widely known as an influential member of an elite group
called the Anglo-American faction, to head the government.
Ikeda, they reasoned, might be able to change the course of
Japan's foreign policy. But Konoe opposed him, declaring to
Yuasa that it was unwise to appoint Ikeda just then, for Japan's
foreign policy would be turned around 180 degrees and would
become pro-British. That might be feasible some day, but it was
still too soon, he said, and the domestic uproar would be damaging. It was bad tactics, warned Konoe, to add insult to injury by
pushing someone so pro-British when the military was already
disgruntled by its own miscalculation. If Ikeda were strong
enough to override opposition even from the military, he might
be worth considering, but Mr. Ikeda was a "gentleman," not a
politician. Konoe expressed doubt that Ikeda could go far enough
to be effective, and, if he could not, that his appointment might
cause a great deal of bloodshed. Since before the conclusion of
the German-Soviet non-aggression pact, Konoe had been behind
Hirota Kōki for prime minister. Konoe believed that because
Hirota was on good terms with the army, he should be able to
perform effectively. But certain groups within the army objected
to Hirota, while the army as a whole backed either Abe Nobuyuki or Hayashi Senjūrō, both senior statesman generals.
True to form, Konoe continued to oppose Ikeda and pressed
Yuasa to recommend Abe instead. Thus, when the Hiranuma
cabinet fell, Saionji gave his consent, and Yuasa submitted Abe
Nobuyuki's nomination to the Emperor.

Almost as soon as the Abe cabinet was formed in August 1939,
the German army overran Poland, and World War II began.
The new cabinet was not equipped to provide the leadership
Japan needed in a world that was changing so radically, and the
army soon withdrew its support. While the Abe cabinet teetered,
Konoe now began seriously pushing Ikeda, of all people, as the
next prime minister, claiming that the failure of its economic
policy had brought the Abe cabinet to a deadlock. By then,
however, the army wanted Konoe back as prime minister and
stood firmly against Ikeda. Hata Shunroku, minister of the army,
told Konoe that army opposition to Ikeda could not be suppressed, even by himself. He said he feared something like

another February 26th Incident if Ikeda tried to form a cabinet. But Konoe backed off from another term as prime minister, claiming lack of expertise in financial and economic affairs. He rejected Privy Seal Yuasa's appeal and insisted on Ikeda. This time, however, Yuasa would not consider Ikeda. In January 1940, the Abe cabinet resigned after only four and one-half months. The Privy Seal, having consulted ex-prime ministers and Saionji, recommended former Navy Minister Yonai Mitsumasa as the next premier.

The situation in China was getting more and more out of control. The Konoe Declaration, issued at the time of Wang Ching-wei's defection from Chungking, proved thoroughly ineffective in inducing the Nationalist government to seek peace. Wang was compelled to abandon his original idea, and he began to consider setting up a new government in Nanking. He hoped that as head of the new regime, formed with Japanese army approval, he could keep Japan to the promises made in the Konoe Declaration and somehow reach a breakthrough in settling the war. Thus Wang opened negotiations with the Abe government for a treaty between his regime, yet to be established, and Japan. During the secret meetings, however, the Japanese negotiators blatantly departed from the statements in the Konoe Declaration by demanding numerous political, military, and economic concessions from China. Shocked and infuriated by the Japanese betrayal, the Chinese balked, and the negotiations were temporarily deadlocked. However, by December 1939, Wang gave in and agreed to virtually all of the demands. The agreement was codified in a document called Main Points Governing the New Relations between Japan and China, and at the end of March 1940, Wang established his regime in Nanking.

Under the Yonai cabinet, the Japanese military came no closer to a solution to the war in China. Military leaders expected little from Wang's new regime and could not, therefore, completely abandon the possibility of a quick and total settlement through direct negotiations with Chungking. In early March, Army Minister Hata discussed the situation with Konoe. At that time, Konoe later related to Harada, Hata was so anxious to terminate hostilities that he suggested sending someone, even

Akiyama Teisuke, to negotiate directly with Chiang Kai-shek. Akiyama, Konoe continued, had once been suspected of being a Russian agent during the Russo-Japanese War of 1904–05, and now he might be collaborating with the Chiang regime. For all we know, Konoe said, he was on Chiang Kai-shek's payroll. In Konoe's opinion, if Japan had bought out Chiang immediately at the outbreak of hostilities, for 100 million or so yen, Japan could have avoided a costly war. Konoe, in fact, had tried to send Miyazaki Ryūsuke to China as Akiyama's deputy, but that attempt was thwarted by the gendarmerie, who arrested Miyazaki in Kobe. When Konoe complained to the army minister that nothing could be done if the army continued to interfere, Hata assured him that the army would stay clear and to go ahead and approach Akiyama, which Konoe did.[1]

Harada reprimanded Konoe for getting embroiled in a scheme that directly contradicted his own pledge not to deal with the Nationalists, when successive cabinets had tried so hard to settle the war in accordance with that pledge. Later, Harada advised Konoe to have Hata inform both the prime minister and foreign minister that as army minister he personally had requested Konoe to promote the Chungking maneuver. Otherwise, Harada added, Konoe would come out very badly, having undercut his own declaration. Konoe followed Harada's advice. Apparently Akiyama did try to approach Chiang directly in the summer of 1940, but he achieved nothing.

Wang's new regime was clearly not going to be of help, and the Japanese military grew more restless. On the very day when the Nanking government was founded, a joint conference of top army officials and general staff members was convened in Tokyo. They decided that if there was no settlement by the end of 1940, all Japanese troops would be withdrawn from China except stationary forces deployed to defend against communism in North China, the Mongolia-Sinkiang region, and in the vicinity of Shanghai, and that the troop withdrawal would commence in early 1941 and be completed within two years. A totally unmanageable war had driven the Japanese military leaders to a despairing standstill.

The depression was, however, suddenly dissipated by the

German blitzkrieg in Europe during May and June 1940. German troops swept over Holland, Belgium, and Luxemburg, and they invaded France. With the fall of Paris, France surrendered. Having swiftly established control over the heart of the European continent, Germany was poised to carry out its long-planned landing operation in England. The entire world was shaken, believing it only a matter of time before the Germans landed in England and then claimed total victory.

With the history of the world moving so quickly, demands from within Japan grew more strident, urging the country to act, and the military was offered a new opportunity to push the advance into southern Asia. The German conquest in Europe had removed the colonial powers from the Dutch East Indies and French Indochina, and England, facing imminent German attack, appeared powerless to defend its rights and interests in Asia. For the Japanese army, now was the time to go ahead with the southern advance and fill the gaps. The navy, which had urged moving south for a long time, was also impatient for action. Both had their sights on the abundant military matériel that could be acquired in Southeast Asia but not within Japan, Manchukuo, or China—the sphere of the New Order.

The drastic new developments in the war in Europe also buttressed the army's argument that an effective southern advance depended on stronger ties with Germany and Italy. The issue of alliance with the two European powers, which had been ignored since the German-Soviet non-aggression pact, thus assumed fresh priority. Having stubbornly opposed strengthening the Anti-Comintern Pact when he was navy minister under Konoe and Hiranuma, Yonai suddenly found himself with many new and determined opponents in the army.

In June 1940, the nation was itching with excitement. Just then Konoe resigned as president of the Privy Council. In a public statement, he said that Japanese must establish a new order of strong national unity if they were to successfuly cope with the kind of changes that were shaking Japan and transforming large parts of the world. He was resigning, he said, so that he could work for that political order. He would support the new party movement, which had become unexpectedly active, if its goals were the same as his, but if it was meant simply as forging alignment among the established parties or turned into a scramble for political power, Konoe would not take part. He said he would seek advice and many opinions and consider them carefully in formulating a concrete program for the new order of national unity.

Complicated circumstances lay behind the position Konoe took. Since about 1935, certain politicians had been trying to form a new party with Konoe as its president, but he had shown no interest. After he installed his first cabinet, however, there was a sudden burst of activity among a wider group in support of a new party led by him. At the same time, Konoe himself now began to want his own political party, partly to back him in handling the Diet, and partly to create a base for control over the increasingly unmanageable army so that he could move toward a quick settlement of the China War. Activities behind this "Konoe new party" were basically of two types. On the one hand were the various schemes and projects of established party members aspiring to rebuild their parties, which had been rendered all but lifeless after the Manchurian and the May 15th incidents. They hoped a new party with the popular Konoe as its president would revive them all. There was also a pro-military movement to establish a "one nation, one party" system with Konoe as president, modeled after the Nazis. Many of those involved participated in both categories of activity.

In the autumn of 1938, Akiyama Teisuke, Diet member Akita Kiyoshi, and the Shakai Taishūtō[2] leaders Asō Hisashi and Kamei Kan'ichirō came forward with a concrete proposal. Their plan for a new party interested Konoe, who was, as ever, apparently drawn to the somewhat peculiar, unorthodox character of the individuals involved. At that time Konoe remarked to Harada that Akiyama was another Mizuno Naoshi, but with broader experience, and an inordinately tough fellow. He found a person like Akiyama much more interesting than the ordinary bureaucrat, and he was attracted to Asō and Kamei, saying that they possessed "a kind of philosophy." Konoe also seems to have hoped that if the Shakai Taishūtō leaders participated, the new party might develop into a popular movement attracting members from the labor-farmer class. This hope may have been all the more intense because of the lack of a mass base in his political background. Konoe was keenly aware and troubled that so far he had virtually no channels to the common people.[3]

Another Konoe new party plan afoot at the same time was actively pushed by Home Minister Suetsugu, Justice Minister Shiono, and Education Minister Kido, who were motivated by the awareness that Konoe now wanted his own party.

However, as so often happened, Konoe could not bring himself to make a solid commitment. Hesitating and vacillating, his response to any concrete proposals was always ambiguous. He told Harada on October 20, 1938, that the Suetsugu plan annoyed him. "Once I took [the party] on, it would be hard to get out, and there is no assurance that it would go well, either. But without some sort of comprehensive national unity the government simply cannot cope with this situation. . . . I don't have the courage to head a new party, and I know that it would be chaos if I accepted the job. So I want to refuse it, but knowing that my refusal will also cause turmoil, I am keeping the issue pending. The chief cabinet secretary tells me, 'You could postpone your decision until the end of this month.' On the other hand, Shiono and Suetsugu tell me, 'The government simply has to formulate a policy platform this week to show that the premier is firm and decisive.' We can procrastinate as long as I refrain from taking a definite stand."[4] He remained in this indecisive state long enough for both plans to wither and die.

Even after Konoe's resignation in January 1939, his public appeal did not diminish, despite the meager accomplishments of his government. Backers of a Konoe new party kept up their activities, and public pressure on him to return to the prime minister's post persisted. In the long run, Konoe's popularity was apparently based largely on the shallow whims of a public whose preferences revolved around personality more than achievement. Around this time Kiya Ikusaburō urged Konoe that the time was right; he should make the move and form a party. He was at the peak of popularity, and the new party movement had reached a climax. But Konoe was only too aware of the ephemeral roots of his appeal, and he equivocated. One cannot rely on popularity, he said. Like a movie star, one is left without it before very long.

Kiya was one of the early supporters of a party organized by Konoe and had been searching for someone qualified to assist the prince as secretary-general. It would be difficult, Konoe told Kiya, to find anyone willing and able to take on the onerous role of party secretary-general. He needed a completely dependable right-hand man, someone who was practical and honest. So many who sought him out told him only what was calculated to please, and more than once Konoe admitted that this was distinctly annoying. He was only human and must have committed a number of mistakes, he said, but no one ever pointed them out to him. He needed someone who would offer forthright criticism, not flattery and platitudes, he told Kiya, but so far had found no one.[5] Perhaps even more, he needed someone to help relieve the loneliness of his isolated pedestal.

As the war continued to change the face of Europe, the political situation in Japan grew progressively more unstable. Konoe was fairly certain that he would be asked to take over the government again in the near future, which is why he resigned from the Privy Council and issued his statement on the establishment of a "political order of national unity."

Konoe's action made a considerable impression on the public. His supporters, who had impatiently waited for his rise, were delighted. As Konoe wrote in his memoirs, he had concluded that "only a government supported by political power based on a nationwide popular organization, not the established parties, would be able to control the military and settle the China War." Since then it had been his goal to establish such an organization.[6] But when he actually proposed a "powerful political order of national unity," he had no concrete program.

What is more, several days after Konoe had made his proposal public, he told Harada that he had suggested to Chief Cabinet Secretary Ishiwata Sotarō that the government take the initiative in this new political order. This is something that must involve not only the legislative, but the executive and, in some ways, the supreme command as well, he said. Konoe then requested Harada to tell Yonai and Ishiwata that if the government wished, he would be willing to become chairman or president of a national unity organization created by the government. Clearly, Konoe was attempting to pass full responsibility for the planning and establishment of a political organization on to the government, he himself being unable to form a concrete program. His very ambivalence points to a lack of confidence in and enthusiasm for the realization of his own proposal. The Yonai cabinet, in any case, judged it improper to take on such a program.

In July, Konoe went to his Karuizawa villa. He invited Professor Yabe Sadaji of Tokyo Imperial University's Department of Law to come to the villa and draft a concrete program for the New Order (Shin Taisei). According to Yabe's recollections of that visit, Konoe expressed how deeply he felt his responsibility for the China War. To settle it, Konoe said, the government had to have unity within the army, but more, the support of a political force backed by the people as a whole and strong enough to counteract the military. Konoe wanted to mobilize that political force, but it could not come out of a realignment of the established political parties, and he had no interest in starting his own. At the same time, any new political order must avoid the pitfall of becoming a one nation, one party system. That would be no more than another bakufu—a government outside the legitimate government. It was along those lines that Konoe asked Yabe to draft a program.[7]

We must note in Yabe's reminiscence, first, that Konoe had already given up the idea of a new party by the time Yabe met him in Karuizawa, but it is not clear when he lost interest in it. Second, Konoe wanted above all to prevent the new political order from developing into a single, autocratic national party. As soon as Konoe announced that he hoped to build a "political order of national unity," the ideological Right began to suspect him of covertly planning to install another bakufu in modern guise. In the name of kokutai (national polity), they launched an attack. A part of the Right even considered eliminating Konoe for having dared promote an idea that undermined the so-called national polity. Konoe, who was firmly committed to the concept of kokutai, was shocked by the reaction, all the more because of his close ties with certain members of the ideological right wing.

Arima Yoriyasu recalled Konoe's deep distress over the attack.

About then, Arima wrote, in a discussion they had shortly before
he became premier for the second time, Konoe confided that of
all the various comments on the idea of a new party, the most
bitter was the accusation that he was out to set up a modern-day
bakufu. Arima noted that a party intended to gain greater political authority than the Emperor and structured to disregard the
imperial family could not be countenanced, but since Konoe's
party would be quite different from the ultranationalist parties
in Germany or Italy, the criticism was totally misplaced. Still,
Konoe was by nature extremely uneasy about terrorism or
possible threats to his life, and rumors that the right wing contemplated his assassination frightened him.

Professor Yabe agonized over Konoe's request, but finally submitted a recommendation. The new political order should be
based on an organization whose functional units were economic
associations, cultural societies, and other vocational groups. The
people would have a direct connection with politics through this
organization, which, by establishing links between political and
occupational activities, would allow popular participation in the
process of policy making and help publicize information regarding
established policies and government decisions. The aims were to
modify the system of bureaucratic control that operated in isolation
from the daily lives of the citizens, and to reestablish channels
between the people and politics, channels that had been cut off
because the political parties never generated nationwide popular
participation.

While Konoe was in Karuizawa, some of the more influential
army officers began pressing harder to have Yonai removed from
office. They backed Konoe for prime minister, believing that his
popularity would make him a useful tool in promoting their
programs. In July 1940, they convinced Army Minister Hata
that he should resign, which brought down the Yonai cabinet.
Yuasa Kurahei had retired the previous month, on account of
poor health, and Kido Kōichi succeeded him as Lord Keeper of
the Privy Seal. Now it was Kido's turn to recommend the next
prime minister. He told the Emperor that he would consult the
senior statesmen and the Genrō, and he convened a conference
of the senior statesmen. Kido informed them that the military

was interested in Konoe and that there was sufficient ground to suspect that the army had caused the collapse of the Yonai cabinet just to get Konoe back in office. He concluded that since no other possible candidate seemed suitable, he would like to nominate Prince Konoe. All the senior statesmen except Konoe agreed. After the conference Kido sent Chief Secretary Matsudaira to Okitsu to talk with Saionji. The Genrō told Matsudaira that he could not offer a responsible opinion, for he had been in poor health and was not sufficiently informed on political developments. Thereupon Kido recommended Konoe to the Emperor.

As it turned out, even before Matsudaira's visit, Harada had apparently remarked to Saionji that there was no one except Konoe who could take over the government. Saionji replied that it would not work; they were still clinging to the idea that the job of governing could be propped up with popularity. The time for that was past, he said. It seems that by then, Saionji's expectations for strong, wise, or decisive political leadership from Konoe had faded and disappeared.

The roster of the second Konoe cabinet, formed on July 22, 1940, read as follows: Konoe Fumimaro, prime minister; Matsuoka Yōsuke, minister for foreign affairs; Yasui Eiji, home minister; Kawada Isao, minister of finance; Tōjō Hideki, minister of the army; Yoshida Zengo, minister of the navy; Kazami Akira, minister of justice; Hashida Kunihiko, minister of education; Ishiguro Tadaatsu, minister of agriculture; Kobayashi Ichizō, minister of commerce and industry; Murata Shōzō, minister of communication and concurrently minister of railways; and Tomita Kenji, chief cabinet secretary.

Matsuoka Yōsuke, the new foreign minister, had been head of the Japanese delegation to the League of Nations in February 1933 when Japan clashed with the other delegates over the settlement of the Manchurian Incident. News of Matsuoka's dramatic announcement at the plenary session that Japan would withdraw from the League and his stormy departure from the assembly created wild jubilation at home. Overnight Matsuoka became a hero to a nation growing feverishly chauvinistic, and his reputation as a strong foreign policy advocate was made.

Personally he was strong-minded, eloquent, and loquacious. He always had a ready supply of ideas, some of which were quite inventive. Once he experienced the sensation of being in the national limelight, Matsuoka's thirst for popular acclaim, and then power, kept growing. He became self-conscious, all too aware of his appeal and reputation, and at the same time he acquired the skills of an uncompromising, opportunistic operator in his pursuit of power. He had a violent temper and could be very difficult to work with. Learning that Konoe was about to make Matsuoka his foreign minister, many, including Kido, had strong reservations. Even the Emperor urged Konoe to reconsider the appointment. But Konoe would not be dissuaded. He was undoubtedly drawn to Matsuoka's unique personality and broad vision, but more, he probably hoped that Matsuoka, whose appointment had been commended by the army, could effectively restrain the officers with his self-assertive arrogance and extraordinary verbal power.

The day after the inauguration of his cabinet Konoe delivered a radio address entitled "Receiving the Imperial Mandate." The old world order, Konoe declared, was collapsing in Europe, and the waves of change were reaching other parts of the globe. Japan, too, must be ready to cope with a radically different world, he said. Their first task was to reorder the internal politics of the nation. The political parties manifested two shortcomings. First, their underlying principle was liberalism, democracy, or socialism, and their fundamental views of the world and life were incompatible with *kokutai*. Second, their primary objective was power, and in this they failed to uphold their original imperative, laid down by the legislature, of assisting the imperial rule. In order to restore the beneficial state of the nation wherein one hundred million people together dedicated themselves to serve their country in accordance with the imperial wish, the shortcomings of the political parties must be eliminated. Not only the political parties, but all the people, civilian and soldier, army and navy, government official and common citizen, everyone high and low shared the duty to assist the imperial rule in obedience to the Emperor's dictates. If the Japanese people could work in unity toward that goal, he announced, the many problems of the nation in these critical times could be resolved.

The new political order was still no more than an idea when Konoe became prime minister again. Now, much sooner than he expected, he had to do something concrete about it. Beginning at the government level, Konoe announced that in basic foreign policy, Japan would stand resolute at the forefront of change and on its own power establish a new order in the world. Japan must, therefore, free itself as soon as possible from economic dependence on other countries and concentrate on heightening economic collaboration with Manchukuo and China and expansion into the southern Pacific regions, both of which would be vital in the future. Those efforts would require new policies for education. Konoe declared that the government would reconstruct the content and goals of education in order to rear a new generation of young people equipped to meet the challenge of supporting the Japanese empire in total dedication to the doctrine of *kokutai*.

On August 1, the Konoe cabinet announced the Outline of a Basic National Policy. Actually this document was drafted by the Military Section of the Army Ministry's Military Affairs Bureau and then was adopted by the Cabinet Council. The Outline stated that the world stood at a historic turning point, and that Japan, too, "faced an unprecedented, great ordeal." To fully implement the national policy, it was urgent to complete fundamental reforms in government and create a strong national defense state (*Wehrstaat*). Japan's basic goal was world peace, firmly established in accordance with the lofty spirit of the nation's founding and with the ideal of *hakkō ichiu*.[8] The first step in realizing the national policy was to construct a New Order in Greater East Asia founded on the solidarity of Japan, Manchukuo, and China.

On the day the Outline was made public, Foreign Minister Matsuoka issued a statement declaring that he had long urged the recognition of Japan's mission to proclaim and demonstrate the "Imperial Way" throughout the world. He believed that the concept of Imperial Way allowed every nation and race to find its proper place in the world. The immediate aim of Japan's foreign policy was to establish, in accordance with that noble concept, a Greater East Asia Co-prosperity Sphere (Dai Tōa Kyōeiken) linking Japan, Manchukuo, and China. At the press conference afterward, Matsuoka declared that the Greater East Asia Co-prosperity Sphere naturally included both French Indochina and the Dutch East Indies. Within minutes, he had coined a term that was soon to become known throughout the world.

The Cabinet Council approved the Outline on July 26, and the next day the Imperial Headquarters–Cabinet Liaison Conference approved another policy statement, Main Principles Governing the Response to Changes in the World. This document was a proposal prepared by a committee of army and navy leaders to be presented by Imperial Headquarters to the Liaison Conference. It stated that Japan would work toward a rapid settlement of the China War and would solidify the nation internally while strengthening its international position. It stressed the need to move carefully, exploiting opportunities to settle Japan's position vis-à-vis southern Asia and the Pacific, while rapidly buttressing ties with Germany and Italy and bringing radical improvement in relations with the Soviet Union.

After specifying policies to be implemented toward French Indochina, the Dutch East Indies, and other areas in the south, the document laid out the general conditions for the use of military force in the south: 1) In the event that a basic settlement for the China War were reached and if conditions at home and abroad permitted, Japan would take the first favorable opportunity to resort to arms; 2) if the China War remained unsettled, Japan would carry out its policies as established so long as hostilities with third powers were not provoked. If particularly favorable conditions were to develop, Japan would use force to solve the southern problem; efforts would be made to limit the use of force to military action against Britain, but since such circumstances might end up in war with the United States, thorough preparations would be made to provide for that contingency. The Main Principles is a noteworthy document. It was drawn up by the military, and it set the course for foreign policy during the second Konoe cabinet, as was proven by the succeeding events.

In September, after lengthy and forceful negotiations, Japan and French Indochina signed a convention allowing Japanese troops to be stationed in northern French Indochina. Japan had two objectives: one was to cut the flow of American and British aid goods to Chungking via French Indochina, and the other to facilitate Japan's operations in South China.

The circumstances leading to the Tripartite Pact among Germany, Italy, and Japan centered on moves made by the United States, and Soviet suspicions toward Germany. Once the non-aggression pact with the Soviet Union was concluded, for a while Germany lost interest in an alliance with Japan. But in the spring of 1940, with the Germans firmly in control over the continent, American assistance to England began to increase dramatically and it seemed more and more certain that the United States would enter the war. The Soviet Union had become extremely uneasy at the prospect of a German-controlled Europe on its southern flank, and relations between them were far from stable. Germany then began to calculate the advantages of an alliance with Japan: to prevent the United States from entering the war, and, at the same time, obtain backing for a confrontation with the Soviet Union. In September, Heinrich Stahmer, special envoy of Foreign Minister Joachim von Ribbentrop, arrived in Japan on a secret mission, armed with a draft of the three-nation pact.

Stahmer began negotiations with Foreign Minister Matsuoka, who kept in touch with Konoe on the major points of the proceedings. The negotiations progressed rapidly, and with approval of the Cabinet Council and the Imperial Conference the Tripartite Pact was signed in Berlin on September 27, four days after Japan's first troops had been sent to northern French Indochina. Its principal stipulations were: 1) that Japan recognize and respect the leadership of Germany and Italy in the establishment of a new order in Europe; 2) that Germany and Italy recognize and respect Japan's leadership in the establishment of a New Order in Greater East Asia; 3) that Japan, Germany, and Italy cooperate in setting up their respective new orders; 4) that all three were bound to assist one another, using all political, economic, and military means possible if one of the signatory nations was attacked by a power not yet involved in the European war or in the Japanese-Chinese conflict; and 5) that the agreement would in no way affect the political status quo currently prevailing between each of the three signatories and the Soviet Union.

At the outset of the negotiations, Stahmer stated that Germany considered it important to end the European war as quickly as possible and that it was crucial to prevent American participation on the British side. At present, Germany did not seek military assistance from Japan to prosecute the war against England; Japan's immediate role was to help keep the United States at bay. Only if Japan, Germany, and Italy joined forces in a treaty or some other kind of alliance and prepared for an emergency could armed conflict between Japan and the United States be prevented. The three powers had to demonstrate their resolution to the world if they hoped to put an effective brake on the United States. Weakness or hesitation at this point was dangerous, Stahmer continued, for it would undermine their credibility. Once the alliance with Germany and Italy was concluded, Germany was prepared to mediate if Japan opened negotiations with the Soviet Union. A Japanese-Soviet rapprochement should not encounter too much difficulty. Stahmer added that his statements represented the thinking of Ribbentrop.

As it happened, Stahmer had voiced the thinking of the Japanese army on most points, but that was not purely coincidence. Most likely the Germans and the Japanese army had made certain beforehand to clarify the points on which they agreed and work out ways to make them palatable to the Japanese government. Then Stahmer was sent to convey these points to Matsuoka, representing them as the German position.

Most of what Stahmer had proposed was acceptable to Matsuoka, who believed that Japan also would benefit by readjusting relations with the Soviet Union through German mediation. The "threat from the north" would be lifted, giving greater leeway to push ahead with the Greater East Asian Co-prosperity Sphere in the course of fighting the war in China. Further, stronger relations between Japan, as an ally of Germany and

Italy, and the Soviet Union, which was formally bound by the non-aggression pact with Germany, would also serve to draw Moscow closer to the Tripartite Pact thus fortifying the deterrent to American military moves against Japan. A stronger alignment would, finally, cause Washington to think twice before going to war for England, and without American interference, a German-Italian victory in Europe seemed almost certain. Matsuoka believed that the Greater East Asia Coprosperity Sphere depended on German-Italian victory. If the United States could be restrained, Matsuoka reasoned facilely, Washington would become more conciliatory toward Japan, and with American mediation Japan might be able to bring the China War to a close.

Matsuoka, however, never completely believed Stahmer. How, he asked, could Germany help Japanese-Soviet relations? Evading the question, Stahmer continued to insist that Japan should trust Germany. Its leaders had confidence that they could mediate successfully between Japan and the Soviet Union. Was not Germany planning to attack the Soviet Union in the future? Would not Germany clash with Russia over the Balkan problem? Stahmer parried Matsuoka's questions simply by answering no.

Konoe was not completely sanguine about the alliance with Germany. He was aware of the danger and could not conceal his own reservations. Several days before the pact was signed, Harada asked him whether he thought the alliance might actually provoke war with the United States, not prevent it. Harada added that he was totally opposed to the alliance. Germany, Konoe replied, had offered not only to mediate a non-aggression pact between Japan and the Soviet Union, but also to help settle the war in China. Harada responded that it seemed extremely risky to conclude an alliance with Germany without full as-surance first that the Japanese-Soviet pact was as good as established. Konoe confided that he also was somewhat uneasy at the speculative nature of the whole proposal, particularly in view of reports that Germany had been deploying troops against the Soviet Union after the fall of Paris. The circumstances did not portend success for any German-Soviet talks. Konoe was even more pessimistic about the consequences for Japan if England came out on top in Europe and then turned toward the Pacific together with the United States.[9]

Konoe and Matsuoka decided that the possible benefits of the alliance outweighed the potential danger. Both held high hopes that Japanese-Soviet relations would improve, and that the Soviet Union would move closer to the Tripartite Pact nations. But their expectations were based not on evidence but on their own assumptions and, more, on the credibility they attached to Stahmer's statements. As far as they knew, Germany and the Soviet Union had maintained a generally friendly relationship since the conclusion of the non-aggression pact. They assumed that Germany, now the military master of Europe, could and would exert influence to improve Soviet relations with Japan and to draw the Soviet Union closer to all the Tripartite Pact nations. In addition, Konoe was being pressured by the army. In later years he attempted to justify his position and actions regarding the Tripartite Pact, but his explanations were mutually contradictory and unconvincing. In his postwar memoirs, how-ever, he squarely acknowledged the military element behind Japan's withdrawal from the League of Nations in 1933. Neither the Emperor nor Prime Minister Saitō personally approved of that action, Konoe wrote; "They were pressured into it by the military, just as I was when I concluded the Tripartite Pact."[10]

Since early 1939, when Hiranuma headed the cabinet, the navy had steadfastly opposed strengthening any alliance with Germany and Italy. About when the second Konoe cabinet was formed in mid-1940, however, some of the younger navy officers veered off in their own direction and began rallying support for the pact. Navy Minister Oikawa Koshirō, who succeeded Yoshida in September 1940, was able to bring the navy as a whole to support the position of the younger officers and back the alliance. This was a drastic change that greatly alarmed Konoe.

Now the navy was behind the pact, too. But there were others who remained opposed or deeply uneasy about it. Once a com-mitment had been made to go ahead and sign the pact, Konoe went to the palace to report the cabinet decision to the Emperor. According to what Konoe later told Harada, during the audience the Emperor suggested that an alliance with Germany was perhaps unavoidable if Japan had exhausted every recourse in efforts to come to terms with the United States. He was seriously troubled by the situation they faced, the Emperor said. What would happen to Japan if they lost the war? Would Konoe share his pains and hardships, the Emperor asked. Konoe reported that while he was usually calm and unemotional, the pathos of that question brought him to tears.

Count Kaneko Kentarō once told Konoe a story about the Meiji Emperor and Itō Hirobumi. After the Imperial Conference had decided to go to war against Russia in 1904, the Emperor had sent for Itō and asked him how he would react if Japan were defeated in the war that was about to begin. The Emperor himself was not at all confident about the outcome. Itō replied that if the war developed badly for Japan, he would relinquish his titles and honors to the throne and go to the battlefield as a rank-and-file soldier to fight to his last breath. The Emperor Meiji, Kaneko recounted, was profoundly moved by Itō's resolution. Konoe apparently reminded the Emperor of that episode and added that he shared his deepest anxieties. Konoe vowed to dedicate himself to carrying out the will of the Emperor. Saionji, sharing the Emperor's anguish, bitterly regretted the conclusion of the Tripartite Pact.

The day the pact was signed in Berlin, a sternly worded imperial rescript was issued in Tokyo that forbade any criticism of the alliance. The next day Konoe delivered a radio message entitled "The Japanese-German-Italian Tripartite Pact," in which he stated that the world was at a grave historic turning point. In accordance with the infinitely vast imperial will, the government had decided to conclude the alliance with Germany and Italy and actively cooperate with them for the cause of lasting worldwide peace and progress. Germany and Italy were moving toward the establishment of a new order in Europe, while Japan was trying to realize a new order in Greater East Asia based on the "inherent nature" of Asia. It was inevitable that the many peoples of the world would some day gather to form spheres of coexistence and co-prosperity. In fact, war had broken out again in Europe and a semi-wartime state of tension had arisen in East Asia only because that inevitable development had been stifled. That Japan, Germany, and Italy had agreed to cooperate and use, if necessary, the might of their military alliance was also unavoidable.

Konoe stressed that Japan was facing the gravest national crisis in its history. In response to the extraordinary circumstances, the government was making every effort to build a new national order based on the unity of the people, in which every subject would participate, carrying out the imperial rule in compliance with the spirit of the nation's founding. In obedience to the imperial wish, the government was taking the first positive steps to resolve the national crisis by perfecting its policies toward other nations and solidifying the national order, which was the base of popular participation in the imperial rule. Konoe declared that the government would tell only the truth to the people, and expect sacrifice and dedication from them. In return, the government would make all efforts to guarantee the people basic security of livelihood and accord them highest honor.

During the ensuing press conference Konoe elaborated on the promise of "basic security of livelihood" and "highest honor" to the people. Their participation in the great program of establishing a new world order, he declared, would bring glory to the people of Japan, Germany, and Italy; they would be remembered with admiration in the history of mankind. The government would, furthermore, use all possible means to provide basic security of livelihood for all the citizens of Japan, avowed Konoe. This last turned out to be an empty promise; from that time onward life became more and more difficult as the people were asked to make ever greater sacrifices in order to fulfill the vast requirements of the military. Year after year their distress intensified as daily necessities grew steadily harder to obtain.

About a month after the conclusion of the Tripartite Pact, on October 12, the Imperial Rule Assistance Association (IRAA, Taisei Yokusankai) was set up. The process of creating this institution was rocky, and from the beginning it was tinged by the irony that the IRAA was meant to provide the operational machinery for a political order of national unity that its author—Konoe—no longer believed to be feasible. When he was appointed prime minister for the second time in July 1940, Konoe still had no concrete plans for putting his national unity order into effect. But the political parties, including the Seiyūkai and the Minseitō, had reacted quickly to Konoe's June statement and vied with one another to dissolve rapidly to clear the way for a brighter future in the new political order. That is why, in mid-1940, Japan's political parties suddenly disappeared from the scene.

This turn of events left Konoe bewildered and dampened his enthusiasm. He told Gotō Ryūnosuke that the new political order could no longer be a popular movement, now that he was head of government, and he wanted to abandon the whole idea. Gotō understood Konoe's logic, but he pointed out that Konoe's defection just then would create widespread suspicion that he had deceived the people and merely used them to grasp power. If he lost the people's trust, he would not be able to govern effectively. Gotō urged Konoe to stand behind the idea of a new political order and to press forward with it. "Well, I might as well stay with it," was Konoe's reply, but clearly his interest was halfhearted, at best.[11]

In August, Konoe set up a preparatory commission to lay the groundwork for the new political order. In place of the customary address at its first meeting, he read a lengthy statement proclaiming that, with much of the world in turmoil, Japan had embarked on the unprecedented, great task of establishing a New Order in East Asia. International developments demanded that the China War be ended quickly and that Japan assume positive leadership in building a new world order. To achieve those objectives, Japan had to prepare itself and build up an advanced national defense state, whose base lay in a powerful new domestic order. Hence it was necessary to create an organization geared for nationwide popular participation, which could mobilize the total energy of the state and enable all one hundred million subjects to act as one in assisting the imperial rule.

The statement outlined how the new organization would be structured. In the first place, since everyone had to be able to participate from their respective places of work, all economic and cultural sectors of society would be organized vertically and integrated into a nationwide network which would allow two-way interaction between the people and the state. Each individual would contribute to the process of formulating national economic and cultural policies; once approved, policy decisions would be disseminated back down to every corner of the national life. Only by providing such channels to convey the popular will to the government and to communicate government policies to the people could the national resources be concentrated on the governing of the nation.

Konoe's inaugural statement contained a section describing the leadership and goals of the movement that would become the underlying support of the new organization. It had to be a mass movement, he said, and ideally it should arise spontaneously from the ranks of ordinary citizens, but events were moving too quickly to stand by and let it develop naturally. Further, a spontaneous popular movement was likely to deteriorate into factional bickering, eventually losing its force as a national program. The government, therefore, would give active encouragement and guidance, which meant that the proposed "movement for a popular organization" would be a state project of government and people together. It would be a distinctly political movement, but never a political party, which by definition was partisan and represented particular interests and sectors. Konoe's movement would embody the united interest of the nation and the public and would aim at transcending factional party politics and the kind of liberalism on which they were premised. But this would not be a one nation, one party movement, which would identify a single part with the whole and would equate party with state. Such a system would turn opposition to the party into treason to the state, and it would perpetuate party dominance, whose head would acquire a permanent monopoly on power. A one nation, one party system would violate *kokutai*, which was premised on one emperor for the entire people. Every subject would have the honorable duty of assisting the imperial rule, and no one person or one party would be permitted to monopolize that role.

Yabe Sadaji drafted the statement, and Konoe touched it up and revised it. While it rejected the proposal sponsored by members of established parties of a new political party under Konoe, it also rejected the one nation, one party structure that the army, pro-military party members, and rightist groups had vigorously tried to promote. Konoe's statement bitterly disappointed a great many people, particularly those on the Right, and their anger presaged some of the difficulties to come.

Characteristically, Konoe recruited a somewhat unusual group to make up the preparatory commission. The members represented assorted interests, sectors, positions, and ideologies, reflecting an attempt to gather the diverse forces of the nation under one roof. Its unruly membership made it difficult to maintain a balance, and no sooner had the commission begun deliberation than sharply conflicting opinions and tumultous arguments destroyed any semblance of constructive order. As usual, Konoe, as chairman, did not even try to guide the proceedings. Worse, he often just walked out in the middle of a meeting when it became deadlocked in interminable debate. Gotō Ryūnosuke, a standing executive member, recalled that the commission was a hodgepodge of individuals without guidance. They argued for as long as ten hours before they settled on a name for the nucleus of the New Order movement.

According to Gotō, the ideological right wingers argued that since the entire population was to participate in the movement, to set up an association would immediately create a distinction between members and nonmembers. This was countered with the idea of including all citizens in the association, in which case the association would be unnecessary. Mutō Akira, chief of the army ministry's Military Affairs Bureau, was so exasperated over these exchanges that at one point he reportedly shouted into the fray that, if no name was necessary, neither was the association, nor the Konoe cabinet, for that matter. Amid chaotic disorder, Gotō said, the commission at last voted to name the organization the Imperial Rule Assistance Association.

The commission managed to settle on a name, but when it proceeded to discuss the proclamation and platform, consensus was virtually impossible. Opinions were so polarized that the group could agree on only one thing: to leave those matters totally up to Chairman Konoe. Arima Yoriyasu, who was a member of the preparatory commission and the first secretary-general of the IRAA, recalled after the war that on the evening of October 12, the night before the inaugural ceremony was supposed to take place, he and Konoe, working at the Tekigaisō villa,[12] tried to draft an address, proclamation, and platform to be announced at the ceremony. "True to form, Konoe kept revising the drafts until they had turned completely red, and at about 2 A.M. we finally decided to give up the cumbersome task."[13]

The inaugural ceremony took place at the prime minister's official residence. In the capacity of chairman of the IRAA, Konoe delivered a brief address in which he expressed the pleasure of the planners at being able to inaugurate the IRAA and begin a movement to assist the great imperial rule based on kokutai, a principle unique among nations. The platform of the movement, Konoe continued, was no more and no less than to realize the Way of the Subject (Shindō)—how ideal subjects should conduct themselves—in assisting the imperial rule. Besides that, neither platform nor proclamation was necessary. Konoe declared that he had decided, therefore, not to issue either one that day. Many of those present were dumbfounded. "No one but Konoe could get away with that," Arima later remarked.

Thus the IRAA was born without platform or proclamation. Without any concrete pegs, the movement turned into essentially the same idealistic, vague campaign (Kokumin Seishin Sōdōin Undō) that was launched during the first Konoe cabinet, with its appeal for "national spirit, total mobilization." While many at the inaugural ceremony were bewildered at Konoe's address, the right wingers greeted it joyfully, for, like others, they understood it to signify Konoe's capitulation to the demands of the ideological right wing.

A few weeks later, on November 10 and 11, cities and towns throughout the nation staged jovial celebrations of the 2600th anniversary of the founding of the Japanese empire. Voices everywhere sang out vigorously, "bathing in the glorious light of the Golden Kite[14] adorning Japan, let us celebrate this morn, marking twenty-six hundred years since the founding of our empire. . . . " But over all the gaiety, especially in Tokyo, hung the pall of the war in China, now over three years old, which continued to claim lives in uncontrolled destruction. At the same time, the Greater East Asia Co-prosperity Sphere and the Tripartite Pact scraped nerves already raw, bringing regional and world tensions that much closer to snapping. Internally, the political parties had disappeared, and, with the founding of the IRAA, constitutional government became a mangled caricature. From that time onward, shortages of daily necessities grew steadily more severe and created suffering that took an enormous psychological and physical toll.

Also unknown to the celebrating throngs, Saionji Kimmochi was then lying ill at his Okitsu villa, Zagyosō. Even as his condition rapidly deteriorated, he still continued to worry about Japan. Unrelieved anxiety about the future hung heavily upon the mind of the 91-year-old Genrō. As he often lamented to Harada, he believed that the ultimate victory would be Britain's. Speaking of the Tripartite Pact, he pronounced it a "grave diplomatic blunder" for Japan to have set itself up against Britain and the United States. When Harada visited in early October, Saionji noted critically that Konoe was spending too much time on "preparations" and could hardly be managing the actual job of government very well. By "preparations" Saionji must have meant the drawn-out process of establishing the IRAA. Some time later, Saionji said somewhat sadly to Harada that he wished Konoe would act with more resolution, but as long as the army could get its way not much could be done, whoever was trying to run the government.

While Saionji's personal affection for Konoe remained strong, he seemed to have lost faith in him as a statesman and worried deeply about the future of Japan. Early in November he told Harada that he thought serious trouble loomed ahead. He felt sorry for Konoe, but wanted some clear answers from him. He asked Harada to try and get full statements from Konoe on his political goals, how he intended to settle the China War, and his views on Japan's foreign policy—was it on the right track? Konoe was confronted with these questions on November 6, and

he told Harada he would consider the answers and then go to see
Saionji personally. He had not seen the Genrō in some time, he
said. It was four days later that Saionji was taken ill. When
Harada reported to the ailing Genrō Konoe's desperate efforts
to make the Chungking maneuver work, Saionji retorted harshly
that it was foolish to expect Chiang Kai-shek to listen to Japan
now, no matter how they tried to persuade him. Several days
later, on November 24, in Zagyosō, Okitsu, Saionji's long life
ended.

On November 30, Japan concluded what came to be known
as the Basic Treaty Between Japan and China with Wang Ching-
wei's regime in Nanking. By this, Japan extended recognition to
Wang's regime as the central government of China. The groundwork for this move had already been laid earlier. During the
latter part of 1939 the Abe cabinet had persuaded Wang to
accept the Main Points Governing the New Relations Between
Japan and China, and the succeeding Yonai cabinet had
opened negotiations with Wang for a treaty based on the
Main Points, which would codify the fundamentals in the relations between the two governments. Negotiations were continued
under the second Konoe cabinet. Although the new foreign minister, Matsuoka, tried out some of his own schemes to settle the
China War by somehow bringing Chiang and Wang together,
he made little headway even after negotiations for the basic
treaty had been successfully concluded. Forced to abandon other
alternatives, Matsuoka signed the treaty recognizing the Nanking
government.

Fukai Eigo was a member of the Privy Council, which had
to ratify the treaty. He recorded in his memoir that the treaty
proclaimed the ideals of a new order based on ethical principles,
amicable relations, mutual help and friendship, mutual respect
for sovereignty and territory, economic cooperation, cultural
harmony, and so forth. The treaty stipulated, therefore, that
Japan's extraterritorial rights and concessions in China would
be nullified. On the other hand, Fukai wrote, virtually everything
Japan had been demanding as it tried to subjugate China over
the years, either through formal negotiations or informally, accommodating the wishes of certain Japanese, had been incor-

porated somewhere in the treaty. Fukai understood the situation clearly. Wang Ching-wei's defection from Chungking left him no other recourse. His original expectation having been totally betrayed, he was left in despair and severely hurt. After the outbreak of the Pacific War, he is said to have lamented bitterly that perhaps National Reconstruction through Peace was, after all, no match for National Reconstruction through War. The Basic Treaty Between Japan and China and Japan's recognition of the Nanking government merely served to strengthen the determination of the Chungking regime to keep up their resistance against Japan. Thus the course of events in China promised to carry both countries deeper into the tragic morass of a protracted war.

Before the 76th Imperial Diet convened at the end of December, Konoe asked Home Minister Yasui and Justice Minister Kazami to resign. They had been advocates of the new party and both had played roles in setting up the IRAA. Konoe appointed the influential right wingers Hiranuma Kiichirō and Yanagawa Heisuke to succeed them, in one more move that revealed his intention of aligning the IRAA to accord with the demands of the right wing. But many Diet members were deeply dissatisfied with the IRAA. While party politicians had precipitously dissolved the parties in anticipation of recouping their political influence through participation in a new party under Konoe, their hopes were dashed when the IRAA was formed instead. Members of the House of Peers and House of Representatives who joined the new association were assigned to a legislative bureau, which was merely a division of the IRAA. They, too, were bitterly disappointed and indignant. Thus the 76th Diet, the first after the inauguration of the IRAA, seethed with resentment.

When questions were raised as to the nature of the IRAA, all government spokesmen deliberately stressed that the IRAA was concerned with public affairs, not politics; it was not intended to promote a specific political program. It was made completely obvious that the government approached the IRAA in the same way as the right wing.

There was also criticism that the IRAA was communistic,

that communist elements had infiltrated the association and were using it as a base for their propaganda activities. Even before the formation of the IRAA, it was suspected by some of possible connections between the New Order movement and the left wing. The right wing was particularly active in stirring debate on that point. In October, just before the IRAA was officially established, Konoe held a press conference in Kyoto. He acknowledged the accusations that the New Order had been influenced by communist ideology and admitted that so-called converts from the Left had joined the movement. He said the movement might consider incorporating some of their views. Indeed, in one respect it was definitely ideological in that it was a movement whose aim was to clarify the essence of *kokutai*. He compared the movement to a huge drum: beat it hard, it sounds strong; beat it lightly, it sounds soft. At times it may sound Nazi, and at other times it may sound Marxist, but its true sound is rooted in Japan's *kokutai*. Konoe explained that the movement must act on the pure concept of the Way of the Subject. If that concept were forgotten, the New Order movement might indeed deteriorate into another bakufu or, as some people feared, a communist movement.

He sounded altogether too glib. Suspicions of possible connections between the New Order movement or the IRAA and communism grew deeper. One result was the suspension of contributions from business to the IRAA. The general anxiety about the IRAA seems to have originated in the proclivity for national socialist ideas and a controlled economy among converts from the Left, the radical Right, and members of the Shōwa Kenkyūkai, Konoe's brain trust, all of whom either joined or participated in the IRAA. When questions persisted during the 76th Diet session on the connections between the IRAA and the Left, spokesmen replied that the government would be very careful in handling this problem and take thorough measures as necessary.

Because the IRAA had caused such controversy and was attacked so bitterly in the Diet, Konoe decided to reorganize the association. First, he had every member in IRAA headquarters, from Secretary-General Arima Yoriyasu on down, resign.

Konoe then created the post of vice-president, to which he appointed Justice Minister Yanagawa. He made drastic changes in personnel and organization, and ended up losing all those who had hoped eventually to transform the IRAA into a new political party under Konoe. It became a public affairs association, attached to the home ministry as an associated body for local administration. Thus, Konoe's New Order, initially hailed with enormous enthusiasm, sagged and went out with a whimper, a miserable failure.

Konoe later wrote, "Upon reflection, I should have tried harder to push a grand union of the political parties without too much concern for idealism. I am now certain that I could have avoided forming that strange creature, the IRAA, if I had only removed the partitions and gathered all the party politicians into one room."[15] Gotō Ryūnosuke, a driving force behind the New Order movement and the IRAA, remarked after the war that it might have been too much to ask of Konoe to show the courage of another de Gaulle. But if he had appealed to the Diet with the courage and tenacity to galvanize the army, navy, and the people in general to rally for a solution to the national crisis, Konoe would have been able to accomplish his original aims. "I cannot overstate my regret," said Gotō, "that the prince so quickly lost his fighting spirit. It was our mistake to expect him to lead a mass movement to begin with, something he was not cut out to do."[16]

One of Japan's primary objectives in concluding the Tripartite Pact was to keep the United States out of the war. But Washington reacted fiercely against the pact and relations with Japan were strained further. Japan also expected the pact to pave the way for better relations with the Soviet Union, as the Germans had promised, and after the pact was signed Japan requested Germany to commence mediation. Foreign Minister Ribbentrop responded by transmitting to Japan the draft of an agreement among Japan, Germany, Italy, and the Soviet Union. Actually, Ribbentrop had already sent a message to Stalin in October 1940, saying that Germany was prepared to mediate in the adjustment of relations between Japan and the Soviet Union, and that the Führer believed the four countries must pursue policies that would not clash in the long run. In order to insure each of the four countries an equal chance at development, they should conclude an agreement delineating their respective spheres of interest in the world. Ribbentrop suggested that Stalin dispatch Foreign Commisar Vyacheslav M. Molotov to Berlin to discuss the matter.

In November, Molotov arrived in Berlin for talks with Hitler and Ribbentrop. The German leaders proposed that the four countries first agree on their respective spheres of influence. Then, on the basis of that agreement, they should conclude a treaty of cooperation among the Tripartite Pact nations and the Soviet Union. Ribbentrop presented to Molotov a draft agreement identical to that he had shown to the Japanese leaders. After Molotov's return to Moscow, the Soviet government sent Germany a formal reply through Germany's ambassador to Moscow. The reply stated that the Soviet government would accept the Ribbentrop draft agreement under certain conditions and asked Germany to recognize assorted Soviet demands concerning Eastern Europe, the Balkan countries, the Middle and Near East, Northern Sakhalin, and other areas. Germany declared the Soviet conditions unacceptable and terminated negotiations. At the same time the German leadership secretly began preparations for war against the Soviet Union.

During the Tokyo negotiations for the Tripartite Pact, Stahmer had promised the Japanese that when the pact was finalized, Germany would mediate between Japan and the Soviet Union; that prospect was now completely lost. Germany told Japan only that negotiations with Soviet Union had ruptured. However, reports later began to reach Tokyo that the German Balkan operation was causing friction between Berlin and Moscow.

Matsuoka was not pleased, but he thought he might be able to save the situation by a strong personal effort. He decided to go to Europe and negotiate directly for the adjustment of Japan's relations with the Soviet Union. If they accepted the Ribbentrop proposal, the Soviet Union would be committed to cooperate with the Tripartite Pact nations in the conquest of Britain. Matsuoka also wanted to discuss diplomatic policy for the future with the German and Italian leaders. In March 1941, Matsuoka left

Tokyo for Europe by the Trans-Siberian railway, going through Moscow. He received an excited, warm welcome in Germany, which gave a lift to his talks with Hitler and Ribbentrop. He took a few days to visit Italy, where he met Prime Minister Benito Mussolini and Foreign Minister Goleazzo Ciano.

During their talks with Matsuoka, the German leaders insisted that the conquest of Britain was simply a matter of time. If Japan immediately opened hostilities against Britain and attacked Singapore, that would be a decisive factor. They could move across the English Channel quickly. They assured Matsuoka that the United States would not enter the war if Japan attacked Singapore, mainly because the government would not risk sending the American fleet closer to Japan. The Soviet Union was immobilized by German forces stationed along the western Soviet border, and, if Moscow dared take any action against Japan, Germany would swifty attack the Soviet Union to secure Japan's back door facing Siberia. The New Order in Greater East Asia could be achieved only when Japan had established control over southern Asia. That furnished another reason for Japan to attack Singapore. Throughout the talks the Germans persisted in urging Japan to take Singapore, hinting more than once that after Molotov's visit, German-Soviet relations had deteriorated so far that war between them was a definite possibility.

After his visit to Germany and Italy, Matsuoka stopped in Moscow on his way home. The upshot of negotiations there was the Japanese-Soviet Neutrality Pact signed in April, and a promise by Matsuoka that he would persuade his government to liquidate Japanese coal and oil rights and interests in Northern Sakhalin. The Neutrality Pact stipulated that if either party was attacked by one or more third power, the other party would remain neutral throughout the conflict. Matsuoka knew by then that he could not expect anything from German mediation. Unable to shift the track of Japan-Soviet relations, he aimed at using the Neutrality Pact to prevent the United States from cooperating with the Soviet Union against Japan. As a result, he hoped, the United States would be compelled to modify its position toward Japan. On the other hand, the Soviet Union was realistically aware of the growing tension with Germany and also of the German war preparations, thanks to information from the American government. The Neutrality Pact gave the Soviet Union some assurance that Japan would remain neutral in case of war against Germany, and also provided the tool to get Japanese interests out of Northern Sakhalin. The Soviet leaders had reason to be eminently satisfied.

Konoe also was pleased with the neutrality treaty. Matsuoka's accomplishment, which he called a diplomatic feat, renewed his optimism that an acceptable modus vivendi might be worked out with the United States. Germany was not happy. No one in Berlin anticipated that Japan would conclude a treaty with the Soviet Union when Soviet relations with Germany were deteriorating so quickly. The German leadership made its displeasure very clear.

5

THE ROAD TO WAR

I n April 1941, Foreign Minister Matsuoka made his way home via the Trans-Siberian railway, exulting in the diplomatic coup that produced the Japanese-Soviet Neutrality Pact. That month in Washington, Secretary of State Cordell Hull and Ambassador Nomura Kichisaburō began formal negotiations on the so-called Japanese-American Draft Understanding, a document whose inception lay in the visit to Japan of two Catholic priests toward the end of the previous year.

In Japan, Bishop James E. Walsh and Father James M. Drought, both of the Catholic Foreign Mission Society of America at Maryknoll, New York, had been able to meet with a number of influential Japanese and learn their views on the main points of friction that were causing Japanese-American relations to deteriorate. One was Ikawa Tadao, a friend of Konoe and an executive officer of the Central Bank of the Industrial Association (Sangyō Kumiai Chūō Kinko). Walsh and Drought returned to the United States in January 1941, and, with an introduction from Postmaster General Frank C. Walker, they reported to Roosevelt and Hull on the results of their visit. The meeting with the president left the two priests feeling optimistic about the prospects for settling some of the problems. Then in February, Ikawa was sent to the United States to begin negotiations, and Colonel Iwakuro Hideo, chief of the military section of the Army Ministry's Military Affairs Bureau, came to Washington in March. The four decided to write up the draft of a plan for the adjustment of relations, and, with some participation by Ambassador Nomura, they produced "A Draft Understanding Between the Governments of Japan and the United

States." Postmaster General Walker, with Hull's approval, remained privately in contact with the group.

In their April 14 meeting, Nomura informed Hull that he knew all about the Draft Understanding and that he had collaborated to some degree with the Japanese and Americans who had composed it. The secretary asked Nomura if he wanted to present the document officially as a first step in negotiations between the two governments. Nomura replied that he did, and added that his government had not yet seen the draft, but he thought they would agree to starting negotiations based upon it.

Two days later Nomura called on Hull and handed him a final copy of the Draft Understanding, the main items in which were as follows:

4/16

I   The Concepts of the United States and of Japan Respecting International Relations and the Character of Nations (omitted—author)

II   The Attitudes of Both Governments toward the European War

The Government of Japan maintains that the purpose of its Axis Alliance was, and is, defensive and designed to prevent the extension of military grouping among nations not directly affected by the European War.

The Government of Japan, with no intention of evading its existing treaty obligation, desires to declare that its military obligation under the Axis Alliance comes into force only when one of the parties of the Alliance is aggressively attacked by a power not at present involved in the European War.

The Government of the United States maintains that its attitude toward the European War is, and will continue to be, determined by no aggressive alliance aimed to assist any one nation against another. The United States maintains that it is pledged to the hate of war, and accordingly, its attitude toward the European War is, and will continue to be, determined solely and exclusively by considerations of the protective defense of its national welfare and security.

III   The Relations between the Two Governments concerning the China War

The President of the United States, if the following terms are approved by His Excellency and guaranteed by the Government of Japan, might request the Chiang Kai-shek regime to negotiate peace with Japan.

  a. Independence of China
  b. Withdrawal of Japanese troops from Chinese territory, in accordance with an agreement to be reached between Japan and China
  c. No acquisition of Chinese territory
  d. No imposition of indemnities
  e. Resumption of the "Open Door"; the interpretation of which shall be agreed upon at some future, convenient time between the United States and Japan
  f. Coalescence of the governments of Chiang Kai-shek and of Wang Ching-wei.
  g. No large-scale or concentrated immigration of Japanese into Chinese territory
  h. Recognition of Manchukuo

With the acceptance by the Chiang Kai-shek regime of the aforementioned Presidential request, the Japanese Government shall commence direct peace negotiations with the newly coalesced Chinese Government, or constituent elements thereof.

The Government of Japan shall submit to the Chinese concrete terms of peace, within the limits of aforesaid general terms and along the line of neighborly friendship, joint defense against communistic activities and economic cooperation.

IV   Naval, Aerial and Mercantile Marine Relations in the Pacific

  a. As both the Americans and the Japanese are desirous of maintaining the peace in the Pacific, they shall not resort to such disposition of their naval forces and aerial forces as to menace each other. Detailed, concrete agreement thereof shall be left for determination at the proposed joint conference.

  (b and c omitted)

V   Commerce between both Nations and Their Financial Cooperation

When official approbation to the present understanding has been given by both Governments, the United States and Japan shall assure each other to mutually supply such commodities as are respectively available or required by either of them. Both

Governments further consent to take necessary steps to the resumption of normal trade relations as formerly established under the Treaty of Navigation and Commerce between the United States and Japan. If a new commercial treaty is desired by both governments, it could be elaborated at the proposed conference and concluded in accordance with usual procedure.

For the advancement of economic cooperation between both nations, it is suggested that the United States extend to Japan a gold credit in amounts sufficient to foster trade and industrial development directed to the betterment of Far Eastern economic conditions and to the sustained economic cooperation of the Governments of the United States and Japan.

VI   Economic Activity of Both Nations in the Southwestern Pacific

On the pledged basis of guarantee that Japanese activities in the Southwestern Pacific area shall be carried on by peaceful means, without resorting to arms, American cooperation and support shall be given in the production and procurement of natural resources (such as oil, rubber, tin, nickel) which Japan needs.

VII   The Policies of Both Nations Affecting Political Stabilization in the Pacific

   a. The Governments of the United States and of Japan will not acquiesce in the future transfer of territories or the relegation of existing states within the Far East and in the Southwestern Pacific area to any European power.
   b. The Governments of the United States and of Japan jointly guarantee the independence of the Philippine Islands and will consider means to come to their assistance in the event of unprovoked aggression by any third power.
   (c omitted)
   d. Japanese immigration to the United States and to the Southwestern Pacific area shall receive amicable consideration—on a basis of equality with other nationals and free from discrimination.

The Japanese-American Conference

   a. It is suggested that a Conference between delegates of the United States and of Japan be held at Honolulu and that this Conference be opened for the United States by President Roosevelt and for Japan by Prince Konoye [sic]. The delegates could number less than five each, exclusive of experts, clerks, etc.

(b omitted)

c. This Conference could be held as soon as possible (May 1941) after the present understanding has been reached.

d. The agenda of the Conference would not include a reconsideration of the present understanding but would direct its efforts to the specification of the pre-arranged agenda and drafting of instruments to effectuate the understanding. The precise agenda could be determined by mutual agreement between both governments.

Addendum

The present understanding shall be kept as a confidential memorandum between the Governments of the United States and of Japan.

The scope, character and timing of the announcement of this understanding will be agreed upon by both Governments.

Having been shown the Draft Understanding, Hull handed Nomura a statement containing four principles which the United States insisted must be honored in any treaty between the two governments: 1) Respect for the territorial integrity and the sovereignty of each and all nations; 2) support of the principle of noninterference in the internal affairs of other countries; 3) support of the principle of equality, including equality of commerical opportunity; and 4) nondisturbance of the staus quo in the Pacific except as the status quo may be altered by peaceful means. Hull informed Nomura that if the Japanese government accepted the four principles and approved the Draft Understanding, and, if Nomura was instructed to propose it to the United States, it would provide a basis for negotiations. The United States would thereupon offer its own, and some independent proposals, and then discuss them with Nomura, together with the Japanese proposals.

The American response to the Draft Understanding was more positive than had been generally expected. It was certainly no panacea, but it offered a possible means of breakthrough at a time when Washington was increasing aid to Britain and did not want to get involved in a war in the Pacific, if it could be avoided. American arms production was rapidly expanding, but the United States still did not consider itself sufficiently prepared to engage in a two-ocean war against Japan and Germany at the same time.

After the meeting with Hull, Nomura telegraphed the Draft Understanding to Tokyo, reporting that Secretary Hull was ready to start negotiations on the basis of the document, and that he had asked Nomura to receive instructions from his government. Nomura added in parentheses that he had "sounded out" the response of the American government to the Draft Understanding. Secretary Hull, he said, had no objections to it generally; they had agreed upon it as it stood through secret intervention and negotiations.

Desperate that Tokyo would agree to their continuing the talks, Nomura said virtually nothing about the four principles that Hull had presented. Only in May, after Japan had decided upon its first counterproposal, did Nomura finally get around to reporting the extent of Hull's demands. Even then, Nomura told his government that, although Hull insisted on acceptance of the four principles as a premise for discussions on the Draft Understanding, Nomura himself sought to soften their impact by proposing that they press on with negotiations without becoming involved in arguments over abstract principles.

By the time the Japanese government received the text of the Draft Understanding, the diplomatic situation had become so tenuous that no one knew what to expect next. Konoe was, therefore, all the more pleased by the Nomura telegram. Hosokawa Morisada, then Konoe's secretary, recalled that he had never seen Konoe so jubilant as when he had finished reading the telegram. Konoe immediately convened the Imperial Headquarters–Cabinet Liaison Conference to discuss the Draft Understanding. The conference decided to accept it "in essence." Even Army Minister Tōjō, Mutō Akira, head of the army Military Affairs Bureau, and Oka Takazumi, head of the navy Military Affairs Bureau, "rollicked with joy," in Tomita Kenji's words. Nomura's misleading report, which made no mention of

Hull's demands, must have made a big difference in the positive way they received the Draft Understanding.

Later, in one of his memoirs, Konoe enumerated several points on which the conference agreed: "1) To accept the American proposal [the Draft Understanding] would be the best way to deal with the China War. Wang's regime has done no good whatsoever, and direct negotiations with Chungking are practically impossible at this time, besides the fact that Chungking is totally dependent upon the United States. Consequently, no effective negotiations can be conducted with Chungking without American mediation; 2) Acceptance of the proposal might not only bring Japan and the United States closer, providing an opportunity to avert war between us, but it might also restore peace in the world by preventing the European conflict from expanding into a world war; 3) Japan's national strength has been considerably depleted. Japan must recoup its losses and rebuild strength by settling the China War as quickly as possible. The Supreme Command is in fact neither prepared for nor confident of success in the southern advance, although some people are pushing it heavily. To increase our national strength and to furnish the necessary materials for the future, Japan must for a time make a reconciliation with the United States."[1]

The conference, however, decided that Japan's response to the Draft Understanding would be determined after Matsuoka's return. At the beginning of the above passage in Konoe's memoirs, he says, "To accept the American proposal . . . " in reference to the Draft Understanding. It seems the original misunderstanding about the United States government's position toward the Draft Understanding persisted long afterward, and this misunderstanding was largely due to Nomura's incomplete communication to Tokyo.

On April 22, Matsuoka arrived at Tachikawa airfield. It had originally been arranged that Chief Cabinet Secretary Tomita Kenji would represent the government and meet the foreign minister. But immediately before Matsuoka's arrival, Tomita later recorded, Konoe called in the secretary to discuss the possibility of going to meet Matsuoka himself. Konoe noted that Foreign Minister Matsuoka, being "unusually emotional," might

react differently to the Draft Understanding depending on who
approached him about it and his mood at the time when he was
told that both the government and Imperial Headquarters had
agreed to accept it. If Konoe took the trouble to meet him at
Tachikawa and briefed him on the way back to Tokyo in the
car, Matsuoka might receive the news with more equanimity
than otherwise expected. Thus Konoe, rather than Tomita,
went to meet Matsuoka. But upon his arrival, Matsuoka requested that they drive to the plaza outside the imperial palace
moat so that he could pay his respects to the Emperor. This was
awkward. Konoe had a strong aversion to rituals, which he considered vulgar and perfunctory, and wanted nothing to do with
them. He decided not to ride back with Matsuoka and instead
asked the vice minister of foreign affairs, Ōhashi Chūichi, to take
over the briefing. During the trip back to Tokyo, as Matsuoka
listened to Ōhashi's report on the Draft Understanding, he
became extremely grouchy. He was quick to indicate strong antipathy toward the whole plan.

That night the Imperial Headquarters–Cabinet Liaison Conference convened at the prime minister's official residence. Those
attending hoped to persuade Matsuoka to start negotiations with
the United States on the basis of the Draft Understanding, but
the foreign minister preempted the opening moments by reporting with great animation on his trip. As he boastfully recounted the details of his visits to Germany, Italy, and the
Soviet Union, the others frowned in growing distaste. The display completed, Konoe brought up the matter of the Draft
Understanding, requesting the foreign minister to inform the
United States government that both the Japanese government
and the Supreme Command approved the plan in principle.
Matsuoka reacted with curt displeasure. His ideas differed considerably from Nomura's, he declared. Demanding ample time to
think about it carefully, he left the meeting, pleading exhaustion.

Matsuoka's opposition to the Draft Understanding might have
seemed out of proportion in its vehemence, except that the
European trip had blown up his already pronounced sense of
self-importance. Now he saw himself as the powerful foreign
minister, ally of Germany and Italy, countries he had visited

just when Nazi military power held Europe in thrall. Reveling
in the grand welcomes he received, Matsuoka fraternized with
Hitler, Ribbentrop, Mussolini, and Ciano. Then on his way
back, he had engineered the Japanese-Soviet Neutrality Pact
with such aplomb—he thought—that Stalin, in an unusual
gesture, had appeared at the railway station the night Matsuoka
left Moscow and had enfolded him dramatically, for all to see,
in a Russian bear hug. The European trip probably left the
elated Matsuoka believing himself indeed to be among the
world's leading statesmen. He was not prepared to be greeted by
the Draft Understanding when he reached Japan.

Because the attempt, through the Draft Understanding, to
improve Japanese-American relations was initiated by private
citizens of both countries, it was officially unrelated to the foreign
ministry until Hull referred to it in his meeting with Nomura.
At that point it became an official matter. With Matsuoka still
away, Amabassador Nomura cabled the plan to Tokyo, requesting instructions from the government; it was received with
serious interest by the government and military leadership, from
Konoe on down. The Draft Understanding seemed to offer them
an unexpected springboard to begin the long-sought negotiations
with the United States. The fact that so much had been done in
his absence put Matsuoka, until then exuberant and triumphant from the European trip, into a mood of dour frustration.
Not only did the Draft Understanding seriously injure his inflated ego, but Matsuoka also had his own definite ideas on how
Japan should approach the United States in order to avert war
between them. He opposed trade-offs and concessions by Japan;
he was convinced that the only way to negotiate and induce the
Americans to concede was to dictate terms and stick resolutely
to them. Matsuoka deeply resented the quick involvement of
both government and military leaders in a document that he
considered to represent unnecessary compromise and mediocre
diplomacy.

Matsuoka's attitude bitterly disappointed and angered everyone concerned, particularly Konoe, who believed they had
finally been given the chance to start negotiating with Washington. He tried his best to convince Matsuoka of the merits of the

document. "Beginning the morning after Matsuoka's return, Prince Konoe repeatedly tried to persuade him," wrote Tomita Kenji, who was then chief cabinet secretary. "On few other occasions did the generally phlegmatic Prince Konoe exert himself that much. He tried badgering with persistence and extreme patience. From anyone else, such extraordinary efforts might have been expected, but not from Prince Konoe. How I sympathized, for I knew it was a very trying thing for him to do."[2] But Matsuoka's unmoving, tough foreign policy argument thwarted anyone who tried to make him veer off. He stubbornly refused to consider negotiating on the basis of the Draft Understanding and remained rigid, declaring that diplomacy should be left up to him.

The next meeting of the Imperial Headquarters–Cabinet Liaison Conference was delayed when Matsuoka, still unmoved, became ill. When it finally met in early May, it ended up giving virtually blanket approval to Matsuoka's revisions of the Draft Understanding. Matsuoka's revisions made it clear, first of all, that Japan would maintain the Tripartite Pact in its original form, in name and in substance. They also stipulated: 1) Japan maintains that its obligations of military assistance under the Tripartite Pact among Japan, Germany, and Italy will be carried out in accordance with the stipulation in Article 3 of the said pact. The United States maintains that its attitude toward the European War is, and will continue to be, directed by no such "aggressive measures" as assisting any one nation against another. Concerning the China War: 2) the United States acknowledges the three principles proclaimed in the Konoe Declaration of December 22, 1938, and the principles set forth in the Basic Treaty with Wang Ching-wei's Nanking government as well as those stated in the Joint Declaration of Japan, Manchukuo, and China of November 30, 1940 [Konoe's three principles were "neighborly friendship," "joint defense against communism," and "economic cooperation," and the Joint Declaration further pledged mutual respect for sovereignty and territorial integrity—author]. Relying upon the policy of the Japanese government to establish a relationship of neighborly friendship with China, the United States shall forthwith request the Chiang Kai-shek

regime to negotiate peace with Japan. All the peace terms between Japan and China that were contained in the Draft Understanding are to be deleted. 3) The provision in the Draft Understanding, "As both the Americans and the Japanese are desirous of maintaining the peace in the Pacific, they shall not resort
to such disposition of their naval forces and aerial forces as to
menace each other," is also to be deleted. Concerning Japanese
activities in the southwestern Pacific, Matsuoka requested a
further deletion that carried highly important implications: 4)
The Draft Understanding provides that such activities "shall be
carried on by peaceful means, without resorting to arms." "Without resorting to arms" is to be deleted.

These revisions fundamentally altered the character of the
Draft Understanding. Any evaluation of the intent behind Matsuoka's revisions, moreover, must take into account Hull's
demand that Japan accept his four principles as a precondition
to negotiations for the adjustment of Japanese-American relations, for the revisions mocked that demand.

One wonders why the Matsuoka revisions were approved,
given the enthusiasm among both government and military
leaders for the Draft Understanding, because, in effect, the revisions doomed the effort to futility. It is possible that Matsuoka
pressured his colleagues into acquiescence. It is also possible
that the creation of the Draft Understanding itself led them to
expect more conciliation than the Americans were ready to offer
and tempted them to demand further concessions. In any event,
following Matsuoka's instructions, Nomura delivered the revised
version to Hull on May 12.

At the time the Japanese government considered the Matsuoka
version, which we shall refer to as the May 12 proposal, to be a
revised counterproposal to the Draft Understanding, which they
assumed had been put forth by the American government. The
American government, on the other hand, regarded the same
document as the first official Japanese proposal prepared on the
basis of the Draft Understanding. When Hull received the May
12 proposal, "Very few rays of hope shone from the document,"
he wrote in his memoirs. It offered little basis for an agreement,
he continued, unless his government were willing to sacrifice

some of their most basic principles, which they were not. But
Roosevelt and Hull agreed, the memoirs recounts, that if there
was the slightest possibility of inducing Japan to withdraw from
the Axis alliance, they should pursue it, for Japan's withdrawal
would be a sharp blow to Germany and a boost to Britain. Thus
they decided to go forward with the negotiations on the basis of
the Japanese proposal.

During the next two months there was a flurry of activity. The
United States government conveyed to Nomura an oral statement dated May 16, a draft proposal dated May 31, and another
oral statement dated June 7. Matsuoka would yield nothing in
response to all three. Thoroughly distressed by Matsuoka's
attitude, Konoe told Kido he was ready to resign. Kido replied
that Konoe could not simply walk out; he had appointed Matsuoka foreign minister in the first place, against the wishes of his
own associates and even the Emperor, and he must see the problem through. These circumstances made it difficult for Konoe to
force Matsuoka out, but to have his entire cabinet resign would
shift the responsibility onto the cabinet. Kido pointed out that
Matsuoka's behavior since his return from Europe had been so
extreme that there was ample ground to request his resignation.
Kido urged Konoe to reconsider. In view of the grave situation
Japan faced, it was especially important that the cabinet not be
permitted to resign because of a problem of Konoe's own making.

On June 21, Hull transmitted to Nomura an oral statement
and a draft proposal. In the oral statement, the secretary of
state said he had no reason to doubt the desire of many Japanese
leaders for understanding between Japan and the United States
and for peace in the Pacific area. But some individuals in high
official positions were committed to a course that bound Japan
to support Nazi Germany and its "policies of conquest." The
only kind of understanding with the United States which they
would endorse was based on the certainty that if, as a consequence of American self-defense policy, the United States became
involved in the European hostilities, Japan would fight on the
side of Hitler. As long as those individuals maintained this
attitude in their official positions and appeared to push public
opinion in Japan toward that position, it was illusory, said Hull,

to expect a proposal such as that under consideration to promise substantial results.

The Japanese proposal contained another element that the American side found objectionable. That element was the government's intention to include in its peace terms a provision permitting Japanese troops to be stationed in certain areas of Inner Mongolia and North China. The proposal was framed in terms of cooperation with China in resisting communist activities, incorporating part of the Konoe Declaration of December 22, 1938. Hull made it clear that the liberal policies to which the United States was committed would not permit the government to associate itself with any course that was inconsistent with those policies. Furthermore, the matter under discussion affected the sovereign rights of a third country, and the United States government had to be highly scrupulous in dealing with such a matter.

Throughout the negotiations on the Draft Understanding, the American government stated its position directly for the first time in the draft proposal of June 21. The main points were, first, that the Japanese government maintained that the purpose of the Tripartite Pact had been, and was, defensive; the pact was designed to help prevent an unprovoked extension of the European War. The attitude of the United States government toward the European hostilities was and would continue to be determined solely and exclusively by considerations of protection and self-defense, its national security and the defense thereof. Second, upon the communication by Japan to the United States of the general terms governing the settlement that the Japanese government would propose to China, those terms having been declared by the Japanese government to be in harmony with Konoe's stated principles of neighborly friendship and mutual respect for sovereignty and territorial integrity, and upon the actual application of those principles, the president of the United States would suggest to the Chinese government that the Chinese government and the Japanese government enter into negotiations.

The June 21 proposal was subjected to further discussion, however, in order to handle the question of cooperative defense against communist activities and stationing Japanese troops in Chinese territory, as well as the issue of economic cooperation between China and Japan. A supplementary document further enumerated the basic terms that the United States government demanded in the Sino-Japanese peace settlement. Thus the American June 21 proposal differed drastically from the Japanese May 12 proposal. Arita Hachirō seems to have been correct when he commented after the war that the April 16 Draft Understanding had been formulated on the basis of the matchmaker's account. The true intentions of Japan and America did not emerge until the May 12 and June 21 proposals, respectively. It was no surprise, Arita remarked, that their views clashed, for the fate of Japanese-American negotiations were already determined by then.

Events allowed little time to relax. On June 22 suspicions of a German-Soviet war finally became fact. The Japanese were shocked, and they rushed into repeated sessions of the Imperial Headquarters–Cabinet Liaison Conference to discuss Japanese policy. Army and navy representatives shrilly demanded that Japan immediately exploit the European situation and occupy southern French Indochina. By occupying that territory, the Japanese military hoped to establish a dominant position in the wide southern region from the Philippines to Malaya and the Dutch East Indies, thus gaining unimpeded access to the necessary raw materials from French Indochina, Thailand, and the Dutch East Indies, and securing a hold that would threaten the southern flank of the Chinese forces. But Foreign Minister Matsuoka countered that the German-Soviet war would probably end quickly in German victory; Japan should immediately attack the Soviet Union in concert with Germany and suspend or postpone the Indochina operation. Matsuoka assured his colleagues that the United States did not like the Soviet Union and would not enter the war.

The foreign minister was voted down. Representing the supreme command, Army Chief of Staff Sugiyama Hajime and Navy Chief of Staff Nagano Osami were firm that southern French Indochina must be occupied immediately. Konoe supported them. "We should go ahead if the supreme command is in a position to do so."[3] The other ministers concurred, and so by the end of June the Japanese government had made the formal decision. A few days later, the Liaison Conference produced the Main Principles of the Empire's Policy for Dealing with the Changing World Situation, which the Cabinet Council and the Imperial Conference both approved by July 2.

The Main Principles presented an unambiguous, positive stand regarding the southern advance and a wait-and-see attitude regarding the next moves vis-à-vis the north. It stated that: Japan is committed to a policy leading toward result in the establishment of the Greater East Asia Co-prosperity Sphere, and that policy will thereby contribute to world peace, regardless of changes in the world situation. Japan will continue its efforts to bring about a settlement of the China War and will seek to establish a solid foundation of security and self-defense for the nation. To do so will require advancing south. Depending on how the situation develops, Japan might also effect a settlement in the Soviet regions north of Japan in order to establish "stability" there. Japan "will not decline" a war with Britain and the United States. Japan will not enter the German-Soviet war for the time being. If that conflict should develop to Japan's advantage, it will resort to armed force to "settle the northern question." Further, in accordance with established policy, Japan will make all-out efforts to prevent the United States from entering the European war. But if the United States should enter the war, Japan will act in accordance with the Tripartite Pact.

After completing the July 1941 Main Principles statement, the Imperial Headquarters–Cabinet Liaison Conference turned to the American June 21 proposal. During the deliberations Matsuoka vented his anger at the implication in a part of the oral statement. Hull clearly meant Matsuoka in his reference to certain individuals who sought understanding with the United States only in context of conflict. Matsuoka declared that Japan could not abandon the Tripartite Pact and that Japan probably would not be able to prevent American entry into the war. Stating that acceptance of the American proposal would almost definitely preclude the establishment of a Greater East Asia Co-prosperity Sphere, Matsuoka demanded that they reject the oral statement and withdraw from negotiations with America. The Liaison Conference decided unanimously to reject the oral statement. But the army and the navy wanted to continue negotiations. Matsuoka conceded. Declaring Japanese-American accord to have been a cherished wish ever since he was young, he agreed to continue the negotiations until the end, although he saw no hope. A Japanese counterproposal was drafted, but it contained no significant new concessions.

Matsuoka wanted Nomura to report Japan's rejection of the oral statement to Hull first and then present the Japanese counterproposal several days later. Konoe, however, feared that such an approach would provoke the United States into terminating negotiations, and so he asked Matsuoka to have Nomura present the rejection of the oral statement and the counterproposal simultaneously. Matsuoka ignored Konoe's request and cabled only the rejection to Nomura. That was more than Konoe could tolerate. He could see that it was impossible to continue negotiations with the United States as long as Matsuoka was foreign minister, but, instead of getting rid of him, Konoe decided to resign. The Emperor and Kido both tried to presuade Konoe to fire Matsuoka and keep the present government intact, but Konoe was convinced that he must take responsibility for appointing Matsuoka in the first place by resigning himself.

The Konoe cabinet resigned on July 16. Privy Seal Kido called a meeting of senior statesmen to hear their opinions on his successor, and they unanimously recommended Konoe. When Konoe formed his third cabinet, he retained some members of the previous cabinet but replaced Matsuoka with Toyoda Teijirō. Toyoda was an admiral and had served in the second Konoe cabinet as minister of commerce and industry directly in charge of material supplies. In addition Toyoda also wished to avert war with the United States. Konoe hoped that making Toyoda foreign minister would gain navy support so that he could somehow lead the Japanese-American negotiations to a peaceful, mutually satisfactory conclusion.

Immediately after the formation of the new cabinet on July 28, Japanese forces occupied southern French Indochina, as had been decided during the last days of the previous cabinet.

The United States government had been warned of the southern advance beforehand and had sternly informed Nomura that if Japan occupied southern French Indochina, further negotiations would be pointless. On July 25, having confirmed that Japan intended to proceed as planned, regardless of the warning, President Roosevelt ordered a freeze on all Japanese assets in the United States. Britain and the Dutch East Indies quickly followed suit. Then on August 1, the United States placed an embargo on oil exports to Japan. This was a very serious, unexpected move; until then Japan's oil production (both natural and synthetic) met only 12 percent of its peacetime needs and four-fifths of the rest came from the United States.

Konoe and the military leadership were caught unprepared for such a quick, hard retaliation from the United States, even though other Japanese had foreseen exactly what would happen. Shidehara Kijūrō recorded after the war that in the summer of 1941 Konoe requested a meeting with him. Konoe informed him that the government had decided to move into southern French Indochina and that the fleet carrying troops and supplies for that purpose had set sail two days before. Shidehara's response was harsh and clear. The troops had not yet arrived at their destination, he said; the prime minister must have them brought back to Taiwan or another appropriate place and retained there. Konoe answered that the troops had been sent only after careful deliberation by the Imperial Conference and he had no power to countermand the decision. Shidehara declared that he was absolutely certain a full-scale war would erupt as a result of the Japanese action. Repeating that war was inevitable unless the fleet was called back, Shidehara urged Konoe to exert all his power to keep the ships away from Indochina and continue the negotiations with the United States. If, however, Japanese troops had already landed at Saigon or a nearby port, Konoe might as well terminate the negotiations, for they would be useless.

Konoe was astounded. He could not see why the Japanese action should produce such dire consequences when the government had gotten the military leaders to agree that the troops would only occupy the area and not become involved in military conflict. The occupation of southern French Indochina was a gross mistake, Shidehara replied, for once that was accomplished, Japanese troops would next march into the Dutch East Indies and Malaya, escalating the situation until Japan could not withdraw. If Konoe wanted his advice, Shidehara said, he had no choice but to categorically oppose the southern advance. "Prince Konoe, as he listened in silence, turned somewhat pale, and asked, 'Isn't there any other way?' " Shidehara declared again that the only recourse was for Konoe to buck the inevitable protest and get an imperial order to recall the troops. This would be hard on his own prestige and the military would lose face, but the situation was too critical to worry about such things. The Konoe-Shidehara meeting broke off in an "unpleasant and irresolute state."[4]

Konoe wrote in a letter to Arita Hachirō dated August 3, after the American embargo and freeze on Japanese assets had gone into effect, "Both the army and navy agreed that while the Dutch East Indies might be a different question, the occupation of French Indochina would not affect our negotiations with the United States too adversely. It is extremely unfortunate that their view was erroneous and has brought such serious consequences." He added that the government was nonetheless determined to exert every effort to resolve the crisis by improving relations with the United States.[5] In this letter, Konoe laid all the blame on the military for the incorrect assumptions that allowed approval of the occupation of southern French Indochina.

The American oil embargo had several immediate repercussions in Japan. First, pressure by the army for war against the Soviet Union (the so-called northern advance) was intensified as prospects for a quick German victory over the Soviet Union—which Germany had noisily and confidently predicted earlier—became more remote. Also, the oil embargo, together with the freeze on Japanese assets by the United States, Britain, and the Dutch East Indies, made any operation against the Soviet Union extremely difficult. The problem of securing enough oil suppressed the argument for the northern advance. On the other hand, it generated heated insistence on a strong posture toward the United States, particularly within the navy. On July 31, Navy Chief of Staff Nagano reported to the Emperor that while the navy still wanted to avert war with the United States, if Japan's main source of oil was cut off because negotiations with the United States failed, Japan would be left with only a two-year stockpile, and that amount would be consumed in eighteen months in the event of war. If war was inevitable, Nagano concluded, the navy wished to start it immediately, even with no assurance of victory. The Emperor was deeply disturbed by Nagano's report, but it represented the thinking of a great many navy personnel.

Konoe knew that the navy was by no means confident of victory in a clash with the United States and wanted to avoid war if at all possible. He had hoped that the navy would restrain the army and actively help to prevent war in the Pacific. For this reason the drastic change within the navy as reflected in Nagano's report distressed Konoe. Now it was with fear and anxiety that he searched for a way to break out of the deadlock in negotiations brought about by the move into French Indochina. His search was in vain, for the United States had lost any real interest in the negotiations. The Americans' main concern was to gain time to push forward their military preparations before inevitable war.

In his memoirs Konoe reviewed the effects of the Tripartite Pact. Germany had made a commitment to act on Japan's behalf and induce the Soviet Union to become an "ally." Japan had agreed to join the Tripartite Pact on the basis of that promise, but then Germany had ignored Japan's advice [Matsuoka's May 28 message to Ribbentrop requesting Germany to make every effort to avoid war with the Soviet Union—author] and had initiated a war against the Soviet Union. It was an "act of betrayal." At the moment, Japan had the "right and justification" to reexamine the Tripartite Pact itself. Konoe believed the pact should be dissolved and consulted the army minister. The army, however, had such faith in the German military that they would not consider breaking the relationship the pact established. Konoe concluded that internal conditions prevented reconsidering the Tripartite Pact, and to dissolve the pact so soon after its conclusion would, in any case, undermine Japan's international credibility, despite the blatant German betrayal. It was inappropriate to question the pact itself. But an important objective of the pact, a Japanese-German-Soviet alliance, had been rendered hopeless by the German-Soviet war. Under these circumstances, it would be extremely serious if the "danger that might arise in the future because of the Tripartite Pact, namely, the danger of war with the United States" became reality; in that event the alliance would become not only pointless, but a liability. Konoe reasoned that the only way to avoid the danger was to bring Japan and the United States closer together. He was determined to pursue the Japanese-American negotiations to a successful conclusion even if it meant "dampening" the effect of the Tripartite Pact.[6]

Thus, at the outbreak of the German-Soviet war, Konoe wrote that he was resolved to bring the negotiations to a successful end, but several important facts cast doubt on the depth of his resolution and his true objectives. As we have already observed, the Main Principles of the Empire's Policy for Dealing with the Changing World Situation stipulated that while Japan would strive to prevent it, if the United States actually entered the European war, Japan would act in accordance with the Tripartite Pact. The document also stipulated that "Japan will not decline a war with Britain and the United States" if that became a necessity in order to advance south in the interests of national security. In another memoir Konoe wrote about the July 2 Imperial Conference, which approved the Main Principles. To have flatly rejected the demands of the military would have produced only a frontal clash with the military, contributing nothing to the solution of the problem. Furthermore, at that time the possibility of success in the negotiations was greatest and he was "most confident of effectively reducing the danger of war." The most urgent task just then, therefore, was to forestall the army's demand for forceful action toward the Soviet Union. That required acceding to pressure by the military and accommodating some of their demands regarding the advance to the south, while approving the decision on the "northern operation." Konoe related that his decision to declare Japan ready to risk a Pacific war for the southern advance was made to palliate the military, but there was still room for maneuver before hostilities became inevitable, and he was "sufficiently confident" that he would be able to avert war. It must also be noted that the southern advance had another, more important purpose: to help bring down Chiang Kai-shek and resolve the China War.[7] In another memoir, Konoe wrote that the government leaders were compelled to approve the occupation of southern French Indochina as a "sort of compensation" to the military, which had been thwarted in their demand for an immediate war against the Soviet Union.[8] His memoirs, of course, contain much more, but here again Konoe's version of these decisions has a self-serving aspect that suggests he was trying to justify his actions as much as explain them.

Deeply anxious to repair the damage done to the negotiations by the move in Indochina and somehow avert war with the United States, Konoe decided to attempt resolving Japan's troubled relations with the United States once and for all, in the most efficient possible way, by having a personal meeting with President Franklin D. Roosevelt. While the navy minister supported the idea, the army minister informed Konoe in writing that the army would consider a summit meeting inappropriate. It would undermine diplomatic efforts based on the Tripartite Pact and would cause disturbing repercussions within Japan. The communication made it clear, however, that the army would not oppose a Konoe-Roosevelt meeting if Konoe undertook this last effort to salvage the negotiations with enough determination: he must uphold the basic principles of Japan's counterproposal and be ready to commit Japan to war against the United States if Roosevelt, failing to "understand" their true intentions, persisted in the current policy. When the Emperor also gave approval, Konoe had Ambassador Nomura convey the proposal for a meeting to the American government.

Tomita Kenji, writing after the war, explained that Konoe had formulated his own strategy to get around army obstruction. If Roosevelt agreed to meet him in the United States, Konoe would cable from there directly to the Emperor and ask for his approval on the points of agreement reached in the conference.

Even if the military opposed some of them—inevitably, the with-drawal of troops from China—Konoe would still sign the agreement using the extraordinary means he had devised.[9] Konoe's plan to visit the United States and return to Japan with the negotiations successfully concluded added up to a dangerous scheme to outmaneuver the army. In confidence Konoe told Izawa Takio of what he was planning to do. "If you go ahead with it you're going to be killed. . . . ," Izawa warned, but Konoe replied that he was not worried about his life. When Izawa added, "It is not simply a matter of your life; they will say that you have sold out Japan to the United States," Konoe answered, "That doesn't bother me, either."[10] With the two nations on the brink of war, Konoe was desperate. This may have been the first time he had been so completely and grimly determined over any matter of state. Terrorism seriously frightened Konoe, but at that point he was willing to risk his life for a summit meeting with Roosevelt.

On August 8, following instructions from Tokyo, Nomura called on Hull and proposed a Konoe-Roosevelt meeting. On August 17, having just returned from the meeting with Prime Minister Winston Churchill during which they drew up the Atlantic Charter, Roosevelt called in Nomura and handed him two documents. One of them stated that if the Japanese government took any further steps in pursuit of a policy or program of military domination of neighboring countries using force or threat of force, the United States government would be compelled to take immediately any and all steps it deemed necessary. The other set out the American position toward the summit proposed by Japan. The document stated that if Japan suspended its expansionist activities and embarked upon a peaceful program for the Pacific, honoring principles to which the United States was committed, the United States government would be prepared to consider resumption of the discussions that had been interrupted in July and would endeavor to arrange a suitable time and place to exchange views. The United States government, however, believed that, in view of the circumstances attending the interruption of the informal conversations between the two governments, it would be helpful to both governments,

before undertaking a resumption of such conversations or pro-
ceeding with plans for a meeting, if the Japanese government
would be so good as to provide a clearer statement than had yet
been furnished of its present attitude and plans. During the
meeting with Nomura, Roosevelt proposed Juneau, Alaska, as
a possible place for the summit meeting and suggested a date
sometime in the middle of October.

Nomura met Roosevelt again on August 28 and handed him a
message from Konoe and a written statement explaining Japan's
position, in response to the above American demands. The
Konoe message stated that, since the situation was changing so
rapidly and in some ways so unpredictably, the mode in which
the negotiations had been conducted until they had broken off
seemed inappropriate. He considered it urgent that the two heads
of government discuss all problems important to their nations
concerning the entire Pacific area from a "broad perspective"
and explore every possibility of saving the situation. Minor items
could, if necessary, be adjusted through negotiations between
competent officials of the two countries after the meeting.

The written statement presented the factors that ostensibly
led Japan to take action in French Indochina. The move was
intended, it said, to hasten a settlement of the China War, and
at the same time to remove the barriers to peace in the Pacific
and secure for Japan an equitable supply of essential materials.
It was an act of self-defense the Japanese government was compelled to take. The Japanese government was prepared to withdraw its troops from French Indochina as soon as the China War
was settled or a just peace was established in East Asia. Japan's
action in French Indochina was not, furthermore, a preparatory
step for a military advance into neighboring territories. Concerning Soviet-Japanese relations, the Japanese government
declared that Japan would take no military action as long as the
Soviet Union remained faithful to the Japanese-Soviet Neutrality
Pact and did not threaten Japan or Manchukuo or take any
action contrary to the spirit of the said pact. In a word, the
Japanese government had no intention of using, without provoca-
tion, armed force against any neighboring nation.

Having read the two documents, an affable Roosevelt repeated that he thought Juneau would be a good location for the meeting and that he should like to talk with Konoe for three or four days. The president then asked Nomura if Prince Konoe spoke English. When the ambassador said he did, Roosevelt said that was good. But Roosevelt proposed no specific date for the summit talks.

Konoe's memoirs state that, during the meeting with Nomura, Roosevelt had been extremely enthusiastic about the summit and that "perhaps at that time Japan and the United States came closest to one another."[11] Konoe had his own reasons for making that assessment, but in reality the state of the Japanese-American relations at that time was far less than promising. While Roosevelt showed interest in the proposed talks with Konoe, most of the State Department officials were suspicious of the proposal from the outset. Hull, deeply distrustful of the Japanese government and Konoe, insisted that before the talks could begin they must prepare a specific agreement between the two governments on the substance of the settlement.

Hull wrote in his own memoirs: "Japan's insistence on holding the meeting and leaving the 'details' to be worked out later was in itself significant. It seemed to us that Japan was striving to push us into a conference from which general statements would issue—and Japan could then interpret and apply these statements to suit her own purposes, as she had always done in the past. Moreover, she could then say she had the President's endorsement of her actions.

"It was difficult to believe that the Konoye [Konoe] Government would dare to agree to proposals we could accept. . . . A substantial opposition existed in Japan to any efforts to improve relations with the United States. . . .

"Even while our preliminary conversations with the Konoye Government were in progress, that Government restricted and narrowed the concessions it had originally been willing to make. It was not likely that Konoye, in a personal meeting with Roosevelt, would be able to move in completely the opposite direction.

"We had no assurance that Konoye himself would desire to carry out an agreement that would turn Japan into the paths of real peace. We could not forget that Konoye had been Premier when Japan invaded China in 1937; he had signed the Axis

Alliance in 1940 and had concluded the treaty with the puppet government in Nanking designated to give Japan the mastery of China.

"We could not overlook the fact that the very holding of the meeting between the President and Konoye, following so soon on the Atlantic Conference, would cause China grave uneasiness, unless an agreement had already been reached that would pro-tect China's sovereignty.

"Unless the President were willing to agree to vague generali-ties that would all be to Japan's advantage, there was every likelihood that the meeting would end in failure. In that event Japan's military officials could declare to the Japanese that the United States was responsible for the failure and proceed to prepare public opinion for war in the Pacific."[12]

Roosevelt himself was soon convinced that Hull's insistence on caution was justified. On September 3, he gave Nomura a reply to Konoe's message plus an oral statement. Roosevelt stated in his reply that while he supported the idea of a meeting between them, he was aware that there prevailed among certain Japanese leaders a pattern of thinking that might obstruct the success of the meeting. Under these circumstances, he continued, it would be desirable to hold preliminary discussions immediately in order to reach agreement on the basic principles. The oral statement referred specifically to the four principles Hull had stipulated as the basis for negotiations and all other relations between the two nations. Having reaffirmed the American position, the oral statement suggested that it would be desirable to resolve the dis-pute on the American June 21 proposal before the meeting, as it had been left hanging since the negotiations were interrupted in July. Actually, the Japanese government had drafted a coun-terproposal, but, with the fall of the second Konoe cabinet, Nomura lost the chance to present it to the American govern-ment.

By September 6 nothing further had been done about the proposed Japanese-American summit. That day the Imperial Conference approved a policy document entitled Main Points in Implementing the Imperial Policy. The basic points were: 1) In the interest of self-defense and self-preservation, Japan would complete preparations for war by the latter part of October and would not "avoid" war with the United States, Britain, and the Netherlands, if that were necessary; 2) Japan also would utilize all possible diplomatic measures in the attempt to attain its objectives. Japan's minimum objectives in negotiations with the United States and Britain and the maximum concessions Japan would make were noted in an annex; 3) If there was no prospect that Japan's demands would be met by early October through diplomatic negotiations, Japan would immediately decide to commence hostilities against the United States, Britain, and the Netherlands.

The annex began by stating the minimum demands Japan expected to be met through negotiations with the United States and Britain. Those demands were: 1) that the United States and Britain refrain from interfering with or obstructing a settlement of the China War by Japan. That meant (a) "not obstructing" Japan's efforts to settle the war on the basis of the Basic Treaty Between Japan and Chinà and the Joint Declaration of Japan, Manchukuo, and China; and (b) closing the Burma Road and withdrawing all military, political, and economic assistance from Chiang Kai-shek. 2) Concerning Japan's national defense, the United States and Britain were to refrain from any action that might threaten the defense of Japan in the Far East. (a) Both countries were to recognize the special relations between Japan and French Indochina based on the agreement between Japan and France; (b) refrain from obtaining military rights in Thailand, the Dutch East Indies, China, and the Far Eastern territory of the Soviet Union; (c) and keep the strength of their military forces in the Far East no larger than their current level. 3) The United States and Britain were to cooperate to allow Japan's acquisition of necessary goods. Specifically, they were to (a) restore commercial relations with Japan and supply from their territories in the southwest Pacific all goods vitally necessary to Japan, and (b) "amicably" contribute to economic cooperation among Japan, Thailand, and the Dutch East Indies.

Next, the annex listed the maximum concessions Japan would make if its own demands were met. There were three: 1) Japan would not advance militarily from bases in French Indochina into neighboring areas other than China; 2) Japan was prepared to withdraw its forces from French Indochina after a "just" peace was established in the Far East; and 3) Japan was prepared to guarantee the neutrality of the Philippine Islands. It was noted in addition that, if the United States and Britain pressed Japan about its position regarding the Tripartite Pact, Japan would declare its determination not to modify its obligations under the pact.

By this time the army regarded the Japanese-American negotiations as essentially futile. Most naval leaders fervently wished to avert war with the United States, but the navy, too, was nervously and angrily aware that time was running out; pressed hard by the American oil embargo, each passing hour reduced Japan's fuel oil stocks further. If they waited too long, Japan would be drained of the power to wage war altogether. Army and navy staff officers met numerous times and finally produced a draft of the Main Points in Implementing the Imperial Policy. Revised slightly in the Imperial Headquarters–Cabinet Liaison Conference, but reflecting the military opinion that war was unavoidable, the document was approved by both the Cabinet Council and the Imperial Conference. In both tone and content, particularly the "minimum demands to be met through diplomatic negotiations with the United States and Britain"—which were much more baldly self-interested than the American demands so far—the document was tantamount to a final decision for war against the United States and Britain.

On September 5, the day before the Imperial Conference, Konoe reported to the Emperor on the new national policy. Kido, who had seen the document before it was reported to the Emperor, was appalled at the ominous implications it carried. It seemed to him particularly dangerous to set a time limit on the negotiations, and he urged Konoe to try to modify at least the early October deadline. Konoe replied that it would be difficult, since the matter had been decided by the Liaison Conference. At best, Konoe said, he could only do whatever was humanly possible to make the negotiations a success.[13]

The Emperor was equally alarmed. He observed that the document dealt with war preparations before diplomatic negotiations, giving the impression that war had precedence over diplomacy. Konoe explained that the order of discussion did not necessarily indicate their relative importance and that the government intended to work until the very end to obtain a settlement through diplomacy. Only if diplomatic efforts became totally hopeless would war preparations begin. Afterward, at the suggestion of Konoe, the Emperor summoned Army Chief of Staff Sugiyama and Navy Chief of Staff Nagano and asked the same question; both answered the same way as Konoe.

At the Imperial Conference of September 6, Nagano stated that clearly Japan must do everything possible to resolve its precarious situation by peaceful means. He pointed out that vital military supplies were dwindling day by day, and that Japan's national defense would be eroded if this went on, particularly in view of the rapid military buildup in Asia by the United States, Britain, and other countries. He concluded that if Japan's minimum demands could not be met through diplomacy, the nation would be compelled to fight.

Next, Sugiyama affirmed the army's agreement with Nagano's statement and said that war preparations would be completed by late October so that Japan could open hostilities while it was still capable of waging war against the United States and Britain. Then Hara Yoshimichi, Privy Council president, spoke. He pointed out again that the plan they had developed indicated greater emphasis on war than diplomacy. Hara requested that both the government and supreme command clearly state their positions on the matter. Navy Minister Oikawa, representing the government, made a reply, Konoe recorded in his memoirs, but no one from the supreme command rose to speak.

Suddenly breaking the silence, the Emperor himself declared that Privy Council President Hara's question was deeply important and how regrettable it was that the supreme command had failed to respond. He then drew a slip of paper from his pocket and read a verse composed by Emperor Meiji:

Throughout the world

Everywhere we are all brothers

Why then do the winds and waves rage so turbulently?

The Emperor said he frequently read that imperial poem in his own effort to uphold in his time Emperor Meiji's dedication to peace. Those present were stunned. Roused by the imperial statement, Nagano finally rose and said that he had not replied to Hara personally, assuming that the navy minister spoke for both government and supreme command. The supreme command, Nagano affirmed, would of course stress diplomacy first, and would turn to war only as an unavoidable last resort. The Imperial Conference adjourned in an atmosphere of greater tension than he had ever experienced, Konoe recalled.[14]

While the document Main Points was being formulated, Konoe wanted somehow to avoid establishing the date when hostilities would begin. But he conceded to the argument of the military that thorough, complete war preparations required a specific deadline. Konoe wrote in his memoirs that the Main Points had specified that "in the event that there is no prospect of our demands being met by the first part of October through diplomatic negotiations, we will immediately decide to commence hostilities against the United States, Britain, and the Netherlands." Consequently, the government could have avoided the decision to commence hostilities by insisting that "some prospect still remained" for successful negotiations. Even if the government made the decision to commence hostilities, that would not have been quite the same as "opening hostilities." Therefore, even if the negotiations failed, the government could have carried on under severed economic relations without resorting to war. In fact, Konoe wrote, the government considered "gradually contriving some such fallback measures" if necessary.[15] That might have been plausible if the wording in the Main Points were taken at face value, but, considering the priorities and intentions of the military at the time, Konoe's argument is not very convincing. He may have tried in his memoirs to minimize his personal responsibility in the formulation of the document.

In any event, as Konoe himself said, as far as Japan was concerned, the policy approved in that crucial Imperial Conference of September 6 placed a definite time limit on the negotiations. "We were all too aware that the matter had entered the final stage," he observed. With the future of Japanese-American relations growing more ominous, Konoe was desperate that the meeting with Roosevelt take place. On the evening of the sixth, just after the Main Points had been approved, in strict secrecy Konoe invited American Ambassador Joseph C. Grew to dinner and talked with him for more than three hours. The only others present were Ushiba Tomohiko, secretary to the premier, and Eugene H. Dooman, counselor at the American Embassy.

During the meeting, Grew recorded, Konoe stated that he and, therefore, the Japanese government, agreed "conclusively and wholeheartedly" with Hull's four principles as a basis for the rehabilitation of relations. (A month later Foreign Minister Toyoda corrected Konoe's endorsement of the four principles by saying that the prime minister accepted them "in principle" on that night; Grew noted in this regard that Konoe's statements had been translated by Dooman, who had a superb command of the Japanese language, and that there was no doubt whatsoever about what Konoe had told Grew.)[16] Konoe further declared strong confidence that he could resolve the points of contention between Japan and the United States through direct talks with the president. Certainly it would take time to work out a detailed agreement, Konoe acknowledged, especially in view of mounting resentment in Japan toward the economic pressure being exerted by other countries. He could not guarantee that domestic conditions would be conducive to widespread acceptance of a detailed agreement by the time it was concluded, but at present, Konoe said, he could carry the Japanese people to the goal he had selected. If difficulties were encountered in working out the details of the commitments, he could overcome them satisfactorily. Thus, Konoe stressed again and again that time was of the essence.

Grew replied that the Japanese government had often failed to keep its promises in the past, and by now the American government trusted only actions and facts, not Japanese promises or assurances. Konoe made no attempt to refute or defend; he simply insisted that his government wished a thoroughgoing reconstruction of American-Japanese relations. Any commitments he undertook from now on, he told Grew, would be honored, unlike the "irresponsible" assurances of the past. He was determined that relations with the United States be improved and placed on a stable, mutually satisfactory footing, regardless of cost or personal risk. Konoe added that the ship waiting to take his party to the meeting with Roosevelt had been equipped with a radio that would let him communicate directly with Tokyo from the meeting place. As soon as he had reached an agreement with President Roosevelt and had reported to the Emperor, the Emperor would immediately issue a rescript ordering the suspension of all hostile actions.[17]

"The fact," Grew observed, "that the peace party led by Konoye [Konoe], and including even influential figures in the Army and Navy, was ready to resort to the unprecedented and highly hazardous device of causing the Emperor to intervene— the device used four years later with complete success to accomplish Japan's surrender—is strong proof that Prince Konoye was ready to use all possible means to accomplish his objectives of avoiding war with the United States and reorienting Japan."[18] Grew wrote further, "Mr. Dooman and I returned to the Embassy from that historic meeting with the firm conviction that we had been dealing with a man of unquestioned sincerity." Grew urged the State Department to approve the Konoe-Roosevelt meeting, but Hull was suspicious and Stanley Hornbeck, the Far East political advisor, was rigidly opposed. In general, the State Department regarded the meeting as meaningless unless the basic issues were worked out beforehand. The summit proceeded no further.

Factors militating against any peaceful solution were even more powerful in Japan. The day before the Imperial Conference, Konoe had told Imperial Prince Higashikuni Naruhiko about the proposal for the summit and the enormous importance he attached to its success, particularly in view of the Emperor's determination that everything possible be done to improve relations with the United States. Venting his frustration that, while the navy was enthusiastic, the army remained divided and at best cool toward the meeting with Roosevelt, Konoe asked Higashikuni to try to persuade Army Minister Tōjō to give his support. Higashikuni summoned Tōjō the day after Konoe's dinner with Grew, but throughout their discussion Tōjō held firm to the army's rigid position vis-à-vis the United States. The talk ended in disagreement.

While Japan's leaders were deadlocked, early October approached with frightening rapidity. When the Imperial Headquarters–Cabinet Liaison Conference convened on September 25, everyone felt the pressure of time. Army Chief of Staff Sugiyama and Navy Chief of Staff Nagano took turns demanding a governmental decision for war or peace by October 15 at the latest. A document that had been prepared for submission to the government with both their signatures gave two reasons that a clear decision was necessary. First, the Main Points stipulated that Japan would immediately decide to commence hostilities if, by early October, there was no prospect of success in the negotiations with the United States. Second, the state of Japan's military resources and American war preparations in progress left no margin; any delay in the opening of hostilities would put Japan at a serious disadvantage once war began. And, since war against Britain and the United States might mean fighting the Soviet Union as well, it would be imperative to achieve all major goals in the southern Pacific area by the following March. The southern operations must be commenced, therefore, by November 15 at the latest. These factors indicated, the document concluded, that the supreme command should begin operational preparations to let Japan open hostilities by early November.

Konoe was shocked. As soon as the conference adjourned, he skipped a luncheon at the Imperial Headquarters and returned to his official residence with all the cabinet ministers who had attended the conference. Konoe turned to Tōjō and asked him if the demand to set October 15 as the "cut-off point for war" was irrevocable. Tōjō replied that the military chiefs had set the deadline in strict compliance with the Main Points, which had been approved by the Imperial Conference; it could not be altered now.

Konoe was driven into a corner. The next day he told Kido that, if the military were determined to start a war on October 15, he had to resign, for he did not accept the necessity for hostilities. Kido had been painfully disturbed about the deadline on the negotiations specified in the Main Points, and now he reminded Konoe that he himself had accepted "early October" as decided by the Liaison Conference and had upheld that decision at the Imperial Conference of September 6. It would be irresponsible to resign without making any move to revise what he thought was an unwise course. Konoe should act with integrity and propose reconsideration of the September 6 decision; only when the army rejected his proposal should he decide his own course of action. Kido strongly urged Konoe to give more careful thought to his resignation.

On October 2, the United States replied to Japan's counterproposal, which had been presented to the American government through Ambassador Nomura. By that time Japan had transmitted two counterproposals to Washington, one on September 6 and the other on September 25. The September 6 draft was intended to open the way to a summit meeting by making some concessions on major issues, thus skirting the earlier debate on principles. The gist of it was that, first, Japan would not advance militarily from French Indochina into any adjoining areas, and would not take unjustified military action in any region lying north of Japan. Second, if the United States joined in the European war, Japan would interpret its obligation under the Tripartite Pact independently. Third, when "general and normal relationships" were resumed between Japan and China, Japan would withdraw its armed forces from China as soon as possible thereafter in accordance with the agreement between Japan and China. Fourth, American economic activities in China would not be restricted as long as they were pursued on an equitable basis. Fifth, Japan's activities in the southwestern Pacific area would proceed in accordance with the principle of nondiscrimination in international commerce. Finally, Japan would take the necessary measures for the resumption of normal trade relations with the United States. In return, the Japanese government would request the United States to suspend any military measures in the Far East and in the southwestern Pacific area and to normalize trade with Japan and lift the freeze on Japanese assets. The September 25 counterproposal was basically a redraft of the main points Japan had presented so far.

The American government found no evidence of a modification of Japan's position in the September 25 counterproposal, and perhaps for that reason ignored it and replied to the September 6 draft. Noting first that Prime Minister Konoe had stated earlier in a conversation with Grew that he "subscribed fully" to the four principles, the American reply iterated the government's disappointment that in the September 6 proposal and subsequent explanatory statements Japan had attached various qualifications to the application of the four principles. The American reply also expressed displeasure with Japan's intention to station troops for an undetermined period in certain areas of China and demanded that Japan further clarify its position regarding the Tripartite Pact. Finally, the document said, while the president was eager to hold the proposed summit, no meeting would be fruitful as long as the two governments held such disparate views. Hull later recorded that it seemed to him there was still no more than one chance in fifty of any success in the negotiations, but he wanted to hold off Japan's next advance as long as possible, for it would probably mean war in the Pacific.

On October 4, two days after Hull had given him the American reply, Nomura reported to Tokyo that although the negotiations appeared to be deadlocked, he did not believe they should be regarded as completely hopeless. The issues concerning the Tripartite Pact and nondiscrimination in trade, he said, were as good as resolved, leaving the problem of Japan's troops in China as the crucial outstanding issue "upon which Japanese-American understanding hung." Compared with Hull's outlook, Nomura's perception of the situation was unrealistically optimistic, and, significantly, Konoe shared his optimism.

Yet the American reply certainly did not inspire optimism among Japanese decision-makers. The dominant core of the army judged that the negotiations had failed and that the early October deadline set out in the Main Points had not been met. In the navy, certain groups were eager to go to war, but as a whole the navy was deeply anxious. They had no confidence in Japan's capacity to wage a successful war against the United States, and the majority supported any efforts at negotiations in order to avoid hostilities.

Thus, when Konoe called in Tōjō on October 7 and tried to

work out some compromise, he had little success. After going over the current state of the negotiations, Konoe stated that the American insistence on the four principles compelled Japan to recognize an open door and equal opportunity in China. But that should be acceptable as long as the United States recognized the special relationship implicit in the propinquity of China and Japan. It might be difficult to settle the Tripartite Pact problem simply by exchanging notes, but Konoe said an agreement could be reached in direct talks with Roosevelt. The remaining large issue was the deployment of Japanese troops in China. What would Tōjō say if, indeed, only the matter of the troops in China remained unresolved? Could the army accept a compromise by which Japan would accept the principle of troop withdrawal but in actuality maintain some troops in China? Tōjō replied that the only way Japan could accept the four principles was to specify exceptions and attach qualifications to them. But the United States, in its October 2 message, had taken issue with the qualifications Japan wanted to apply, because of its geographical proximity to China. The army could make no concessions on the issue of troops in China.

He found it impossible, Tōjō continued, to answer a hypothetical question and state what the army would do if the only problem left unresolved through negotiations was the matter of troops in China. He would consider it when the situation demanded, but even then he doubted the possibility of any concession. Konoe then brought up the key point. The next of the Main Points, he noted, stipulated that, if there was no prospect that their demands would be met by "first ten days of October through diplomatic negotiations," Japan will "*immediately* decide to commence hostilities against the United States, Britain, and the Netherlands" [emphasis author]. Konoe declared that "immediately" posed a serious problem and that setting a time limit should be reconsidered. Tōjō wondered if it was really necessary to reconsider the original decision, insofar as any attempt to revise a decision of the Imperial Conference would be a very serious move. If at this date there was any doubt about the decision, Tōjō persisted, those who had advised the Emperor in the Imperial Conference bore heavy responsibility.

The Konoe-Tōjō meeting ended as it began, without agreement.[19]

Konoe agonized over the matter. Finally he decided to try to enlist the navy in a last attempt to override army pressure for the immediate opening of hostilities. Konoe set up a meeting to discuss Japan's next move—for war or peace—at his villa, Tekigaisō, in Ogikubo, for October 12. He called the army, navy, and foreign ministers and Cabinet Planning Board President Suzuki Teiichi to attend. The night before the meeting, Chief Cabinet Secretary Tomita called on Navy Minister Oikawa. Tomita told the navy minister that the negotiations with the United States had almost reached the breaking point; if the army refused to concede on the issue of troops in China, war would be inevitable. Tomita tried to push Oikawa to act. If the navy genuinely wanted to avert war, he said, their most positive move would be to back Konoe at the conference the next day and press for continuation of the negotiations with Washington. Oikawa's reply was ambivalent. He understood Tomita's intent, he said, but the military could not decide for war or peace. That was the job of the government. Once a decision for war had been made, the military was bound to fight, however unfavorable the odds. Oikawa said he would make it clear at the meeting that the navy left the decision totally up to the prime minister, but, he added, he hoped that Konoe would push hard for continued negotiations.

October 12 was a clear, crisp Sunday, and it happened to be Konoe's fiftieth birthday. The meeting, which came to be known as the Ogikubo conference, was convened in the afternoon. Tōjō stated the army position at the outset. Successive concessions by Japan, he said, had failed to produce any change in the American demands, and he believed further diplomatic negotiations would be useless. Oikawa stressed consistency. Japan, he declared, stood at the critical juncture of war or peace. If they opted for diplomacy at this point instead of war, they must pursue it to a successful conclusion, even if it meant further concessions. They could not change that policy midstream in the negotiations. Much depended on the conditions Japan set, Toyoda replied; at present the snare in relations with the United States was the deployment of troops in China. If the army made absolutely no concession, there was no hope for a peaceful solution. But if the army were willing to give a little, the negotiations still had a chance. Tōjō retorted that the army could concede nothing on that issue.

Konoe then intervened, stating that both war and peace carried great risks, and the question was which was Japan best equipped to handle successfully. Konoe had more confidence in diplomacy, he said, and that was the course he believed Japan should take. If the army held to their demand for war, he would not take the responsibility. After a four-hour discussion, the conference adjourned, but no consensus had been reached.

As in his talks with Tomita, Oikawa had once more evaded a clear expression of navy opposition to the war with the United States, frustrating Konoe's gamble that navy support would restrain the army. A final recourse was to appeal directly to Tōjō. Two days after the Ogikubo conference, and immediately before a cabinet meeting, Konoe called in Tōjō and put before him the request to reconsider the army stand on the troops issue. He was mistaken, but Konoe was convinced that this was the main barrier to a diplomatic solution. Japanese troops on the continent would ensure the end of the China War, Tōjō had argued at Ogikubo, and the Basic Treaty between Japan and the Nanking government stipulated their presence in China for an indefinite period. When he tried once more to persuade Tōjō to modify his stand, Konoe used the China War to strengthen his argument. He himself bore serious responsibility for the war in China, Konoe told Tōjō, and that he could not possibly commit Japan to another major military engagement, particularly when the outcome was so uncertain, while the China War remained unsettled.

Japan must temporarily yield to America, Konoe argued, and accept in principle the withdrawal of troops from China in order to avoid war in the Pacific. The nation's strength and the people's morale both demanded that the China War must be settled first. For a nation to grow, it is sometimes necessary to retreat a little and recoup its energy, he admonished. Tōjō retorted that if Japan yielded now, that would only give America's heavy-handed arrogance more room to grow. As for Japanese troops on the mainland, the army had been asked to make the greatest sacrifices so far, and even to agree in principle to withdraw would destroy army morale. This meeting with Tōjō also ended inconclusively. During their talk, Tōjō had remarked to Konoe, "I think you are too pessimistic. It is probably because you know our weaknesses too well. Doesn't America have weaknesses of its own?" Toward the end, he blurted out, somewhat emotionally, "All this is a matter of differences in our personalities, isn't it?"

Thus, at the cabinet council meeting of October 14, Tōjō announced that no hope remained in the negotiations with Washington and declared that they should be terminated in accordance with the early October deadline. Toyoda protested that the biggest obstacle to a diplomatic solution was the issue of the Japanese troops in China, drawing a vehement retort from Tōjō. To yield to the American demand and withdraw their troops, he exploded, would wipe out all the fruits of the China War, endanger Manchukuo, and jeopardize the governing of Korea. To accept troop withdrawal in name only would not benefit Japan either, he said. Withdrawal would mean retreat. It would depress morale. A demoralized army would be as worthless as no army. Our troops in China are the "heart of the matter," he persisted. Having made one concession after another, why should Japan now yield the "heart"? "If we concede this, what is diplomacy? It is surrender . . . a stain on the history of our empire!" No one in the cabinet argued. The council adjourned after deciding a few other matters.

Now in his worst predicament yet, Konoe saw little he could do but resign. On the night of the 14th, by previous appointment, he met Kaya Okinori and Uchida Nobuya at Uchida's residence. Originally they had planned to exchange views on current developments and also to discuss candidates for president of the North China Development Company. "As I waited for Prince Konoe and Mr. Kaya, I hadn't the faintest idea that Army Minister Tōjō had made his crucial statement at the cabinet council that day," Uchida recollected. "At the appointed time, 6 P.M., Prince Konoe arrived, calm as usual and dressed in Japanese attire. Entering the parlor, he said, 'Our discussion

tonight is no longer necessary. My cabinet is about to fall.' "
Konoe related how the army minister had demanded that they
terminate the negotiations, and he explained that the navy,
refusing to come out and acknowledge its lack of confidence to
fight a war with America, left the matter of war or peace to the
prime minister. Remarking that the next cabinet meeting would
go through the same, fruitless debate, "Konoe gave a lonely
smile. 'I am here tonight only to enjoy your kind hospitality,'
he said. After dinner the prince picked up a brush and wrote the
character for 'dream' and muttered darkly, 'Two thousand six
hundred years. It's been a long dream.' Even now I can envi-
sion the prince just as he was at that moment."[20]

When Konoe returned that night to his private residence,
Suzuki Teiichi, the Cabinet Planning Board president, came to
see him with a message from Tōjō. Tōjō reportedly said that he
had investigated and learned that the navy was very reluctant
to go to war against the United States. Why, Tōjō wondered,
had not the navy minister openly told him so? If indeed the navy
was not behind a war, Tōjō had to reconsider the whole question.
The navy minister should not have left the decision of war or
peace entirely up to the prime minister. If the navy was uncom-
mitted, the decision of the September 6 Imperial Conference
had been fundamentally wrong, and, if so, it would mean that
all those who had attended, including the prime minister, army
and navy ministers, and army and navy chiefs of staff, had
failed in their duty to properly advise the Emperor. The only
option would be resignation en masse, and then the policy decision could be reconsidered in its entirety. At this point, however,
Tōjō continued, there was no commoner who could control the
army and the navy and conduct a thorough policy review.
Therefore, it would be advisable to ask Imperial Prince Higashikuni to take over as prime minister. It was hard to ask Konoe to
resign, Tōjō said, but since there was no alternative, he would
like Konoe's cooperation in recommending Prince Higashikuni
to the Emperor. Tōjō added that he would rather not meet
Konoe again, for fear that he might lose his temper.

Throughout the night of October 14, Konoe struggled, sleep-
less, to think of some way to avert war. He seriously contemplated

"getting out" of the country, heading for America, and meeting Roosevelt face to face.[21] But in the end, Konoe decided to support Prince Higashikuni as prime minister. Prince Higashikuni was against the war, and he might, Konoe thought, be able to restrain the army and avert hostilities. On October 15, Konoe attended court and advised the Emperor to order Imperial Prince Higashikuni to form a cabinet. Konoe met Kido also and told him that his relationship with Tōjō had deteriorated so far that he could not continue as prime minister. He asked Kido to cooperate in getting a Higashikuni cabinet off the ground. That night Konoe called on Prince Higashikuni and pressed him to form a cabinet. Higashikuni promised that he would seriously consider it.

Kido saw clearly that both Tōjō and Konoe were pushing Higashikuni to accept the post that so he could use the prestige of an imperial prince to solve the differences between the army and navy. What Kido feared most was that, depending on the consequences, if an imperial prince made the decision for war or peace, the act might bring the "wrath of the people" upon the imperial family. Thus Kido was opposed to the choice of Prince Higashikuni, and on October 16, he told both Konoe and Tōjō his opinion. Thereupon, Konoe later wrote, "believing the situation to be so critical as to allow not even a moment's delay," he resigned. Kido had been convinced that Konoe and Tōjō could still come to some kind of agreement, and so he was shocked and bitterly displeased.

At the sudden fall of the Konoe cabinet, Kido was faced with the agonizing task of recommending the next prime minister. The events leading to the end of the Konoe cabinet made it clear that the September 6 decision had to be revised. He was equally aware of how difficult that would be, given the army's rigid refusal to compromise. The next prime minister had an intricate job. While conforming to the Emperor's wishes, he had to keep as close rein as possible on the military, particularly the army, and at the same time establish effective coordination between the army and navy. Konoe's successor had to be someone thoroughly familiar with the course of events up to then, someone who had explored all their possible ramifications. Kido concluded that only Navy Minister Oikawa and Army Minister Tōjō were qualified.

Konoe agreed with Kido's thinking. The most urgent task was to keep the army under control, he told Kido. If that failed, everything, particularly the precarious negotiations with Washington, would collapse in disarray. For that reason, Tōjō was the best choice, Konoe thought. If he could rely on what Tōjō had told him during the past few days, Konoe added in his talk with Kido, Tōjō would not necessarily jump into the war upon assuming office, and probably he would hold back further if the Emperor were to advise caution.[22]

On October 17, the day after Konoe's resignation, a senior statesmen's conference was held in the palace to discuss who should be recommended as the next prime minister. Pleading illness, Konoe did not attend. Kido nominated Tōjō and the majority of the senior statesmen supported the nomination. Immediately after he had received the imperial order to form a cabinet, Tōjō was informed through Kido that the Emperor wished him to reexamine the entire domestic and foreign situation and decide carefully upon the affairs of state without regard to the September 6 decision.

Japanese-American negotiations continued after the formation of the Tōjō cabinet, but they made no progress. On November 26, Secretary Hull handed to Ambassador Nomura and Kurusu Saburō, a career diplomat sent to assist Nomura, the so-called Hull note. Shortly afterward Japan terminated the negotiations, and war came to the Pacific on December 8, 1941 (Japan time).

6

TURBULENT CLOUDS OF WAR

The surprise attack on Pearl Harbor was followed by a succession of fast, efficient victories that sent the Japanese people into wildly excited jubilation.

On December 8, Konoe was in Hakone. He heard the news that the war had begun on the radio. His initial dumbfounded shock turned into rage, and he quickly returned to Tokyo, unusually perturbed. That day, when Hosokawa Morisada met him at Kazoku Kaikan (Peers Club), "Everyone around him was reveling in excitement over the success at Pearl Harbor." Hosokawa continued, "But Konoe was despondent. Before I entered the room, he stood up slowly and walked out to the hallway. In a voice filled with dread and sadness, he said, 'It is a terrible thing that has happened. I know that a tragic defeat awaits us at the end. I can feel it. Our luck will not last more than two or three months at best.' I will never forget Konoe as I saw him that day."[1]

The year 1942 began with one Japanese victory after another. On New Year's Day, Konoe went to the palace to give New Year's greetings to the Emperor. When he returned to his villa, Tekigaisō, Konoe related to Tomita with thorough disgust how "everybody at the palace was celebrating the success of the Pearl Harbor attack. Even Admiral Okada [Keisuke] was carrying on, giving toast after toast. Okada's a soldier, too, after all. He literally heaped praise on Yamamoto [Isoroku, commander of the combined fleet], going on about how magnificently he had come through. He said that if Suetsugu [Nobumasa] had commanded the attack on Pearl Harbor, he would have reserved a few aircraft carriers, but Yamamoto put the lot into this battle.

Okada gushed on about the champion gamesman Yamamoto, who used his best poker strategy in the Pearl Harbor attack and won. A number of other old fellows who understand nothing at all started singing boisterously with Okada. What an unpleasant spectacle! How vulgar they are! At this rate, they will push us all the way to defeat."[2]

The following day Konoe went to Uchida Nobuya's villa in Atami. He repeated to Uchida his description of the mood at the palace on New Year's Day. "Even the old men on the Privy Council seemed utterly carried away. They all came up to greet me, voicing sympathies! 'What a pity it is, Mr. Konoe. We wish you had the honor. . . . Indeed, what a shame.' What could I say? Do these old fellows really believe that we will keep on winning and actually come out on top in this war? I wonder how they will greet me next New Year's Day." Konoe firmly predicted that Japan would not hold the advantage for more than a year.[3] While everyone else exulted in each successive victory, Konoe remained pessimistic and detached.

Konoe's attitude was not well received among the majority. He became the target of insults and ridicule as a coward who had exerted himself to avert the war by drawing out the negotiations. Some saw his detachment as negativism and began to watch him with deep suspicion. At one point, Kiya Ikusaburō called on the prince at Karuizawa to report a rumor that Prime Minister Tōjō himself was beginning to wonder about Konoe. Konoe seemed to be aware of it, but he was unconcerned. After Kiya returned to Kyoto, where he had moved after the war started, Kondō Hongen of Kōyasan Temple came to visit him. Kondō told Kiya that because Prince Konoe was president of the advisory council of Kōyasan, the temple seemed also to be under suspicion of being non-cooperative with the war effort. He thought it would be wise to hold a Buddhist mass for victory, which he hoped Konoe would attend. This surprised Kiya; he had not been aware of the wide ramifications of Konoe's alleged unenthusiasm. And so he approached Abe Nobuyuki, president of the Imperial Rule Assistance Political Association and a close associate of Tōjō as well as an advisor to Kōyasan, about the mass. As a result, Konoe and Abe attended a victory mass at

Kōyasan in August 1942 and a memorial service for men who had died in action.[4]

The overwhelming military supremacy Japan had displayed during the initial stage of the war began to crack before long. With the Battle of Midway in June 1942 and the Allied landing on Guadalcanal Island in August, the balance shifted, and the American side gained the advantage. Japan's position grew steadily weaker from then on, its forces repeatedly defeated and forced to retreat. Konoe remained cool as the war in the Pacific went on. Freed from government responsibility and with more time to himself now, he reflected on the turbulent days of the past. It seemed ironic to him that having learned of the navy's reluctance to fight the United States, and then counting on navy support, he ended up being betrayed by it. Once he acknowledged to Tomita, "Prince Saionji was truly a great man. Throughout his life he remained a liberal and a believer in party politics. I created that monstrosity, the Imperial Rule Assistance Association, but I see now that I should have supported the political parties. They were not perfect, but our only real choice was to keep them going and improve them."[5]

One day in June 1945, when Japan's imminent defeat was clear to everyone, Tomita and Konoe talked until midnight about the future of Japan. At the time, Konoe quipped, half-seriously, "I would like revenge; I would like to make a sweeping roundup of all the intriguers who have brought Japan to this defeat and the selfish profit-seekers who have accused us as traitors. I am better qualified than you to perform such a cruel job. I don't think you would be able to do it. Maybe I should be home minister." Konoe looked "serious and resolute." Tomita later recounted the strong impression Konoe's expression left upon him then. "Prince Konoe certainly had that sort of cruelty in him."[6]

More important for the interpretation of history, he seemed to have a very short-sighted view of who, and what, were actually responsible for the conditions that led to war. Konoe was convinced that he himself had done his utmost to avert war, and so when certain defeat loomed ahead, his anger toward the people he believed were responsible was redoubled. Yet apart from who was immediately responsible for starting the war, the longer train of events leading up to it does not necessarily exempt Konoe, prime minister several times over, from responsibility.

During the war Konoe thought of renouncing his title and honors and retiring from public life to live in seclusion in Kyoto. He had a villa built there, and in 1944, when it was completed, he went there for a visit. One day while he was still in Kyoto, Konoe met Kiya Ikusaburō, who suggested that he set up some educational project upon his retirement, much like the Tōa Dōbun Shoin (East Asia Common Culture Academy), which his father, Atsumaro, had founded in connection with Tōa Dōbunkai. Konoe replied that he, too, had been thinking of the same thing. The next morning it rained, but with umbrella in hand, Konoe went out to inspect a piece of land near his villa where he was planning to build a school. He told Kiya that if he retired to Kyoto, he wanted to have all the members of the Konoe family reside near the Omuro area of Kyoto, close to the family library, the Yōmei Bunko.[7]

By April of 1944, Japanese forces were losing their grip all over Asia. Konoe met Imperial Prince Higashikuni Naruhiko to discuss the situation. He said that he thought Tōjō should remain as prime minister, despite the deteriorating war situation. In Hosokawa Morisada's view, if Konoe had thought a new prime minister could reverse the direction of the war, he would have advised replacing Tōjō, but since he believed the war was as good as lost, better to put all the blame on Tōjō, who now stood with Hitler as the two most hated men in much of the world. The United States might raise the question of the Emperor's responsibility for the war. But Americans had little knowledge of the imperial family or how the imperial institution worked in Japan, and, if Tōjō could be made a convincing scapegoat, his culpability might draw American attention away from the question of the Emperor's responsibility.[8]

Hosokawa and Tomita discussed the idea of retaining Tōjō in office to the end, but they came to the conclusion that keeping Tōjō would be the same as simply sitting back to wait for national ruin. For Konoe, a senior statesman, to advocate such a policy was a highly unsuitable move; Prince Konoe's own interests demanded that he show willingness to meet the national crisis positively and try to save the country, even if he alienated the people in the process. To back away now would be to invite personal tragedy in the confusion of defeat. If Konoe took some immediate action, even to try to mitigate the disaster, he might be hated by some, but the more thoughtful would be grateful. This might be the only way for Prince Konoe to survive the coming crisis.

Hosokawa and Tomita decided to put their arguments before Konoe and try to persuade him to take resolute action. Hosokawa called on him soon after that and told him, "In the future when the people know the truth about our nation's situation, in the worst case Tōjō will certainly be assassinated; it will be chaotic enough that you will probably not escape assassination either. You may die whatever you do, whether you sit and do nothing or get up and march forward. That is why at this juncture, you must go forth in confidence, mustering all your courage and might." The prince only smiled, Hosokawa recorded.[9]

The war situation continued to slide closer to catastrophe. In June, as the desperate battle on Saipan was being fought out, Hosokawa told Konoe that at this point the overwhelming majority of the people would probably be grateful if the Emperor terminated the war immediately by an imperial edict. But the public response might be completely different if surrender were put off until the Allied Powers began bombing or landing on Japanese soil. Hosokawa urged Konoe to exert all his influence to bring about an immediate "change of course," but the prince showed little vigor in his response.[10]

When Saipan fell in July 1944, Japan's war was hopeless. Since that spring, four senior statesmen, Konoe, Wakatsuki Reijirō, Hiranuma Kiichirō, and Okada Keisuke, had been meeting from time to time to exchange opinions on how to deal with the increasingly serious situation. After the fall of Saipan, they and other senior statesmen met and agreed that they had to install a powerful "national unity" cabinet which had the support of the entire country. They presented their decision to the Lord Keeper of the Privy Seal Kido, who by this time was also very eager to replace Tōjō. For some time Tōjō himself had been planning a cabinet reshuffle, but he had not made solid progress, and then he was cut short by the senior statesmen's recommendation for a cabinet change, which forced Tōjō to resign. Kido called a conference of the senior statesmen to seek their opinions on Tōjō's successor, and they decided to recommend the governor general of Korea, General Koiso Kuniaki.

Konoe was unusually outspoken during the conference. His presentation of his views on the danger of a communist revolution was particularly memorable for the deeply earnest way he spoke. He held to the same view from this time on. It is not clear exactly when he began to develop the attitude that emerged then, but in a letter to Kido dated November 1943, Konoe wrote that recently he was able to fully understand the "renovation policy" that "a certain group" within the army was promoting. There had been a number of "renovation policy" proposals while he was prime minister, and, in his personal experience in negotiating with the army on foreign policy issues, he had been aware of others. But they had not been altogether clear. Now the army group's scheme brought them all into sharp focus. "When one holds up against this mirror the movements at home and abroad, from the Manchurian Incident to the present, everything seems to fall into place."

The renovation plan originally was drafted to accompany a five-year plan to increase production that Ishiwara Kanji of the army general staff requested Miyazaki Masayoshi to prepare in 1936 and 1937. Even after Ishiwara and Miyazaki had lost their influence within the army, the draft policy was not only retained, but it was steadily radicalized, and now its substance was "hardly different from Soviet-style communism." The various policy plans proposed to Konoe when he was in office were part of the total scheme, but it seemed to Konoe that since then they had been unified and gradually and skillfully put into practice.

Almost everyone recognized the need for basic institutional domestic reform and the construction of a highly advanced national defense state (*Wehrstaat*) for the prosecution of a successful war. The majority of military men must have believed in this, Konoe continued. It was clear that such an idea had motivated

Ishiwara and others. But a small number of people within the military regarded domestic reform itself as the ultimate objective and the war merely as a means for realizing it. These few regarded the "forces supporting the status quo," as they called them—those that were not toppled in the May 15th or February 26th incidents—as obstacles to radical renovation. The radicals had been compelled to "remove by force" the status quo advocates by plunging the country into war. This was the aim of the "communists," and to them winning or losing the war was of no consequence. They even preferred defeat.

Konoe could not believe that this national renovation faction within the military harbored a "red ideology." Yet his experience in dealing with the military during both his first and second cabinets convinced him that the military had purposely escalated the incident in China and had tried to delay the negotiations with the United States. It was also hard to believe that the top army leadership, including the minister, moved with such deliberate intentions, but, if indeed this group was willing to use any means at all to realize their "renovation policy," it would not be unthinkable that they purposely inflated the China War and provoked the Pacific War. The ringleader of the faction seemed to be Ikeda Sumihisa, who came from Ōita prefecture. Minami Jirō and Umezu Yoshijirō, somewhat older than he, were also from Ōita. Konoe considered Ikeda and others supporting the die-hard Umezu position to be a "renovation faction that must be watched most carefully," and if Umezu became prime minister or army minister, "there is the dire possibility that the most extremist course of renovation will be pursued. Even without such a development, the situation now, in Japan and the world, seriously threatens to invite the rise of communism. The matter requires scrupulous attention."[11]

In May 1944 Konoe told Hosokawa of reports about a Soviet military attaché who complained that recent Japanese actions were so communistic that even the Soviets were uneasy: "We are going to have to defend ourselves from Japanese communism," the Soviet officer reportedly said. "The trend in Japan is definitely toward communism."[12]

In June, Konoe invited Hata Shigenori, chief of the first section of the Special Police division of the Metropolitan Police Board to Tekigaisō, with Hosokawa and Takamura Sakahiko, where Hata spoke at length about recent communist movements in Japan. His comments heightened Konoe's growing anxiety about a communist revolution. Hata explained that since no communist party existed in Japan, communist movements were unorganized, but the communists were active at their places of work, carrying on as they considered appropriate under the particular circumstances. The deterioration of the national economy during the war had provided a seedbed for communist movements. The activists did not openly reveal their ideology, but most of them were trying to cultivate and train new communists in anticipation of defeat. In short, the situation was a "pile of dry hay" that would flare up as soon as anyone set a match to it. The Metropolitan Police Board classified those who rejected the national polity (*kokutai*) as leftists and those who supported it as rightists, but it was clear that the so-called rightists included many leftists. In the right-wing cry to "restore industry to the throne," for example, could be heard the voice of the Left, and, moreover, most of the so-called converts from the Left were not true converts.

In July, Konoe called in Matsudaira Yasumasa, chief secretary to the Lord Keeper of the Privy Seal, and handed him a written statement he wished Kido to consider. This was five days before the fall of Saipan. Konoe wrote in the statement, "Since the Battle of Saipan, navy authorities say that the Japanese Combined Fleet has been rendered powerless. . . . The army authorities seem to agree that the war situation holds no hope at all for improvement. In short, both the army and the navy conclude that defeat is inevitable, but under the circumstances neither has the courage to declare the obvious." Konoe advised having the Emperor order both army and navy leaders to confirm their conclusion, replace Tōjō with Higashikuni, and with the assistance of the new cabinet, immediately issue an edict to terminate the war. He should tell the people, "Considering the grave turn of events in the war situation, and in view of the close and affectionate relationship between the Emperor and his subjects throughout the generations, the Emperor finds it intolerable to demand the people to make further sacrifices." Konoe calculated that an edict to that effect, by reaffirming the ties between the imperial family and the people, would boost the deteriorating popular morale to some extent and ward off a "crisis of the national polity in case a revolution breaks out."

Konoe, whose primary concern now was to prevent a communist revolution, advocated an immediate termination of the war, commanded by imperial edict if necessary, as the only feasible way to resolve the crisis, above all, to "preserve the national polity." Once the American forces had an airbase on Saipan, Japanese soil would be within bombing range, and the Japanese Combined Fleet would be powerless to prevent American forces from landing on the shores of Japan any time. Such possibilities were deeply threatening to the national polity. The authorities were reporting a rapid increase of incidents of lèse majesty, and "left-wing elements" were waiting in quiet corners throughout the country until defeat gave them the change to start a revolution. Besides, the so-called rightists, the most fervent advocates of a fight to the bitter end and destruction of the Anglo-American forces were mostly converts from the Left. One could imagine the many ways they would exploit the confusion of defeat. Konoe concluded that to continue a hopeless war when defeat was inevitable was to gamble recklessly with the national polity. The war had to be terminated immediately.[13]

Soon after Konoe submitted his statement to Kido, the Tōjō cabinet collapsed. At the conference of senior statesmen that followed, Konoe brought up the same arguments he had presented in the statement on the danger of a communist revolution. "For more than a decade," he said, "certain groups in the army have harbored 'leftist thoughts' and right now they are scheming to bring about a leftist revolution in collusion with like-minded elements in the military, the bureaucracy, and among the people." There was no lack of indicators, he said, that Japan was marching straight toward a leftist revolution. Defeat would be dreadful, but more dreadful would be a leftist revolution. The hardship of defeat in war would be temporary and the nation could recover, but a leftist revolution would permanently destroy everything, including the national polity. A possible leftist revolution, therefore, required the "closest watch." He warned that left-wing supporters included "not only those who are engaging openly in leftist activities; many soldiers and bureaucrats who pretend to be rightists are actually leftists, and many others who do not see themselves as such are involved in thoroughly communist activities. We must enlist someone who can eradicate these leftist elements."

Konoe was not alone. Hiranuma, Wakatsuki, and Kido were all strongly behind him.[14] Harada Kumao, Hosokawa Morisada, Yoshida Shigeru, and Ueda Shunkichi were among others who were also frightened at the specter of a communist revolution.

The fear that gripped Konoe and others of the "communization" of the army and a possible communist revolution may seem paranoid, but it had deep roots in events over the past decade and a half. Since the Manchurian Incident and particularly the outbreak of the China War, some among the ruling elite suspected that leftist forces were penetrating the army, and that triggered deep fear of a communist revolution. For one thing, they were aware that since before the Manchurian Incident some of the young army officers had been promoting political renovation and national reconstruction movements in collaboration with civilian national socialists. Then, against this background, the Kōdōha and the Tōseiha factions emerged out of the young officers' movement. The two factions clashed explosively, the Kōdōha demanding above all the absolute sanctity of the national polity and the "unique" Japanese spirit, while the Tōseiha pushed toward a highly advanced national defense state. With the February 26th Incident, the Kōdōha collapsed.

The China War broke out, escalated, and was protracted, creating tensions for Japan that finally could not be contained and led to the outbreak of the Pacific War. Throughout this period, the defense state structure was strengthened formidably, while an expanded and rigidly controlled wartime economy steadily eased out the free market economy. Daily necessities became extremely scarce, which had a leveling effect on the standards of living of the different social strata. The fact that the army, directly and indirectly, vigorously promoted the leveling of economic differences intensified the anxiety of some in the ruling elite, who saw this development as a sign that the army was being communized and communist revolution was approaching. In addition, among the planners of the wartime economy were converts from the Left. On top of that, some adherents of the fallen Kōdōha, in an attempt at a Kōdōha revival, had approached Hiranuma, Konoe, and others in or close to government with reports of "communization" in the army that were designed to frighten and alienate the civilian political leadership from the dominant army groups.

In October 1944, American forces landed on Leyte Island and began their advance on the Philippines. In November, B–29s swept in, on the first round of air raids over Tokyo. It was on one of those hectic days, November 10, when Wang Ching-wei, in Japan for medical treatment, died at a hospital in Nagoya, closing his turbulent and fateful career. At the news of Wang's death, Konoe immediately left Kyoto for Nagoya to make his condolences and, at a suburban airfield, said farewell as Wang's remains were flown back to China.

American operations in the Philippines were stepped up with increasing vigor from the beginning of 1945. In early January, American forces attacked the Lingayen Gulf and then landed in Luzon. Manila fell in early February. As the situation grew more and more ominous, the Emperor decided to ask each of the senior statesmen for his opinion. Konoe attended court on February 14 and presented a memorial, the main points of which can be summarized as follows:

"Unfortunate though it is, defeat is inevitable. However, since American and British opinion apparently have not yet considered demanding that we totally revise the national polity, I do not think we need worry too much about the effects on the national polity of defeat itself. Of much greater concern is a communist revolution, which could very well occur in the aftermath of the defeat. If that happened, it would be extremely difficult to preserve the national polity. I believe that conditions inside and outside our country are rapidly moving Japan toward a communist revolution. The Soviet Union is pushing revolution worldwide, and there is good reason to fear that someday Japan will be pressured by Russia to recognize the communist party, place communists in the cabinet, and abolish the peace preservation law and the Anti-Comintern Pact. When one considers our domestic situation also, it becomes more apparent every day that the conditions for a communist revolution are there. The people already suffer from poverty, the voice of the workers is growing more strident, and an increasing hostility toward Britian and the United States is accompanied by rising pro-Soviet sentiments. Further, we are faced with the renovation movement led by a strong segment of the military, moves by the so-called new bureaucrats to take advantage of that, and clandestine maneuvers of leftist elements who are manipulating them quietly from behind the scenes. The most threatening is the renovationist movement within the military. The majority of the younger military personnel seem to believe that communism is compatible with Japan's national polity, and I believe that the renovationist argument within the armed forces is made on the same premise. The majority of our professional soldiers come from below middle-class families, and their circumstances make them receptive to communist doctrine. Communist elements seek to lure the soldiers to their side with the claim that the national polity and communism can stand side by side. It is now clear, I think, that the Manchurian Incident and the China War and their expansion into the Greater East Asia War were deliberately plotted by this group within the military. At the time of the Manchurian Incident, they publicly declared that the purpose of the incident was the domestic reform of Japan. Again, at the time of the China War one of the leaders of the renovationist group publicly declared that the longer the war lasted the better, for a settlement would doom domestic reform. Even if the military renovationist group does not necessarily aim at communist revolution, certain officials in the bureaucracy and civilian sympathizers with influence within the military are consciously intent upon bringing about a communist revolution. Whether they are called right wingers or left wingers is immaterial; these so-called right wingers are communists clothed in the garb of the national polity. I think it is safe to assumed that ignorant and simple-minded soldiers have been manipulated by them. All this I conclude only after having thought a great deal about the events of the past decade, ten years during which I had continuous contact with the military, the bureaucracy, the right wing and the left. Only recently have I understood the true significance of many of the events and incidents that occurred during that time. Twice I formed a cabinet. In order to avoid domestic conflict, I acceded to the demands of the renovationists as much as I could, and in my eagerness to achieve national unity, I was unable to perceive all their true intentions. I deeply regret and feel responsible for my lack of foresight.

"As the war situation daily grows more critical, we hear the call 'One hundred million die together heroically' growing louder. Ostensibly the strongest advocates of this stand are right wingers, but I believe that the hidden instigators are the communists, who wish to throw the nation into disorder and achieve revolution. While some urge the total destruction of the United States and Britain, on the one hand, a pro-Soviet atmosphere seems to be spreading, on the other. Apparently some in the military now are even urging rapprochement with the Soviet Union and the Chinese communist regime in Yenan. With each passing day, the conditions necessary for a communist revolution are growing, both at home and abroad and if the war situation deteriorates much more, it will only accelerate their growth. Therefore, if defeat is inevitable, I am convinced that we should seek to end the war as quickly as possible. This we should do for the sake of preserving the national polity. I think that the greatest obstacle to ending the war is the renovationist element in the military that has driven the country ever since the Manchurian Incident. Once this group is eliminated, opportunistic bureaucrats and civilians on both Right and Left also will be left powerless. Reconstruction of the military by eliminating the renovationists is a prerequisite to saving Japan from a communist revolution. I must urge Your Majesty to make an extraordinarily bold decison toward that end."[15]

The Emperor queried Konoe on several points in his memorial. In his answers, Konoe insisted that the only way to clear the army of its leftist tendencies and thus prevent revolution was to appoint persons who had been Kōdōha supporters. However, the Emperor and his aides strongly distrusted the Kōdōha, as they had since the February 26th Incident, and this attitude came out in the questions the Emperor raised. Konoe was bitterly disappointed. Later he groaned to Tomita that the way things were, "Japan may have to go all the way to ultimate ruin."

By February 19, the American forces had advanced to Iwō Jima, and on March 17 the island fell. Americans landed on the main island of Okinawa on April 1 and launched a fierce attack on the Japanese resistance. All the while, B-29s were pummeling mainland Japan with air raids. The Koiso cabinet could not handle the situation, and it resigned on April 5, upon which the senior statesmen conference recommended Privy Council President Admiral Suzuki Kantarō as the next premier. During the last days of the Koiso cabinet, Konoe and the other three senior statesmen who had been most instrumental in effecting Tōjō's resignation had already settled on Suzuki as the best person to head Japan's last wartime cabinet, and Kido had consented.

About a month later, on May 2, Berlin fell and Germany surrendered unconditionally. Italy had capitulated in September 1943, and so the war in Europe was finally over, ending in Allied victory. In the middle of May, the Supreme War Guidance Council (Prime Minister Suzuki, Foreign Minister Tōgō, Army Minister Anami, Navy Minister Yonai, Army Chief of Staff Umezu, and Navy Chief of Staff Oikawa) drew up a plan of action to prevent Soviet participation in the war against Japan and, if possible, entice the Soviet Union into friendly neutrality. If they were successful, the war could be terminated on terms favorable to Japan using Soviet mediation. Accordingly, Tōgō requested former Foreign Minister Hirota to approach the Soviet ambassador to Japan, Yakov A. Malik, for talks which would take place in Hakone.

Shortly afterward, however, the Supreme War Guidance Council approved a document entitled Fundamental Policy on Conduct of the War Henceforth. By June 8, the document was approved by the Cabinet Council and the Imperial Conference.

Its basic premise was that Japan would engage in a decisive final battle on Japanese soil, which made it crystal clear that not even imminent disaster could knit the government and military together in agreement on a coherent policy. Privy Seal Kido decided that he could wait no longer for a firm government policy, and on the day of the Imperial Conference he drafted another document. This, called simply Measures for Managing the Situation, stated that by the second half of 1945, Japan would have virtually no fighting capacity left. If American planes continued bombing the Japanese islands into middle and late 1945, food and clothing shortages would be severe, and as winter brought new hardships the government might be faced with uncontrollable popular unrest. It was therefore imperative that decisive measures be taken immediately to end war. As a concrete step, Kido suggested opening negotiations with the Soviet Union by using a personal letter from the Emperor seeking Soviet mediation in terminating the war, and he outlined the substance of the proposed imperial letter and the terms of peace.

Kido submitted his draft plan to the Emperor and then consulted the prime minister, and the foreign, army, and navy ministers, finally persuading them to approve it. Then, concerned about the conflict between his draft plan and the decision reached at the June 8 Imperial Conference, Kido made a request for special action on the part of the Emperor. The Emperor responded by summoning the members of the Supreme War Guidance Council on June 22 and ordered them to immediately work out specific measures to end the war and implement them quickly, their policy decision on conduct of the war notwithstanding.

The day before, on June 21, Okinawa had fallen. Now the Pacific War had only one possible outcome, and an American landing in Japan appeared to be simply a matter of time. The Hirota-Malik talks had made no progress in the meantime. The Emperor, increasingly impatient, finally requested Prime Minister Suzuki to seek Soviet mediation outright by dispatching a special envoy to the Soviet Union bearing a personal message from him. The Supreme War Guidance Council gave formal approval, and so after consulting Tōgō, Suzuki recommended

Konoe as the Emperor's special envoy. On July 12, the Emperor summoned Konoe and asked him his views on the termination of the war. Konoe replied that even statements from the military indicated serious doubt about Japan's ability to continue fighting. The morale of the people was low, and there was a growing sense among them that their only hope in ending the war was the Emperor. But there were also frequent rumors of people speaking ill of the Emperor. He believed, therefore, that the war should be terminated as quickly as possible. The Emperor then informed Konoe that he might be asked to go to the Soviet Union as his special envoy. That reminded Konoe of the time during his second cabinet when Japan joined the Tripartite Pact and the Emperor had asked if he would share his joys and suffering in the future. Now Konoe immediately declared that in the present crisis he would undertake any command the Emperor chose to bestow upon him, even if it meant risking his life. After Konoe had withdrawn, the Emperor told Kido, "I think he is rather determined this time."[16]

Konoe personally distrusted the Soviet Union and was very much opposed to seeking Soviet mediation. When he returned to Hakone after the imperial audience, Konoe told Tomita of the Emperor's order. He said that he was opposed in principle to requesting the Soviet Union for good offices, but "I could say nothing when I saw the Emperor. He had come out of an air-raid shelter to the temporary audience room, with his usually neatly combed hair unkempt, looking pale and terribly haggard." Konoe also appreciated Kido's painful efforts so far to end the war. To suppress the military's almost fanatic appeal for a final battle on Japanese soil, when one hundred million might "die together heroically," and somehow bring about peace without losing face altogether, perhaps there was no other choice but neutral Soviet mediation. So thinking, Konoe accepted the role of special envoy.[17]

Konoe wrote in his postwar memoirs that at the time Ambassador Satō Naotake advised from Moscow that in negotiating with the Soviet Union, Japan had to be prepared to accept terms tantamount to unconditional surrender. This quickly hardened the army's attitude, which convinced Konoe that he must take "extraordinary measures" similar to his aborted plan of action immediately before the outbreak of the Pacific War. At that time he had intended to settle the China question in direct talks with President Roosevelt and, knowing that the army would not approve the terms of settlement, to sign the agreement after cabling to the Emperor directly for his sanction. Konoe was prepared to resort to the same method on his mission to the Soviet Union. He would communicate no terms prior to his arrival and would obtain imperial sanction for the terms agreed upon in the talks in Moscow. Konoe added that he had received special permission from the Emperor to follow such a procedure.[18]

Shortly after Konoe had accepted his appointment, Tōgō instructed Ambassador Satō to inform Foreign Commissar Vyacheslav M. Molotov that the Emperor wanted to terminate the war immediately and wished to send Prince Konoe to Moscow as a special envoy bearing a personal imperial letter. Satō was to obtain Soviet approval of the Konoe mission. Molotov refused to see Satō, saying that he was too busy, and so Satō communicated his government's request to Vice Foreign Commissar Alexander Lozovsky. A few days later, on July 17, the Potsdam Conference opened. On July 25, in reply to an inquiry by Lozovsky, the Japanese government stated that the purpose of the Konoe mission was to request the Soviet government to mediate in ending the war and to discuss matters relating to the promotion of friendly relations between Japan and the Soviet Union.

The Potsdam Declaration was made public the very next day. The Suzuki government made another miscalculation by publicly responding to the Declaration with nothing but contempt, which clinched the final decision to drop atom bombs on Hiroshima on August 6, and Nagasaki on August 9.

Still there was no Soviet reply on the Konoe mission, despite Japanese urging. Finally, on August 9, Molotov called in Satō. He handed him an official communication, but it was not the reply on the Konoe mission; it was a Soviet declaration of war against Japan. The idea that Konoe might have convinced the

Soviet Union to mediate suddenly became sour irony. On August 14, the government notified the Allied Powers that Japan would accept the Potsdam Declaration, and on the 15th the Emperor issued the edict of surrender. At last the Pacific War came to a close, leaving Japan in humiliated defeat.

7

KONOE'S LAST DEFEAT

On August 15, 1945, following the imperial proclamation of surrender, the Suzuki cabinet resigned. Stalwart, sober Kido, his first concern being the public morale at the moment of Japan's worst defeat in recorded history, immediately set about installing a new prime minister. Broken lines of communication and crippled transportation made it almost impossible to follow the normal procedures, and so Kido obtained special permission from the Emperor to dispense with a conference of the senior statesmen and to nominate a candidate after consulting only President of the Privy Council Hiranuma Kiichirō. He recommended Imperial Prince Higashikuni Naruhiko. Prince Higashikuni assented but requested that Konoe, whose assistance would be valuable to the politically inexperienced new prime minister, join his cabinet. Kido was in favor of the appointment, and thus Konoe became a minister without portfolio. The new cabinet's first and most serious task was to maintain public order. As soon as he was asked to join the cabinet, Konoe considered taking the post of home minister, mainly in order to keep an eye on any developments that seemed to indicate a possible communist revolution. Since midway through the war, this had become almost an obsession with him. In the end he did not become home minister, but Obata Toshishirō, a Kōdōha man, also joined as minister without portfolio, apparently because of prompting from Konoe. It seems that Konoe expected Obata to help suppress the renovationists within the army if the necessity arose.

The public regarded Konoe as second in command in the Higashikuni cabinet, but his swift political comeback, notwith-

179

standing, the defeat of Japan marked the end of his once great popular appeal. Now he was bitterly criticized, attacked for having instigated the China War and blamed for the developments that led into the Pacific War. People who once welcomed everything he said or did now looked around at their devastated land and resented—or hated—Konoe for it.

The Supreme Commander for the Allied Powers (SCAP), General Douglas MacArthur landed at Atsugi airbase on August 30, and on September 2 the ceremony of surrender was held on the U.S. battleship *Missouri* in Tokyo Bay, when Japanese representatives signed the surrender documents. Thus began the Allied occupation of Japan.

Konoe went to General Headquarters (GHQ) in the Daiichi Seimei Building, Hibiya, on the afternoon of October 4, for what was to be his second meeting with the supreme commander. He was surprised, therefore, when an aide greeted Konoe and told him that because of conflicting appointments the general could not see him, but Chief of Staff Richard Sutherland would. The aide left the reception room, and Konoe, deeply disappointed, turned to Foreign Ministry Counselor Okumura Katsuzō, who had accompanied him as interpreter, saying, "This is not what I was led to expect." Simply left in the room to wait indefinitely, Konoe fidgeted with rankling frustration while Okumura looked on, helpless to assuage the prince's wounded pride. Finally, after more than twenty minutes, the aide reappeared and led him to another room, where he was met by Gen. MacArthur, flanked by Chief of Staff Sutherland and Political Adviser George Atcheson, Jr.

In the interview, Konoe explained that during his first meeting with the general he had been unable to express his thoughts as fully as he wished, but now he was prepared to do so. He went on to say that the Japanese military clique and ultranationalists had indeed destroyed world peace and led Japan into the catastrophic situation before them, but he feared that the Americans misunderstood the role and the merits and demerits of the zaibatsu, as well as the feudal structure of the imperial institution. The power of the imperial throne and its ramifications in society did not converge with the forces of the militarists to bring on the disaster; they had always acted as a brake upon the military clique. The fact that so many outstanding figures representing the imperial order and civilian government had been targets of assassination by radical military groups surely disproved any collusion. Beginning with the Manchurian Incident, the military clique and ultranationalists had pushed harder and shouted more violently for radical national renovation, but in the background was the "leftist element." It was the leftist element, exploiting the military clique, that drove Japan to war. Disaster was brought to Japan by the combined forces of the military clique and the Left, but, while the military clique was devastated by the defeat, the leftists, elated, were given a prize opportunity to make deep inroads into a country of defeated, weary people. If the established institutions of the court and zaibatsu were liquidated along with the military clique and ultranationalists, the country would be an easy target for communism. To prevent communism from dominating Japan and to build a democratic nation, the militarists must be eliminated, but the court and zaibatsu were vitally necessary to provide a solid frame within which democracy could gradually sink deep roots in Japan. Konoe averred that, even if he himself was considered inseparably part of the so-called feudal forces, still he was no mere apologist for them or the zaibatsu. His only purpose was to stress that if the stabilizing elements of the society were destroyed, too, Japan would quickly become a communist country.

MacArthur interrupted several times with questions, and at the end he commented that the talk was useful to him, declaring that it was urgent to encourage free public discussion in Japan. Konoe then asked for the general's opinions on or instructions regarding the organization of the government and the structure of the Diet. MacArthur abruptly assumed his "characteristic soldierly tone" and announced to Konoe that the Imperial Constitution had to be revised and made liberal, and, second, that suffrage had to be expanded to destroy the monopoly of reactionaries in the Diet. Konoe responded that while he had failed to achieve his own aims, he was prepared to serve his nation to the best of his ability with the general's encouragement and advice. MacArthur said Konoe's determination was a good sign, adding that although the prince was indeed a part of Japan's so-called feudal establishment he was a "cosmopolitan" and still young. MacArthur urged him to stand resolutely among the national leadership. If the prince could mobilize the liberal forces in the nation and then publicize his ideas on constitutional reform, the Diet would follow his lead.

At the conclusion of the meeting, Konoe asked if he might regularly consult the general on constitutional and other matters. Or, since the general would be extremely busy, he asked if a representative might be appointed to meet him on a regular basis. MacArthur replied that they would always be happy to see him. By the time Konoe left General Headquarters after the one and one-half hour meeting, the autumn evening had already closed in. As his home-bound car sped along the imperial moat, Konoe uttered half to himself, "Those were momentous words we heard today."[1] He was pleased and encouraged by what MacArthur had said.

By that time, in any case, Konoe was feeling somewhat more personally secure than he had just after the surrender, and MacArthur's remarks bolstered his reemerging optimism. Immediately after the war, Konoe apparently never thought he would be considered a war criminal, but as public criticism mounted and debate on his responsibility in the war heated up, he began to worry that he, too, might be designated as a suspected war criminal. This thought had been hanging heavily over him until September 11, when SCAP designated 39 wartime leaders, including former Prime Minister Tōjō, as suspected war criminals and ordered their arrest. This was the first of the directives concerning war crimes, and it left Konoe clear, at least for the time being.

On the day Konoe met MacArthur, SCAP ordered the Higashikuni cabinet to dismiss Home Minister Yamazaki Iwao, the chief of the Metropolitan Police Board, and all the prefectural police chiefs. Higashikuni resigned on October 5, on the grounds that the SCAP order had crippled his government. For the same reasons as before, Kido again consulted only Hiranuma before recommending Shidehara Kijūrō as the next prime minister. Before the Shidehara cabinet became final, however,

Tomita, in collaboration with Obata Toshishirō, state minister under Higashikuni, had been pressing Konoe to form a cabinet. For some time Tomita had been urging Konoe to remember his duty as a senior statesman and exert himself for the national reconstruction. Konoe should found a new political party, he said. Tomita also believed that as prime minister Konoe would less likely be designated as a suspected war criminal. When Tomita finally suggested this to him directly, Konoe expressed his willingness to resume office again, with "unexpected enthusiasm." But Shidehara had informally agreed to form a cabinet by then, and there was nothing Tomita could do.[2] It is interesting to note, nonetheless, that Konoe's "unexpected enthusiasm," although it came too late, seemed to be a result of his October 4 talk with MacArthur. Until then, Konoe had put Tomita off, pleading the need for more time to think. He seemed to have been very doubtful that he could start a new political party and form another cabinet when public opinion was so clearly critical of his role in the war.[3]

But Konoe was buoyed up now, and he began to work actively on constitutional revision. On October 8, accompanied by Takagi Yasaka, Matsumoto Shigeharu, and Ushiba Tomohiko, Konoe called on SCAP Political Adviser George Atcheson to discuss the Constitution. Atcheson pointed out a number of points in the current Constitution he thought should be revised. SCAP seemed perfectly willing to cooperate. Shortly afterward, Konoe visited Kido and described his October 4 meeting with General MacArthur and the details of his meeting with Atcheson. They must work with speed, he told Kido, for if they waited too long before starting the constitutional revision on their own, SCAP would impose it on them, and that would disgrace the Imperial Constitution.

The possible necessity of constitutional revision had been worrying the Emperor also, and he asked Kido about it on several occasions. Kido had to give him some answer, and so after talking with Konoe, he decided to create a constitutional revision study committee within the Privy Seal secretariat, under Konoe's leadership. Thus on October 11, Konoe was appointed as unattached official in the secretariat. On the same day he had an audience with the Emperor, who ordered him to investigate whether accepting the Potsdam Declaration meant that the Constitution must be revised, and if so how extensive the revisions would be.

A few days later, Kiya Ikusaburō called on Konoe to ask for a decision on the long-pending issue of organizing a new party. Konoe first said, "Shall we kick off, at long last?" but then mumbled that he would not be able to say anything definite until the war criminal question was settled. Kiya kept prodding him, until Konoe muttered, "Well, pulled by you or by someone else, in any event, the time has come for me to set out," and grinned. Kiya later recollected that Konoe sounded then as if he had finally made up his mind.[4] He seemed more positive about everything after his meeting with MacArthur, but the war criminal question still threatened and he continued to vacillate. In the meantime others moved in ahead. On November 9, Hatoyama Ichirō, whose cooperation Konoe had counted on in a new Konoe party, inaugurated the Nihon Jiyūtō, and the Nihon Shakaitō and the Nihon Shimpotō came into being at about the same time.

Konoe's committee to study the constitutional revision was no sooner underway than the new cabinet decided that this was a vital affair of state. The cabinet ruled that the government must take full responsibility for the investigation and drafting of a revised constitution. On October 13, the cabinet announced that a Constitutional Problem Investigation Committee was to be set up, which would begin its work in late October. Kido saw Konoe soon after that. It was pointless and damaging to have both the Privy Seal secretariat and the cabinet engage separately in the constitutional revision question, he said, and so the Konoe study group should limit their work to the preparation of a report to the Emperor on the necessity of revising the Constitution.

From the outset, the Konoe group had gone ahead with planning for the revisions in consultation with SCAP, incorporating their ideas. Konoe was relieved to find that the Allied Power had no objection to a constitutional monarchy in itself, as long as it encouraged a democratic political system. Until then, Konoe had been deeply apprehensive about the Allied Powers' attitude toward the emperor system, partly because of the centuries-old relationship of his own family with the imperial family. He also undoubtedly believed, as he stated during his meeting with MacArthur, that the emperor system would be a powerful bulwark against communism.

On November 1, without warning, GHQ issued a statement declaring that there seemed to be a serious misunderstanding on Konoe's role in the revision of the Constitution of Japan. The Allied authorities had not chosen Prince Konoe for that task. Because he was acting premier before the resignation of Higashikuni, SCAP had simply conveyed a message through Prince Konoe that the Japanese government would be ordered to revise the Constitution. But the following day Higashikuni had resigned, terminating the relationship between the Allied authorities and Prince Konoe concerning the constitutional revision, and MacArthur had then sent a directive on the matter to Prime Minister Shidehara. The Japanese government was conducting preliminary studies directed at eventual constitutional revision, and so Konoe's work on the revisions was being carried out only from personal loyalty to the imperial family, not because of any request from GHQ.

Thus Konoe was completely unprepared when, a few days after the statement was issued, GHQ instructed his group to terminate all contact with the Allied authorities. This move seemed incomprehensible, particularly insofar as GHQ had cooperated with them even after Higashikuni was replaced. What apparently happened, which Konoe did not immediately appreciate, was that GHQ was receiving enough pressure from the growing attacks on Konoe for his responsibility in the war that they felt compelled to withdraw all support, and even disassociate themselves, from him. Konoe entered the Higashikuni cabinet in the capacity of deputy prime minister. Then as an unattached official of the Privy Seal secretariat he began work on the constitutional revision. It was also rumored that he was planning to start a new party. This was too much for a public already wary of any wartime official, particularly Konoe, and the critics, in increasing numbers, only thrust deeper. Hosokawa Morisada wrote on November 3, two days after the GHQ statement, "The newspapers will not let up in their attacks on Prince Konoe; they seem almost to be in daily collusion to make sure they keep the bombardment going."

Konoe was not very popular in the foreign press, either. The *New York Times* bitterly denounced him, stating that no one would be surprised if MacArthur threw Konoe into prison as a war criminal. If Konoe were allowed to draft a new constitution, they might as well make Quisling the king of Norway, Laval the president of France, and Göring the chief of the Allied Powers. Excerpts from this *New York Times* article also appeared in the October 29, 1945 issues of the *Asahi Shimbun* and the *Mainichi Shimbun.*

Being repudiated by GHQ must surely have intensified Konoe's anxiety about his status as a possible war criminal suspect. But he was dealt a more immediate blow on November 9 when he was summoned by the United States Strategic Bombing Survey Mission. The mission stayed in Japan from October to December, 1945, to investigate the damage that the United States Air Force bombing had caused in Japan proper, and during that time they called in numerous political leaders as well as former military men as witnesses. When Konoe was asked to appear before the mission, he was highly reluctant to comply, for he considered anything that amounted to an interrogation humiliating beyond tolerance. But he could not put it off indefinitely, and so he finally consented to meet the mission at Kazan Kaikan in Kasumigaseki, Tokyo.

On the day of his appointment, a car from the mission came to his home and took him and Ushiba Tomohiko, who would act as interpreter, to Shibaura pier, and then Konoe and Ushiba were carried by launch to an American gunboat anchored in Tokyo Bay. This in itself was exceptional; other witnesses were interviewed by the mission in the Meiji Seimei Building. Worse, during the questioning on board the ship, the mission members addressed him as Mr. Konoe. This gave him a very uncomfortable jolt, for the members of GHQ had always addressed him as Prince Konoe. But the most serious threat lay in the mission members' attitude; clearly they regarded him as one of the leaders responsible for the China War and a major participant in the planning for war against the United States. Starting from that premise, they put Konoe through a grueling three hours of rapid-fire questioning.

During the interrogation Konoe became so restless and unhappy that Ushiba had to abandon any impartiality and try to cheer him up. In addition to his severely wounded aristocratic pride, Konoe was also dismayed to learn how he was regarded by the Americans. Now it seemed that the ominous possibility of being designated a war criminal might actually materialize. He said to Tomita, "The inquiry was horrible; like a prosecuting attorney taking a deposition from a criminal. America must have made up its mind already. I will certainly be arrested as a war criminal." Tomita observed that it would be unthinkable to charge someone who had been attacked as a defeatist and escapist peace-seeker during the war with war crimes, but Konoe replied unhappily, "I thought so, too, until now, but I was unrealistic. Maybe America once thought as I did, but we must now conclude that its attitude and policy have changed."[5]

Several days later, on November 13, Hosokawa met Konoe at his Hakone villa. Hosokawa recorded that Konoe was "worrying about the growing trend toward communism, and the prince said that perhaps because there are so many Jews in MacArthur's headquarters, they are not just antipathetic toward the imperial family, but seek some pretext to destroy it. They seem also to be plotting the communization of Japan. It is said that Katō Kanjū, for instance, is a constant visitor at GHQ."[6] Konoe had warned MacArthur about the danger of communism in Japan, but by then GHQ itself appeared to him to be in collusion with the leftist forces. In this Konoe found further justification for his fear of a communist revolution.

Still, the Konoe group continued their study until November 22, when Konoe went to the imperial palace to submit an outline for the constitutional revision. Their outline had incorporated many American ideas that the group had absorbed through contact with GHQ, and its substance turned out to be actually more democratic than the draft revision prepared by the cabinet Constitutional Problem Investigation Committee.

In a memorial to the Emperor dated November 22, Konoe requested to be allowed to relinquish his peerage. The memorial stated that soon after he had received the imperial order and formed a cabinet in 1937, the Lukouch'iao Incident erupted. "My most strenuous efforts to prevent the incident from expanding were in vain. The fighting eventually spread all over China and created an unbreachable break between the two nations." In 1940, when he became head of government again, his primary objectives were to effect a resolution of the China War and maintain peace across the Pacific by improving relations between Japan and the United States. Toward this end, "your humble subject dedicated all his public life and mobilized every possible means to ensure success in the Japanese-American negotiations in 1941. But the domestic political situation prevented its realization, forcing him to resign. . . . With meager talent and little power, your humble subject failed to achieve what he believed in and failed to rescue your imperial state from the crisis; he merely increased the anxiety of Your Imperial Majesty regarding the future of the state. Thereafter, each succeeding cabinet endeavored to do its best, while the power of state gradually declined and in the end sank to a level of humiliation that could never be wiped out. Your humble subject's family, through the generations, has basked in imperial favor. Your humble subject is profoundly ashamed before the gods. Respectfully returning my titles and honors to the throne, I wish to express my deepest gratitude for the incalculable imperial favor that I have enjoyed."

Five days later, on November 27, Konoe went by car to his Karuizawa villa. For many years he had delighted in the scenery of Karuizawa, and once he wrote, as a poem, "Climbing to the summit/Usui mountain path/How refreshing is the evening breeze/Here in Shinano plain." But in late November, winter had already come to Karuizawa. The leaves had fallen, the wind was cold. As far as the eye could see the area was bleak and desolate. He probably could not escape the dark worry of the war crimes question. In Karuizawa Konoe invited *Asahi Shimbun* reporter Kosaka Tokusaburō and dictated a memoir on the basis of random notes he had kept from time to time. Konoe told Kosaka that the memoir was an "honest political confession" and his "political will."[7] After Konoe's death, this memoir was published as *Ushinawareshi seiji* [Politics that failed], together with another memoir Konoe had written during the Pacific War.

On November 19, just before Konoe presented the memorial relinquishing his title, GHQ designated 11 people as suspected war criminals, including former Prime Minister Koiso Kuniaki and Araki Sadao, and ordered their arrests. On December 2, arrests were issued for 59 more, including Imperial Prince Nashimoto Morimasa, Hiranuma Kiichirō, Hirota Kōki, Ikeda Shigeaki, Arima Yoriyasu, and Gotō Fumio. Konoe heard this in Karuizawa; he was shocked at the news that even Imperial Prince Nashimoto had been charged. Particularly upsetting was the possibility that the Nashimoto case might have been a trial balloon signalling the eventual arrest of the Emperor. When the newspapers printed a photo of Prince Nashimoto with a blanket in his hand being taken to Sugamo prison, Konoe burst out at Tomita, "They have freedom of speech and freedom of press, and look how indiscreetly these newspapers use it! Does not the government do anything when an imperial prince is imprisoned? The way things are, the government would do nothing even if the Emperor were arrested! I must ask Prince Nashimoto why he did not kill himself, for the sake of the Emperor and Japan."[8]

On December 6, GHQ issued arrest orders for nine more men, including Konoe and Kido. When he heard it in Karuizawa, Konoe did not appear particularly surprised, because he had been tormented by the possibility for months. Takamura Sakahiko, once Konoe's secretary, heard of the arrest in Nagoya, and he immediately left for Karuizawa. Takamura went to Konoe's villa that night and some years later he recounted the two-hour conversation that took place then. He urged Konoe, he wrote, to place Japan's case squarely and with conviction before the military tribunal and make it clear that responsibility for the war must be shared by other countries as well. Since both Konoe and Kido had been included among the suspected war criminals, Takamura added, it seemed more and more possible that even the Emperor would be charged. Konoe was the best qualified to vindicate the Emperor; he must do everything he could to make sure the Emperor was not charged.

Konoe replied that America was not interested in determining a defendant's guilt on the basis of his statements before the military tribunal. Since the trial was politically motivated, there was really no way he could accomplish what Takamura was urging on him. He was prepared to do anything to assist the Emperor, but he would be powerless at the military tribunal. If he tried to explain his own responsibility as prime minister, that role would be interpreted as falling within civilian state affairs, while the responsibility of the supreme command would still lie with the Emperor as commander in chief of the army and navy. If America had already decided to punish the Emperor, Konoe concluded in anguish, he felt helpess to defend him. Several times during the conversation Konoe said that he did not think he could bear the humiliation of standing in court as a suspected war criminal. But, Takamura wrote, the prince showed no sign of contemplating suicide.[9]

One wintery night a newspaper reporter whom Konoe had known for a long time visited him at the villa. Konoe invited him to the fireside and said, "Before the war I was ridiculed for being indecisive, during the war rebuked as an escapist peace-seeker, and after the war accused of being a war criminal. I am a child of fate." He sighed deeply, and went on, "A man's life cannot be judged before his death. It will be decades, even centuries, after my death before the historian finally judges my career objectively. . . . I am a child of fate. All kinds of people have come and gone within my circle of associates. I have been surrounded by rightists and leftists, and those in between . . . no, I have allowed them to surround me, and that is what has brought this fate upon me. It is my own fault, but it is also tragic reality."[10]

Konoe was to appear at Sugamo prison on December 16. He spent six days following the arrest order in meditation, and on the night of the 11th he left Karuizawa by car. Traveling down through the plains in the cold moonlight of early winter, he arrived at the Nagao Kin'ya residence in Setagaya. The following day, Konoe invited Tomita to the Nagao residence and asked him if international law allowed the victors to try representatives of the vanquished after a war, or if the trials were a "consequence" of the unconditional surrender. Konoe said he believed that the victor had no such right. He requested Tomita to have Itō Nobubumi look into the question immediately. If the right to try war criminals was not recognized by international law, Konoe said, he would not appear at Sugamo prison. Itō told Tomita that in theory Konoe's argument might be valid, but the reality of a defeated Japan did not allow Konoe to ignore the summons. Itō nevertheless promised to study the matter, adding that the idea was worthy of a prince who bore the proud traditions of *sesshō* and *kampaku*. Shortly afterword, he repeated his initial opinion to Konoe.[11]

Some of Konoe's relatives wondered if he could delay his appearance on account of ill health. Tomita contacted GHQ through a foreign ministry official, Nakamura Toyoichi, who was in charge of consigning war criminal suspects, and learned that no delay was permitted on any account. Tomita told Konoe exactly what GHQ had said to Nakamura, and added, "It seems that GHQ attaches a great deal of political significance to your summons. Any further action which looks like delaying tactics may cause all sorts of public misunderstanding. I hope you will tell your relatives that it is your wish that they discontinue negotiations for delay." Tomita's report bitterly disappointed Konoe. Tomita wrote that "the prince nodded silently. At that moment, although it might have been my imagination, the prince's countenance suddenly lost all sign of hope. Throughout my long association with him, I never saw him in such despair as he seemed then."[12]

On the day Konoe's arrest order was issued, Hidemaro, his younger brother, returned to Uraga on a repatriation ship. He had been in Berlin pursuing a musical career as a conductor and had fled the city before its fall, but he was captured by the American army and was not sent back to Japan until early November. At one time many years ago he had dreamed of restructuring the Tokyo College of Music, but his brother had been adamantly opposed. They had quarreled and had been estranged for all these years. When Hidemaro returned home, he quickly learned of the order for his brother's arrest. Wishing to see him again, Hidemaro went to the Nagao residence. It was December 12 or 13, he later wrote. After nine long years, his brother looked truly dejected. Konoe asked Hidemaro if the Germans also used the term "war criminal." "In English it is 'war criminal,'" Hidemaro replied, "but in German, '*Kriegs verbrecher*,' and sounds definitely more infamous." The elder Konoe was silent and seemed deeply discouraged. That evening they had dinner together with Kojima Kikuo and Yamamoto Yūzō. Then their guests requested the elder Konoe to demonstrate his calligraphy, which he did, on sheet after sheet of formal writing paper. As Hidemaro observed, calligraphy was a means for his brother, who could not drink down his worries, to forget himself. Later that night when the brothers could talk alone for a short time, the elder Konoe did not say much, but at one point he declared seriously, "When I think of it now, you chose the right career," and he said several times, "I envy you now. You did the right thing. The right thing." When Hidemaro told him that he had received cultural merit medals from Finland and Bulgaria, but managed to avoid one from Nazi Germany, the elder brother expressed sympathy. "We can see now that you were right, but it must have been very trying then." Their quarrel faded into the past as they talked on as two close brothers would.[13]

On December 14, Konoe invited Gotō Ryūnosuke to the Nagao residence. He was very grave and began by saying that because America was after important figures with "name value," he would surely receive a heavy penalty, although he might escape execution. Gotō was surprised, for when he visited Konoe in Karuizawa earlier, the prince sounded as if he expected a light penalty of three to five years' imprisonment. Now he was saying, in deep discouragement, that he had made repeated blunders since the China War, but he could not forget his unfulfilled goals. He had wanted to see Gotō that day to ask a favor—to tell the world someday what his true intentions were. Gotō said of course he would. Then, assuming that Konoe was prepared to appear at Sugamo, Gotō gave him detailed advice on taking care of himself in prison. But Gotō suddenly realized that Konoe was now hardly listening and was completely indifferent to the prospect of life in prison. After he left, Gotō had his wife and son call upon Konoe immediately to bid their last fare-wells. Gotō wrote about this time that when his wife and son went to see him, Konoe came out to the entrance parlor to greet them, saying that he had other visitors inside. "Perhaps because he was drinking sake, the prince was flushed and seemed excited." Mrs. Gotō told him sadly how much they regretted that he had to face such a situation. Konoe seemed barely able to suppress his profound emotion. He answered, "Such is history." Then he repeated, "Such is history." Gotō's wife and son had never seen him as dignified as he was then. They were moved to tears when they exchanged their last greetings.[14]

On the evening of the 14th, Konoe moved to his Tekigaisō villa. The following evening, Nakamura Toyoichi came to dis-cuss Konoe's appearance at Sugamo, which was to be the next day. Konoe said he had given up requesting a postponement on account of ill health, and so there was no problem on that point. By night-fall the visitors had thinned out. Only Konoe's family and close associates remained. A little after nine o'clock, Konoe met Gotō Ryūnosuke and Yamamoto Yūzō in his livingroom. He told them, Gotō wrote, that doctors had offered to write a medical certificate requiring him to enter Tokyo Imperial University Hospital for a rest, but he had declined the offer. When Yamamoto asked Konoe what he would do then, the prince replied in a low but definite tone, "I am going to reject the trial." "Are you not thinking of the worst?" Yamamoto prod-ded, but Konoe shook his head slightly, enough to indicate clearly that he was not.

At that point Gotō declared that Konoe, as a statesman, was duty bound to state his case openly and with conviction in court, like Marshall Henri Pétain and serve as a shield for the Emperor. Konoe replied with his earlier argument that no matter what he said in court, it would not help the Emperor's defense, to which Gotō responded with a final caution. Referring to Tōjō's awkwardly unsuccessful attempt to shoot himself and his subse-quent hospitalization in custody, he warned Konoe to avoid making the same kind of "unsightly mess." Konoe remained silent. The three presently went into the reception room to join the others. Quietly drinking whiskey, Konoe listened to the random discussion around him. He gave no appearance of a man who knew he was about to face death.[15]

As the night wore on, the visitors left one by one until the villa was completely quiet. At about 11 o'clock Konoe went back to the livingroom. When Michitaka, his second son, suggested that he sleep in the same room with his father, Konoe said no, he did not sleep well when another person was in the same room, and he preferred to be alone. But he asked his son to stay a while to talk. They talked together until midnight. Konoe spoke of his fear that communism would spread in Japan, now that it seemed impossible to maintain *kokutai*, the unique national polity that he had devoted himself to defending. Indeed, the defense of *kokutai* was the irrevocable duty of anyone born into the Konoe family. Michitaka requested his father to write something, and Konoe asked for a brush and paper. With no brush at hand, Michitaka handed his father a pencil and a piece of paper cut from a larger sheet. "Can't you find something better than this?" Konoe asked, and his son produced some of the Konoe family stationery. Konoe wrote the following in pencil, lying on his bedding with the paper laid on the lid of an inkstone case. And then he told his son, "Keep this to yourself; I'm writing too quickly to be able to polish it sufficiently."

I have made many political blunders beginning with the China War, and I feel my responsibility for them deeply. I find it intolerable, however, to stand in an American court as a so-called war criminal. The very fact that I did feel responsible for the China War made the task of effecting a settlement all the more crucial to me. Concluding that the only remaining chance to achieve a settlement of the war in China was to reach an understanding with the United States, I did everything in my power to make the negotiations with the United States a success. It is regrettable that I am now suspected by the same United States of being a war criminal.

I believe those who know me well know what my aspirations were. I believe that even in America I have friends who understand me. The fervor and hatred that accompany war, the excessive arrogance of the victors and the extreme servility of the losers, the rumors born of intentionally false accusations and misunderstanding—all these together are now called "public opinion." But I believe that some day public opinion will once more become calm and return to normal. Then I hope that in the court of the gods, a just judgment will be passed on me.

A little after 2 A.M. Michitaka left the room, telling his father to call on him if he wanted anything, for he would be in the next room. About four hours later, at dawn on December 16, Konoe was found dead in his bed. He had taken potassium cyanide. He was 54 years old.

After Konoe's death, GHQ interfered with the publication of this last testimony and ordered that the entire second paragraph, starting with "I believe those who truly know me . . ." be deleted. Chief Prosecutor of the Far Eastern Military Tribunal Joseph B. Keenan issued the following statement: "No one in custody or to be in custody as a war crime suspect need fear anything, except those whose consciences convince them of being guilty."

The *Asahi Shimbun* discussed Konoe's death, commenting that his activities since the surrender had aroused doubts about him. Why did he visit General Headquarters so soon? He took part in the important business of the constitutional revision; to many, this seemed dubious behavior for a man in his position, particularly when he seemed to assume the task as a matter of course and acted "as if he were the Emperor's regent" when talking to an American reporter about the imperial family, the Constitution, and other major national issues. Prince Konoe did not demonstrate the sense of responsibility for the war that he should have. The senior statesmen bore heavy responsibility for allowing Tōjō and the military clique to grow uncontrollably powerful, and Konoe was the leading senior statesman. What is more, the China War, which ultimately made the Pacific War inevitable, had broken out under a government led by Konoe. It was well known that Konoe, by nature, was averse to war, but his weak character was ineffectual in doing anything to prevent it. In a political leader, weakness of character in effect constituted a "crime against the nation." In that sense, Prince Konoe was guilty of a political crime and must be considered a war criminal. Since the surrender, not one of Japan's highest ranking leaders had faced his responsibility like a man. It was considered tragic that when the Ching dynasty fell in China, not a single true loyalist stood up to face the end, and now Japan seemed to be repeating that tragedy. A few, cornered by GHQ arrest orders, had committed suicide, while others have been arrested at the end of a desperate, vain attempt to prolong their lives. They make us feel all the more intensely the virtueless state of a ruined nation.[16]

The *Mainichi Shimbun* observed, "In the final analysis, Prince Konoe's death is tragic. At least it presents a contrast to the comical case of General Tōjō. We recall that during the China War the prince adjured us in a flowing and flowery speech that the war was the tragedy of East Asia and that our generation must endure the hardship for the sake of future generations. With his weak and introspective character, the prince was perfect for the main role in a tragedy. As a politician in an extremely turbulent era, he displayed all of his defects. His responsibility for the outbreak of the China War, the rise of the Imperial Rule Assistance Movement, and the conclusion of the Tripartite Pact cannot be minimized. But the people have a share in that responsibility because they allowed Prince Konoe the presumption of a great statesman. We can only say that he tried to take on a role for which he was not made."[17]

The funeral of Konoe Fumimaro took place on December 21 at the Yōseikan, Arisugawa Park, in Azabu. It was a chilly day. "A number of people who should have been there excused themselves," Hosokawa Morisada wrote. "Under different circumstances, tens of thousands would have attended the ceremony, but only several hundred gathered that day. The unhappiness and anxiety surrounding his death, as well as difficulties in transportation—many of those who had evacuated the capital during and after the air raids had not returned—probably kept large numbers away. It was singular that an officer of the United States Bombing Survey Mission offered a branch from a sacred tree to the altar." After the funeral, Konoe was buried in the family cemetery in Daitokuji temple, Murasakino, Kyoto.

On December 25, the tenth-day anniversary of Konoe's death was held according to Shintō rites. That night, with more than thirty funeral committee members present, Tomita Kenji recalled some remarks Konoe had made after he had been named as a suspected war criminal that supposedly reflected his thoughts during his last days. According to Tomita, Konoe believed that the China War was without question the result of blundering, an unplanned, de facto war. The Pacific War was different. But Konoe himself remained consistently opposed to opening hostilities and did everything he could to facilitate successful negotiations with the United States. Crime, he believed, must be accompanied by the will to commit it. Tomita said that while Konoe fully acknowledged his responsibility for failing to achieve his aims, he had no intent to commit any act leading to or prolonging the war that could be called criminal. He had, in fact, devoted himself to ending the war as soon as possible. Thus, declared Tomita, Konoe saw no reason for being designated a war criminal, and on that ground he was convinced that he must refuse arrest.

Konoe said at one point that he could not tolerate the humiliation of being labeled a war criminal. He also disagreed with those who urged him to stand before the military tribunal for the sake of the Emperor's defense, firmly stating that he was actually powerless to help. Some pressed him to reveal the truth before the military tribunal and then await fair judgment from the public, but Konoe replied that "the air is ringing with false charges and misunderstanding now. Whatever you say, people accuse you of evasion or lying. I refuse to engage in mud-slinging with people who will say anything to boost themselves. I will not stoop to mud-slinging. It makes no difference to me if people do not understand me. I am convinced that some time in the future I will be judged with justice and exonerated. I am prepared to wait for the next hundred years for the historian's verdict."[18]

From what Konoe said to Tomita, it seems fairly clear that

Konoe chose death over the debasing submission to arrest and trial as a war criminal in the court of the victorious nations. In the same act of self-immolation, he almost certainly sought to retain to the very end the intense pride of nobility that had always been central to the way he saw and conducted himself.

His longtime friend Arima Yoriyasu wrote, "If Konoe had the strength of will to choose death, why did he not display that courage earlier? The prince believed that Japan had to avoid war with the United States at any cost. If, indeed, there were ways to avoid the war, why did he not move with more positive determination to prevent it, even if it cost him his life? His failure to act is Japan's loss, and the prince's also." Other friends asked the same questions. But what they may not have appreciated was the possibility that while Konoe could take his own life, if the alternative was unbearable personal humiliation, to sacrifice himself in a national crisis was perhaps a totally different matter.

But how did it happen that Konoe, who was at one time the most widely respected, even loved, statesman in Japan, ended up being charged by the Allied Powers with war crimes and consequently driven to suicide? Before his death, he had become the target of harsh accusations and intense hatred. His radical fall from grace as a politician was not simply the bitter fruit of turbulent times, nor could it be dismissed as the consequence of a frivolous and fickle public. Konoe spent New Year's Day, 1945, in Atami together with Shigemitsu Mamoru and Kase Toshikazu. At that time Konoe asked to borrow Kase's copy of Oscar Wilde's prison memoirs, *De Profundis*. After Konoe's death, it was discovered that he had underlined the following passage: "People used to say of me that I was too individualistic. . . . Indeed, my ruin came not from too great individualism of life, but from too little."[19] These few words seem to provide a piercing revelation of the political life of Konoe Fumimaro and a poignant rationale for the fate he encountered.

NOTES

Chapter One

[1]The Gosekke, the five Fujiwara houses, are elite families among court aristocrats. They include the Kujō, Konoe, Nijō, Ichijō, and Takatsukasa families.

[2]Seiyūkai was a political party founded in 1900 by Itō Hirobumi. A major party until 1940, when Konoe's New Order movement brought an end to political parties. The majority of its supporters went on to support the Imperial Rule Assistance Association.

[3]Konoe Fumimaro, "Chichi no koto," in *Seidanroku*, Konoe Fumimaro, Itō Takeshi, ed. (Tokyo: Chikura Shobō, 1936), pp. 28, 38.

[4]Konoe Fumimaro, "Shimpen sadan," in *Seidanroku*, p. 2.

[5]Konoe Hidemaro, "Ani Fumimaro no shi no kage ni—Konoe-ke no kyōdai," *Bungei Shunjū* (March 1952): 78.

[6]Arima Yoriyasu, *Seikai dōchūki* (Tokyo: Nihon Shuppan Kyōdō, 1951), p. 93. Tomita Kenji, *Haisen Nihon no uchigawa—Konoe kō no omoide* (Tokyo: Kokon Shoin, 1962), p. 311.

[7]Konoe, "Shimpen sadan," pp. 2-3.

[8]Ibid., pp. 3-4.

[9]"Kazami Kenjirō danwa," in *Konoe Fumimaro kankei monjo*. Papers which were in the possession of Konoe Fumimaro and sources concerning him (hereafter cited as *Konoe Fumimaro kankei monjo*) are kept in the Konoe family library, Yōmei Bunko, in Kyoto.

[10]Tomita, *Haisen Nihon no uchigawa*, p. 212.

[11]Konoe, "Shimpen sadan," p. 5.

[12]Ebina Kiku, "Konoe Fumimaro kō no kage ni ikite," *Fujin Kōron* (April 1967): 280-81.

[13]Konoe, "Shimpen sadan," pp. 6-7.

[14]Kensei Yōgo Undō, the Movement for Constitutional Government, began in 1912 in support of constitutionalism, as opposed to politics based on clanship (*hanbatsu*) and affiliated bureaucrats.

[15]The Kuseiga, the nine Seiga families, consist of nine aristocratic houses that rank lower than the Gosekke.

[16]Konoe Fumimaro, "Saionji kō no koto," in *Seidanroku*, pp. 8-10.

[17]This article, with minor deletion, is in *Seidanroku*.

[18]Konoe Fumimaro, "Kōwa kaigi shokan," in *Seidanroku*, pp. 97-101.

[19]Konoe Fumimaro, "Rain no tabi," in *Seidanroku*, pp. 147, 148-49.

Chapter Two

[1]Genrō, a term usually translated as elder statesman, is an informal appellation signifying the non-institutional seniority in political decision-making retained by persons who held high positions during the Meiji era. Saionji Kimmochi and Yamagata Aritomo were the last two *genrōs*.

[2]"Izawa Takio shi hōmon shuki," in *Konoe Fumimaro kankei monjo*.

[3]A phrase that Izawa used in talking with the Konoe biographer Yabe Sadaji. Yabe, *Konoe Fumimaro*, vol. 1 (Tokyo: Kōbundō, 1952), p. 106.

[4]Kenseikai, along with Seiyūkai, was one of the two leading parties during the Taishō era. It was established in 1916 from three earlier parties, Rikken Dōshikai, Chūseikai, and Kōyū Kurabu, and in 1927 merged with Seiyūhontō to become Minseitō. Kakushin Kurabu was a liberal political group established in 1922 from former Kokumintō and non-affiliated members.

[5]Oka Yoshitake and Hayashi Shigeru, eds., *Taishō demokurashii ki no seiji—Matsumoto Gōkichi seiji nisshi* (Tokyo: Iwanami Shoten, 1959). Entry for May 28, 1924. Hereafter cited as *Seiji nisshi*.

[6]Ibid, entry for October 27. See also entry for November 11, 1924.

[7]"Motoko bodō no danwa," in *Konoe Fumimaro kankei monjo*.

[8]Matsumoto, *Seiji nisshi*, entry for March 3, 1925.

[9]Minseito was founded in 1927. Its first President was Hamaguchi Osachi. Most of its supporters came from the Kenseikai and Seiyūhontō. Along with Seiyūkai, it was one of the two largest and most powerful prewar parties, until 1940, when it was dissolved. Rather progressive, urban middle-class base.

[10]"Izawa Takio shi hōmon shuki," in *Konoe Fumimaro kankei monjo*.

[11]The March Incident of 1931 was an unsuccessful coup plotted by the Sakura-kai of the army. It attempted to place War Minister Ugaki Kazushige as prime minister.

[12]Arima Yoriyasu was a politician and personal friend of Konoe. He supported the establishment of a party lead by Konoe, but when this failed, he supported Konoe's New Order movement and later became secretary-general of the Imperial Rule Assistance Association.

[13]Konoe Fumimaro, preface to *Mori Kaku* by Yamura Kan'ichi (Tokyo: Takayama Shoin, 1941).

[14]Kōdōha, Imperial Way Faction, was a faction within the army, led by Araki Sadao and Mazaki Jinzaburō. It emphasized the national polity of Japan and used direct action, including coups d'état, when necessary. It was a highly fanatical group of officers who rivaled the Tōseiha (Control Faction), but lost influence after the February 26th Incident in 1936, for which it was responsible.

[15]Idealist right wingers, *kannen uyoku*, is a term applied to political activists, for example those in the Kōdōha, who had no concrete program, but acted on fanatic sentiments.

[16]*Kokutai*, literally national polity, but in connotation conveyed the official orthodoxy of the pre-World War II years that determined the function and limits of constitutionalism. *Kokutai* expressed the widely inculcated idea of Japan's uniqueness among and superiority to other nations, based on the virtually sacred quality attributed to the imperial institution.

[17]The October Incident of 1931 was an abortive plot by field-grade officers, the same group as those behind the March Incident. The plot was suppressed after a leak.

[18]The May 15 Incident in 1932 was an unsuccessful coup by ultranationalists and young navy officers. Assassinated Prime Minister Inukai Tsuyoshi.

[19]In *Seidanroku*.

[20]Harada Kumao served Saionji as his private secretary for fifteen years. On intimate terms with Konoe and Kido.

[21]Konoe Fumimaro, "Dai ichiji Konoe naikaku, Shina jihen, oyobi Taisei Yoku-sankai setsuritsu ni tsuite," in Konoe Fumimaro, *Ushinawareshi seiji* (Tokyo: Asahi Shimbunsha, 1946), pp. 1-3.

[22]Shidehara Kijūrō served as foreign minister from 1924 to 1927 and again from 1929 to 1931. Under his liberal leadership, "Shidehara diplomacy" emphasized foreign policy of internationalism, peaceful diplomacy, and trade.

[23]Konoe Fumimaro, "Genrō, jūshin to yo," *Kaizō* (December 1949): 34. Konoe seems to have written this article before his second cabinet and during the Yonai cabinet.

[24]Teikoku Jinken Incident was a graft scandal in 1934 involving several high-level politicians which brought the Saitō Makoto cabinet down.

[25]Both "The Basic Issue in International Peace" and Konoe's reply to Colonel House, which I shall refer to later, are included in *Seidanroku*. There is a separate small volume under Konoe's authorship also entitled *The Basic Issue in International Peace*. It contains the above two pieces, the House treatise, together with pieces showing the worldwide repercussion which it caused, as well as Konoe's two other articles, "Reject the Anglo-American–Centered Peace," and Improving Our World."

[26]The Emperor-as-an-Organ Theory and its foremost exponent, the legal scholar Minobe Tatsukichi, held that the Emperor was the highest organ of the state. It reduced the divine character of the Emperor by placing him subordinate to the law and thus came under opposition from rightists and nationalists.

[27]The February 26th Incident of 1936 was the most devastating of prewar abortive plots and involved several hundred army soldiers who attempted to effect a "Shōwa Restoration." Several important establishment figures were either killed or injured, and key centers in Tokyo were occupied before the troops withdrew.

[28]Konoe, "Genrō, jūshin to yo," p. 34. See also "Atsuji (Morishige) hisho no hanashi," in *Konoe Fumimaro kankei monjo.*

[29]Konoe, "Dai ichiji Konoe naikaku, Shina jihen, oyobi Taisei Yokusankai setsuritsu ni tsuite," p. 8.

[30]Harada Kumao, *Saionji kō to seikyoku*, vol. 5 (Tokyo: Iwanami Shoten, 1951), p. 129. See also pp. 124-25.

[31]Emperor Godaigo's Kemmu Restoration in 1333 sought to restore the imperial authority that had been usurped by the bakufu.

[32]Harada, *Saionji*, vol. 5, pp. 129-31.

[33]Ibid., p. 152.

[34]Ibid., p. 243.

Chapter Three

[1]Uchida Yasuya served as foreign minister under the Saitō Makoto cabinet in 1932. He had been president of the South Manchurian Railway. Supported the Kwantung army after the outbreak of the Manchurian Incident. As the foreign minister, he advocated the recognition of Manchukuo and provoked Japan's withdrawal from the League of Nations.

[2]See also a memorandum Konoe prepared at that time. It was published together with the above-cited "Genrō, jūshin to yo" and Yabe Sadaji's commentary in the December 1949 issue of *Kaizō.*

[3]Ketsumeidan was an ultrarightist terrorist group led by Inoue Nisshō, a Buddhist priest. The incident referred to here, which occurred in 1932, was a plot to assassinate political and economic leaders and succeeded in killing Inoue Junnosuke of the Minseitō and Dan Takuma of Mitsui.

[4]Tōseiha, Control Faction, was a rival faction of the Kōdōha in the army. Its policy sought to transform Japan into a highly organized national defense state

(*Wehrstaat*), as opposed to Kōdōha's fanatic policies that involved terrorist activities and insurgencies.

[5]The Shimpeitai Incident in 1933 was an abortive coup instigated by Amano Tatsuo and his nationalistic Aikoku Kinrōtō.

[6]This appears in the December 1949 issue of *Kaizō*.

[7]The reference to Mukden is to the Manchurian Incident when a bomb exploded on the tracks of the South Manchurian Railway outside Mukden in September 1931 and Japanese troops used this as a pretext to run over the city and moved on to conquer all of Manchuria.

[8]Harada, *Saionji*, vol. 6, p. 30.

[9]Nashimoto Yūhei, *Chūgoku no naka no Nihonjin*, part 1 (Tokyo: Heibonsha, 1958), pp. 239-40.

[10]Kiya Ikusaburō, *Seikai no urakaidō o iku* (Tokyo: Seikai Ōraisha, 1959), p. 142.

[11]Tōyama Mitsuru was an influential rightist; one of the founders of Gen'yōsha.

[12]Kazami Akira, *Konoe naikaku* (Tokyo: Nihon Shuppan Kyōdō, 1951), pp. 42-43, 45-46.

[13]Koyama Kango, *Koyama Kango nikki* (Tokyo: Keiō Tsūshinsha, 1955). Entry for September 20, 1937. Koyama Kango was formerly a journalist and one-time head of Jiji Shimpō. Later, he held positions in several large industrial companies.

[14]Konoe Fumimaro, "Shina jihen ni tsuite," in *Heiwa e no doryoku* (Tokyo: Nihon Dempō Tsūshinsha, 1946), p. 105.

[15]Kido Kōichi, *Kido Kōichi nikki*, vol. 1 (Tokyo: Tokyo Daigaku Shuppankai, 1966). Entries for November 15 and 16, 1937. Harada, *Saionji*, vol. 6, pp. 142–43.

[16]Gotō Ryūnosuke, "Konoe Fumimaro o kataru," in Ozaki Yukio Kinen Zaidan, *Kōen*, no. 137 (December 15, 1968), p. 15.

[17]Arima, *Seikai dōchūki*, pp. 120, 128.

[18]Ishii Itarō, *Gaikōkan no isshō* (Tokyo: Yomiuri Shimbunsha, 1950), p. 299.

[19]Harada, *Saionji*, vol. 6, pp. 208-9.

[20]Kiya Ikusaburō, *Seikai gojū nen no butai ura* (Tokyo: Sekai Ōraisha 1965), p. 202. Kiya Ikusaburō was a political commentator.

[21]Ugaki Kazushige, *Ugaki Kazushige nikki*. Tsunoda Jun, ed., vol. 2. (Tokyo: Misuzu Shobō, 1970), pp. 1240-41.

[22]Inukai Takeru, *Yōsukō wa ima mo nagarete iru* (Tokyo: Bungei Shunjūsha 1960), p. 219.

[23]Kiya Ikusaburō, *Konoe kō hibun* (Wakayama: Kōyasan Shuppansha, 1950), p. 16.

[24]Konoe, "Genrō, jūshin to yo," pp. 33-34.

Chapter Four

[1]Harada, *Saionji*, vol. 8 (1952), pp. 191-92.

[2]Shakai Taishūtō was formed in 1932 on an anti-communist and anti-fascist platform. Later, its ties with the army made it increasingly more rightist in inclination.

[3]See Arima Yoriyasu, *Yūjin Konoe* (Tokyo: Kōbundō, 1948), p. 21.

[4]Harada, *Saionji*, vol. 7 (1952), pp. 163, 164–65.

[5]Kiya, *Konoe kō hibun*, pp. 62-63.

[6]Konoe, "Dai ichiji Konoe naikaku, Shina jihen, oyobi Taisei Yokusankai setsuritsu ni tsuite," p. 25.

[7]"Yabe Sadaji shi danwa," in *Konoe Fumimaro kankei monjo*.

[8]*Hakkō ichiu*, a slogan used in Japan's policy for a Greater East Asia Co-prosperity sphere. From *Nihon Shoki*. Literally, all eight corners of the world under one roof.

[9]Harada, *Saionji*, vol. 8, pp. 349-51.

[10]Konoe, "Dai ichiji Konoe naikaku, Shina jihen, oyobi Taisei Yokasankai setsuritsu ni tsuite," pp. 4-5.

[11]"Gotō Ryūnosuke shi danwa sokkiroku," *Naiseishi kenkyū shiryō*, nos. 66-69 (1968), pp. 160-61. Shōwa Dōjinkai, ed., *Shōwa Kenkyūkai* (Tokyo: Keizai Ōraisha,1968), pp. 47, 280-81.

[12]Tekigaisō was Konoe's villa in Ogikubo in the western suburb of Tokyo.

[13]Arima, *Seikai dōchūki*, p. 203.

[14]The Golden Kite is a reference to a bird that, according to the mythological founding of Japan, led Jimmu eastward on his conquest to the plains of Yamato where he founded the first Japanese state.

[15]Konoe, "Dai ichiji Konoe naikaku, Shina jihen, oyobi Taisei Yokusankai setsuritsu ni tsuite," p. 27.

[16]Gotō, "Konoe Fumimaro o kataru," in *Kōen*, no. 137, p. 24.

Chapter Five

[1]Konoe Fumimaro, "Dai niji oyobi dai sanji Konoe naikaku ni okeru Nichi-Bei kōshō no keika." This memoir is contained as a supplement in Konoe's *Konoe nikki* (Tokyo: Kyōdō Tsūshinsha, 1968), pp. 173-251.

[2]Tomita, *Haisen Nihon no uchigawa*, p. 143.

[3]Sanbo Hombu [Army General Staff], comp., *Sugiyama memo—Daihon'ei seifu renraku kaigi tō hikki*, vol. 1 (Tokyo: Hara Shobō, 1967), pp. 248-50.

[4]Shidehara Kijūrō, *Gaikō gojū nen* (Tokyo: Yomiuri Shimbunsha, 1951), pp. 202-4.

[5]Arita Hachirō, *Hito no me no chiri o miru—Gaikō mondai kaiko roku* (Tokyo: Kōdansha 1948), p. 141.

[6]Konoe Fumimaro, "Sangoku dōmei ni tsuite," in *Heiwa e no doryoku*, pp. 25-26. See also Konoe, "Dai niji oyobi dai sanji Konoe naikaku ni okeru Nichi-Bei kōshō no keika," pp. 182-83.

[7]Konoe Fumimaro, "Oboegaki," in *Heiwa e no doryoku*, pp. 106-7.

[8]Konoe Fumimaro, "Nichi-Bei kōshō ni tsuite," in *Heiwa e no doryoku*, p. 84.

[9]Tomita, *Haisen Nihon no uchigawa*, pp. 172-73.

[10]Yabe, *Konoe Fumimaro*, vol. 2, pp. 340-41.

[11]Konoe, "Nichibei kōshō ni tsuite," p. 79.

[12]Cordell Hull, *The Memoirs of Cordell Hull* (New York: Macmillan,1948). p. 1024.

[13]"Kido hikoku nin sensei kyōjutsu sho[Defendant Kido's affidavit]" to the International Military Tribunal for the Far East. Kido Kōichi's memoir, "Sensō kaihi e no doryoku," in Kido Kōchi nikki kenkyūkai, comp., *Kido Kōichi kankei monjo* (Tokyo: Tokyo Daigaku Shuppankai, 1966), p. 29. Kido penned this memoir after the war in Sugamo prison.

[14]Konoe, "Nichi-Bei kōshō ni tsuite," pp. 87-88.

[15]Ibid., p. 34. See also Tōdai Seiji Kenkyūkai, comp., "Dai yonkai Suzuki Teiichi danwa (April 28, 1963) sokkiroku."

[16]Konoe wrote in his memoir, "Because the United States assumed that Japan had no objection to the 'four principles,' and I myself told Ambassador Grew, '*In principle* I find them acceptable. . . .' Some in the army and the foreign ministry persisted in their strong opposition to an agreement even in principle" (emphasis author). Konoe, "Nichi-Bei kōshō ni tsuite," pp. 89-90.

[17]Joseph C. Grew, *Turbulent Era: A Diplomatic Record of Forty Years, 1904-1945.* Walter Johnson, ed., vol. 2 (Boston: Houghton Mifflin, 1952), pp. 1324-29.

[18]Ibid., p. 1329.

[19]Tanaka Shin'ichi, *Taisen totsunyū no shinsō.* (Tokyo: Gengensha, 1955), pp. 109-10.

[20]Uchida Nobuya, *Fūsetsu gojū nen* (Tokyo: Jitsugyō no Nihonsha,1951), p. 288-89.

[21]"Takamura shi memo," in *Konoe Fumimaro kankei monjo.*

[22]Kido, "Sensō kaihi e no doryoku," pp. 34-35.

Chapter Six

[1]Hosokawa Morisada, "Konoe kō no shōgai," in *Konoe nikki,* p. 150. Hosokawa is Konoe's son-in-law.
[2]Tomita, *Haisen Nihon no uchigawa,* p. 208.
[3]Uchida, *Fūsetsu gojū nen,* pp. 296-97.
[4]Kiya, *Seikai gojū nen no butai ura,* pp. 334-39.
[5]Tomita, *Haisen Nihon no uchigawa,* pp. 111-12.
[6]Ibid., p. 311.
[7]Kiya, *Konoe kō hibun,* pp. 82-85.
[8]Hosokawa Morisada, *Jōhō tennō ni tassezu—Hosokawa nikki,* vol. 1 (Tokyo: Isobe Shobō 1953), entry for April 12, 1944.
[9]Ibid., entries for April 13 and 15, 1944.
[10]Ibid., vol. 2, entry for June 28, 1944.
[11]Konoe Fumimaro's letter to Kido Kōichi, dated January 1943, in *Kido Kōichi kankei monjo,* pp. 591-93.
[12]Hosokawa, *Jōhō tennō ni tassezu,* vol. 1, entry for May 3, 1944.
[13]Konoe, *Konoe nikki,* pp. 32-38.
[14]Ibid., pp. 92-93. Kido, *Kido Kōichi nikki,* vol. 2, entry for July 18, 1944, and the attached document therein.
[15]Gaimushō [Foreign Ministry], comp., *Shūsen shiroku* (Tokyo: Shimbun Gekkansha, 1952) contains this document, pp. 195-98.
[16]Kido, *Kido Kōichi nikki,* vol. 2, entry for July 12, 1945, and the attached document therein.
[17]Tomita, *Haisen Nihon no uchigawa,* pp. 229-30.
[18]Konoe, "Shūsen ni tsuite," in *Ushinawareshi seiji,* pp. 152-53.

Chapter Seven

[1]Gaimushō kiroku[Foreign Minstry record]. Okumura Katsuzō, "Konoe kōshaku to Makkāsā gensui," in *Himerareta Shōwashi,* Hayashi Masayoshi, ed. (Tokyo: Kajima Kenkyū Shuppansha,1965), pp. 266-79.
[2]Tomita, *Haisen Nihon no uchigawa,* p. 256.
[3]Ibid., pp. 251-52.
[4]Kiya, *Konoe kō hibun,* pp. 116-17.
[5]Tomita, *Haisen Nihon no uchigawa,* p. 278. Also, talks by Takamura Sakahiko in "Hensan iinkai ni okeru danwa," in *Konoe Fumimaro kankei monjo.*
[6]Hosokawa, *Jōhō tennō ni tassezu,* vol. 2, entry for November 14, 1945.
[7]Tomita, *Haisen Nihon no uchigawa,* p. 279. Preface by Kishi Isao, chief of the political and economic division, Asahi Shimbun, to Konoe, *Ushinawareshi seiji,* pp. 3-4.
[8]Tomita, *Haisen Nihon no uchigawa,* p. 278.
[9]Takamura Sakahiko, *Shinjitsu no ue ni tachite—Sensō to senryō jidai* (Tokyo: Hakubundō, 1954), pp. 105-7, 108.
[10]*Mainichi Shimbun,* December 17, 1945. An article fly the reporter Itō Harumasa.
[11]Tomita, *Haisen Nihon no uchigawa,* pp. 282-83.
[12]Ibid., pp. 283-85.
[13]Konoe Hidemaro, "Ani Fumimaro no shi no kage ni—Konoe-ke no kyōdai," *Bungei Shunjū* (March 1952): 84-85.
[14]Gotō Ryūnosuke shuki," in *Konoe Fumimaro kankei monjo.*
[15]Ibid., and Gotō Ryūnosuke, "Konoe Fumimaro o kataru," in *Kōen,* no. 137, pp. 27-31.
[16]*Asahi Shimbun,* December 17, 1945. An editorial, "Jisatsu seru Konoe kō."

[17]*Mainichi Shimbun*, December 18, 1945. Column, "Kenteki."

[18]Tomita, *Haisen Nihon no uchigawa*, pp. 300-307.

[19]Kase Toshikazu, *Mizūrigō e no dōtei* (Tokyo: Bungei Shunjūsha, 1951), pp. 277, 279. Oscar Wilde, *De Profundis* (New York: Philosophical Library, 1950), p. 117.

BIBLIOGRAPHY

I   Konoe Fumimaro's major writings and memoirs:
Konoe Fumimaro. "Genrō, jūshin to yo," *Kaizō*, December
1949, pp. 32–36
————. *Heiwa e no doryoku.* Tokyo: Nihon Dempō Tsūshin-
sha, 1946.
————. *Konoe nikki.* Tokyo: Kyōdō Tsūshinsha, 1968.
————. *Seidanroku.* Tokyo: Chikura Shobō, 1936.
————. *Ushinawareshi seiji.* Tokyo: Asahi Shimbunsha, 1946.

II Major sources on Konoe Fumimaro:
Harada Kumao. *Saionji kō to seikyoku.* Vols. 5–8. Tokyo:
Iwanami Shoten, 1951–52.
Hosokawa Morisada. *Jōhō tennō ni tassezu—Hosokawa nikki.*
2 vols. Tokyo: Isobe Shobō, 1953.
Kido Kōichi. *Kido Kōichi nikki.* 2 vols. Tokyo: Tokyo Dai-
gaku Shuppankai, 1966.
Konoe Fumimaro kankei monjo. For details see Note 9, Chapter
1, Fumimaro's Youth.

III Representative biographies and recollections of Konoe
Fumimaro:
Arima Yoriyasu. *Seikai dōchūki.* Tokyo: Nihon Shuppan
Kyōdō, 1951.
————. *Yūjin Konoe.* Tokyo: Kōbundō, 1948.
Gotō Ryūnosuke. "Konoe Fumimaro o kataru," Ozaki
Yukio Kinen Zaidan, *Kōen.* No. 137, December 15, 1968,
pp. 1–34.

"Gotō Ryūnosuke shi danwa sokkiroku," *Naiseishi kenkyū shiryō*. Nos. 66–70, 1968.

Kazami Akira. *Konoe naikaku*. Tokyo: Nihon Shuppan Kyōdō, 1951.

Kiya Ikusaburō. *Konoe kō hibun*. Wakayama: Kōyasan Shuppansha, 1950.

Takamura Sakahiko. *Shinjitsu no ue ni tachite—Sensō to senryō jidai*. Tokyo: Hakubundō, 1954.

Tomita Kenji. *Haisen Nihon no uchigawa—Konoe kō no omoide*. Tokyo: Kokon Shoin, 1962.

Yabe Sadaji. *Konoe Fumimaro*. 2 vols. Tokyo: Kōbundō, 1952.

INDEX